CLASSICS IN THE HISTORY AND DEVELOPMENT OF ECONOMICS

General Editor: Michio Morishima, *Emeritus Professor of Economics, London School of Economics*

In the postwar years the discipline of economics has become highly advanced by focusing upon issues which can be expressed in mathematical terms and ignoring issues upon which it is difficult to make axiomatic analysis. This series aims to make available in English texts which might well have played a major role in the development of a more balanced – not exclusively mathematical – economic theory but for the fact that they were written in a language other than English. However, the series' interest will also embrace mathematical and English-language works where these appear to have been unduly neglected. The series will also seek to make available in English important works that present the experiences of non-English-speaking economies; it is hoped that these will contribute greatly to making economics more comprehensive and more widely applicable to a range of world economies in the future.

Titles include:

Marco Fanno
A CONTRIBUTION TO THE THEORY OF SUPPLY AT JOINT COST
THE MONEY MARKET

Hiroshi Hazama
THE HISTORY OF LABOUR MANAGEMENT IN JAPAN

Hiroshi Okumura
JAPANESE CORPORATION CAPITALISM

Alfonso de Pietro-Tonelli and Georges H. Bousquet
VILFREDO PARETO: Neoclassical Synthesis of Economics and Sociology

Joseph A. Schumpeter and Yasuma Takata
POWER OR PURE ECONOMICS?

Yasuma Takata
POWER THEORY OF ECONOMICS

Giulio La Volpe
STUDIES ON THE THEORY OF GENERAL DYNAMIC ECONOMIC EQUILIBRIUM

Classics in the History and Development of Economics
Series Standing Order ISBN 0–333–71466–0
(*outside North America only*)

You can receive future titles in this series as they are published by placing a standing order. Please contact your bookseller or, in case of difficulty, write to us at the address below with your name and address, the title of the series and the ISBN quoted above.

Customer Services Department, Macmillan Distribution Ltd
Houndmills, Basingstoke, Hampshire RG21 6XS, England

Power or Pure Economics?

Joseph A. Schumpeter
and
Yasuma Takata

Edited by Michio Morishima

Translated by Cyprian P. Blamires and Janet Hunter

First published in Great Britain 1998 by
MACMILLAN PRESS LTD
Houndmills, Basingstoke, Hampshire RG21 6XS and London
Companies and representatives throughout the world

A catalogue record for this book is available from the British Library.

ISBN 0–333–74636–8

First published in the United States of America 1998 by
ST. MARTIN'S PRESS, INC.,
Scholarly and Reference Division,
175 Fifth Avenue, New York, N.Y. 10010

ISBN 0–312–21955–5

Library of Congress Cataloging-in-Publication Data
Schumpeter, Joseph Alois, 1883–1950.
Power or pure economics? / Joseph A. Schumpeter and Yasuma Takata ; edited by Michio Morishima ; translated by Cyprian P. Blamires and Janet Hunter.
p. cm. — (Classics in the history and development of economics)
Includes bibliographical references and index.
ISBN 0–312–21955–5 (cloth)
1. Equilibrium (Economics) 2. Power (Social sciences) 3. Distribution (Economic theory) 4. Economics. I. Takata, Yasuma, 1883–1972. II. Morishima, Michio, 1923– . III. Title. IV. Series.
HB145.S297 1998
330—dc21 98–34978
CIP

This book is printed on paper suitable for recycling and made from fully managed and sustained forest sources.

10 9 8 7 6 5 4 3 2 1
07 06 05 04 03 02 01 00 99 98

Printed and bound in Great Britain by Antony Rowe Ltd, Chippenham, Wiltshire

Contents

General Editor's Introduction

This series, with its designation 'development of economics', has at least four areas of focus, though it would be too restrictive to call them aims.

Since the last war economics has become 'mathematicised' to what could be deemed an excessive degree, so much so that mathematical models are incorporated into the analysis even of questions where there is no need for mathematical argument. As a result, those issues which cannot be expressed in mathematical terms have been all but forgotten. Moreover it has become almost impossible to establish links between economics and other social sciences, in which mathematics are little used. This increasing use of mathematics has thus meant that economics has become isolated; the isolation has in its turn promoted mathematical inbreeding.

The net result is that the discipline of economics has lost many of the capabilities which it formerly possessed. Moreover, since such capabilities have been dispensed with in the selection of specialists, it has become more and more difficult to shift economics away from the path along which it is now proceeding.

One effective means of correcting this tendency, and of giving the contents of economics a better balance, is to dig out some of the economics of the past, and to learn again from those who have gone before us. In the earlier decades of this century economics was not the overwhelmingly English-language-dominated discipline that it has become in the postwar period. There were top-class economics achievements in French, German, Italian and other languages as well. My intention, therefore, is to select from the papers and books written in other languages some which I consider to contain useful knowledge and suggestions, which may help to promote a more balanced economic theory. By translating these works into English, they will be made available to all. This is the first point we will take account of. It is also added that the series' interest is not confined to non-English works; wherever unduly neglected English works are found, proper consideration will be given to them. Secondly, I will try to annex to the series wherever possible critical biographies of scholars active in a wide variety of fields, apart from mathematical economics, in order better to learn from them.

This series is not, however, necessarily 'anti-mathematical'. It is also the intention to include in the series works which might well have played a major role in the mainstream development of economics in the postwar years, but the misfortune that they were written in a language other than English has caused them to remain unknown. The first volume in the series is one such work. This, therefore, is the third point we have in mind.

Finally, modern national economies have not all evolved in an identical fashion. In Japan, for example, and in some other non-English-speaking economies, there have developed perfectly viable and, indeed, efficient economic systems. Work to clarify the structures of these kinds of economic system has been accumulating, but mostly in the language of the country itself. I am also anxious, therefore, to incorporate into the series translations of works in this area, and also research on the historical experience of these economies.

Given the four areas of focus which I have outlined above, the series as a whole will inevitably have a somewhat 'motley' character. While the works may be somewhat disparate, though, I want to build up series in which all the volumes will prove enjoyable and interesting to read. The endeavour involves a great deal of translation work, meaning that publication at regular intervals is likely to be impossible. In addition, there are many candidates whose work must be considered for inclusion. This, of course, makes a great deal of work for a single editor, and therefore it will take time for him to put the project into orbit. My fervent hope, however, is that this series, which, among other things, expresses my own philosophy on the need for a more balanced economics, will succeed in arousing the interest of both students and specialists in a wider economics, and educate them in that economics.

MICHIO MORISHIMA

Foreword: Joseph A. Schumpeter (1883–1950) and Yasuma Takata (1883–1972)

Michio Morishima

I

Following the publication in 1914 of E. von Böhm-Bawerk's 'Macht oder ökonomisches Gesetz',[1] there appeared other works expressing similar opinions to those of Böhm-Bawerk. The work published by Schumpeter in 1916 and included in this volume, which asserted with clarity and intensity that the fundamental law of distribution must follow economic principles, marked a line from Böhm-Bawerk through Schumpeter which established the basic line of what was subsequently to become the main school of economics, the Neo-classical school.

Yasuma Takata sought to reconsider this line of thought. In 'Power and the Economy', the third essay in Part I of his *Power Theory of Economics* (already included in this series), Takata challenged Marx's materialist perspective, the idea that economics determines politics. Through making it clear how in the feudal period power had controlled the economy, he claimed that the materialist perspective was not something which held true throughout history. However, in a capitalist age, when all political forces have to be regarded as the outcome of economic competition, where the often inconsistent plans of all agents are regulated by the market and entrusted to the judgement of the market, the role of politics and sociological elements in explaining economic phenomena has gradually diminished, until finally pure economics (the Neo-classical school) has come to be regarded as the most important tool for elucidating economic problems.

In this respect the difference between the anti-Marxist economists and Marx himself is not all that great. Of course, for Marx pure economics was Marxist economics, and not the theories of

Neo-classicism, but even so such theory is in theoretical terms pure Marxist economics, in as far as it adheres to Marx's basic idea that economic problems are not under the sway of political phenomena – i.e. the phenomena of the superstructure – and must be explained through pure Marxist economics. (It is, of course, the case that some – or even many – Marxist economists have felt this explanation to be inadequate, and have espoused a form of political economy in that they have taken a broader approach to the study of economic problems, an approach which has included political trends – in effect, movements in the superstructure.)

However, although we have reached the stage of a capitalist society, society has certainly not become classless, nor is society constructed of atoms each possessing the same power. Every individual succeeds to the power possessed by his or her parent and the power of his or her class, according to their parentage, or the class into which they are born, and this distribution of power influences the working of the markets for capital goods. (labour, land and capital), and the results of that operation. This results in conclusions reached on the basis of economic theory being modified. Takata regarded conclusions based on pure economics as nothing more than a first approximation in relation to the distribution problem.

This kind of distortion in the producer goods market also extends to the markets for the products themselves, resulting in distortion there as well. Thus all the subjects investigated by pure economics are influenced by power. Takata saw this kind of departure from the competitive mechanism in Keynes' imperfect employment equilibrium. In the Foreword to the volume of writings by A. de Pietri-Tonelli and Georges H. Bousquet published in this series (1994), I called economics in the narrow sense, or pure economics, 'economic theory', while 'economics' must be used to refer to broad economics, or the second approximation of economics which incorporates the influence of power. This, at least, is what Takata maintained. Apart from that, things such as wage relations, enterprise groupings, enterprise takeovers and mergers are all phenomena that have to be discussed by economics, but they are regarded as problems which are very hard to discuss in a pure economics manner, and so they are dealt with, and have to be dealt with, under the remit of broad economics, in which some role is allocated to sociological elements.

To this extent how Takata stands in relation to Schumpeter in the strict sense is clear and straightforward. For Takata a second approximation based on the operation of power is essential to a true clarification of the problem of the market, whereas for Schumpeter it is not. However, in Schumpeter's case we do not have to follow such a strict interpretation – indeed, we ought not to do so. As the title of his work shows, he is merely seeking to emphasise that 'the fundamental principles of distribution theory' were the sovereignty of the consumer and the marginal productivity of each producer, so a recognition of the existence of other forms of power or subsidiary factors would hardly be a departure from the point that he was making. Looked at from this perspective, Schumpeter, too, can be seen as acknowledging a kind of broad economics, removing this as an issue between Takata and Schumpeter. Takata met Schumpeter in 1931, and they did discuss the theory of power, but because Takata subsequently expressed opinions against Schumpeter, it must be the case that at least at the time of the meeting, Schumpeter did not regard the role of power in broad economics as being as important as Takata did. It is likely that at that time his position was fairly close to – if not identical with – that of 'Schumpeter in the strict interpretation'.

There are other problems as well. The degree to which Neo-classical economics has taken over society has varied according to the area of study. As far as the domestic economy is concerned, the influence of the Neo-classical school is, of course, dominant in the developed capitalist countries at the present time, but it was also already conspicuous in 1914–16 in the countries of Western Europe, including Germany and Austria, where Böhm-Bawerk and Schumpeter produced their works. The situation in Japan from the late 1920s through the 1930s, when Takata was writing, can be regarded as not so different. Where international economic relations are concerned, however, not just at that time, but even now we have yet to reach a situation in which we can honestly state that there has been a complete takeover by the Neo-classical school. If anything, it can be said that there are an increasing number of situations in which the international distribution of power influences economic issues, because there are more and more economic problems that have an international dimension.

The question of the international distribution of power – something to which Takata himself seems to have paid little attention – was becoming of increasing importance in the interwar years. By this I am not referring to the sharp change in relations between the winners and losers of the First World War. After the war it became impossible for Britain to maintain the dominant position it had held in its colonies and other territories prior to 1914, and it was compelled to engage in more conciliatory policies. Britain's weakness meant that it had to acknowledge the loyalty, sacrifices and cooperation shown by these territories during the conflict, and to make some sort of corresponding response. Along with the payment of substantial reparations by the defeated nations, the victors were forced to take on the huge political burden left by the war, and its legacy to international confidence. This constituted a major blow to the framework of the British Empire, bringing about a major change in the relative positions of the world powers.

The result was that in the years after 1918 the position of Britain grew weaker, and it became increasingly difficult for it to maintain peace under its supremacy: the era of *Pax Britannica* was over. Britain sought to create a 'federation' independent of its empire, and, by moving the colonies away from the empire and towards the federation, weakened the former and strengthened the latter. The aim was where possible to substitute a federation marked by more equal relations between the two partners for an empire characterised by unequal relations, in order to help minimise the political and economic burden on Britain. Britain thus began to abandon the top position and moved into the second best position.

Such seismic changes in international politics produced vacuum in both Europe and Asia. This was filled by the advance of the so-called 'fascist' powers, notably Germany, Italy and Japan. In particular the China market, hitherto a treasure house for the British, was now exposed, naked and unprotected, to the Japanese. In order to impede the advance of Japan, a series of disarmament conferences aimed at naval limitation were held between Britain, the United States and Japan, but these attempts served only gradually to instil in Japan a greater measure of self-confidence. Immediately following the failure of the London disarmament conference (1930), Japan initiated an advance into mainland China (the 1931 so-called 'Manchurian Incident'), which led to a strengthening of collaboration between the three fascist countries, and finally developed into a full alliance between them.

The structure for maintaining peace agreed in 1919–20 – the Versailles Treaty and the League of Nations – was almost totally destroyed, and in 1933 Japan withdrew from the League, to be followed soon afterwards by Germany and Italy. The free trade economy which the League had been expected to protect received a devastating blow, and all countries (but in particular those which possessed colonies or concessions, and hence the British Empire and federation) were forced to rush headlong in the direction of trade protection. A series of retaliatory actions took place between the advanced industrial economies, the volume of trade shrank and the world economy headed towards major depression. All this was the result of the dramatic changes in international power relations which accompanied the First World War.

In conjunction with the changes described above, there were also dramatic shifts in the power relations between classes within individual countries. The First World War was the first total war, the first war to be fought not just by standing armies. Many, while neither soldiers nor sailors, participated in the war and laid down their lives for their countries; moreover, those who worked on the home front were fighting not just for their own interests, but for something more. After the conflict governments had not merely to show conciliation towards the colonies, but to recognise the efforts of those who had cooperated in the war effort, above all workers and women. The social position of workers and women rose considerably after the war, resulting in their increased influence in society, and governments and ruling classes were obliged to make considerable concessions.

Takata disregarded international power relations, concentrating his attention on domestic power relations. His aim was to explain the depression of the 1930s – a depression which had begun for Britain in the first half of the 1920s – by means of the high real wages which accompanied the increased power wielded by the working class. There is certainly an element of truth in this explanation, and I am not totally opposed to his attempt, but on the other hand I do believe that it was a serious failing on Takata's part to ignore the major changes that had occurred in international power relations, in particular those affecting Britain and her colonies.

Colonies had ceased to be 'branch offices' of the main country, they had become independent (or semi-independent) organisations capable of autonomous actions in their own interest. This shift dealt an economic blow to the imperial power, reducing the effective demand for its products. Even without the high wages resulting from workers' increased power to fight for their interests, it is likely that the parent country would have been plunged into recession by the fall in effective demand, and the existence of the Great Depression could probably be explained by means of a theory of power rather different from that espoused by Takata. So-called theories of imperialism – in particular those of the Marxists – have explained the depression of the interwar period by reference to exactly this shift in the international relations of power.

Takata had been concerned with Marxism since his youth. Like Pareto, and like Schumpeter, Takata had become a strong anti-Marxist. If Takata himself had reacted sensitively to the major shifts in the international relations of power that accompanied the First World War, and developed his own particular power theory of international relations, he would not just have been able to make a major contribution to developing theories of imperialism, which had been virtually monopolised by the Marxists, he would also have perfected his own theory of the great interwar depression. That he did not do so must be a source of regret. What must be emphasised here, however, is that this kind of power theory – whether Takata's or that associated with an international theory of power – is absolutely indispensable in any explanation of a problem which is specifically located within economics, the problem of slump. For that reason it is a problem which lies within the 'broad economics' I have talked about above, and analysis of the sociological elements necessary for any explanation must be inherent in that economics. To construct a pure economics which rejects such analysis, resting only on analyses of utility and marginal productivity and rejecting sociological observations as heresy, is nothing short of a retreat on the part of economics itself. Of course, it may remain essential to hole up in the citadel of purity for a while to stabilise things internally, but if at the same time this results in abandoning the outer protective wall, economics is likely to become an isolated castle within the social sciences to which, while it may be impregnable, no one is going to pay much attention.

If the value of economics, and the confidence placed in it, is to be increased, it is absolutely imperative that the pure economists move away from their isolated stance and make a positive advance into the areas covered by broad economics. There is also something else, which I have chosen to call a far broader economics. This area of study consists of those problems which lie outside historically proper areas of economics, and cannot be solved by the skills of economists alone, but in whose solution the participation of economists is indispensable. These are interdisciplinary problems, one well known recent example of which might be the environmental issue. The issue of social power stressed by Takata has, as we shall see later, a major possibility to be able to become a focal concept of a certain category of interdisciplinary problem. As a broad economics, Takata's power theory embraces the possibility of development into one part of a far broader, or comprehensive economics.

II

The trade liberalisation measures adopted to stabilise the position of British industry (i.e. the repeal of the Corn Laws in 1846) extended a decisive and deadly blow to the British economy, although the effects became conspicuous only about thirty years after the abolition. The volume of production of wheat had by this time shrunk to 60 per cent of what it had been at the time of abolition, and fifty years later it had fallen to around one-third of the same figure. Conversely, imports of wheat increased sharply, by a factor of around 6 during the first thirty years after abolition, and around 11 after around 50 years. Production of barley and oats was not that much affected, but here, too, there was a sharp increase in imports. Since the result of the trade liberalisation was the import of cheap agricultural products, the nominal wages of industrial workers fell, and the policy could be said to have achieved its stated objectives. But because it was countries such as Russia, Germany and the United States which supplied these cheap agricultural products, the previous agricultural producers – the colonies and territories of the British Empire – had little to be thankful for in the repeal.

The British government had to win over the colonies – the fact that they were members of the Empire did not mean that they would necessarily go along with policies that were disadvantageous to themselves and would benefit only the mother country. The colonies had to be given special treatment when it came to trade, and the Empire thus had to establish a tariff union to give them economic protection. Since outside the sphere of the economy Britain and her colonies were all part of a collective unit, tied together by a common destiny of coexistence and coprosperity, the imperial power had to be able to possess the military capability sufficient to defend them. This kind of imperial consciousness, combined with the policy of giving economic priority to the colonies of the empire, was advocated by the rural landlord class at home who had suffered from the same free trade policies. This kind of 'Imperialism' appealed to the nationalist sentiment of the British people in general, and from the latter half of the nineteenth century through to the beginning of the twentieth was a time during which Britain – then the workshop of the world, and its most powerful country – was typified by the operation of a two-party system, within which one party advocated free trade and the other trade protectionism.

The protective tariff policies of the Conservative Party called for retaliatory measures by other countries (including Germany and the

United States), and these countries secured their export markets through dumping. Illegal actions of this kind undermined the international goodwill existing between the capitalist countries. As a result of trade liberalisation, the price of agricultural goods fell, leading to a rise in real wages, workers together with industrialists supporting the liberalisation policies. By contrast, the rural landlords and farmers supported the Conservative Party. Since the power of each side was more or less equally balanced, political power was handed back and forth between the parties. At its best this period saw the realisation of a model two-party system; at its worst it marked the continuation over the long term of a situation in which there was no consistent political line, with the opposed political aims and policies of the two parties cancelling each other out. The result was that the country was always able to avoid confronting any catastrophe head on.

The great powers engaged in bitter disputes to protect their respective empires, and in order to achieve the most favourable solution in economic competition mobilised all conceivable nationalist elements in their struggles. The publication of Schumpeter's 'Zur Soziologie der Imperialismen' (Towards a Sociology of Imperialisms) (1918–19) was sparked off by an interest in this era. He did not overlook the fact that economic conflict between the industrial powers was escalating, but at the same time clearly highlighted the fact that, notwithstanding the loud voices of the English Conservative Party calling for the protection of empire, there was very little resort to military force. With the exception of the Crimean War and the Boer War, England was little engaged in war for the period of seventy years from the repeal of the Corn Laws up until 1914. This depended not only on the existence of two parties with very different political views holding each other in check, but also on the existence of a disjuncture between economic conflict and military action which had to be crossed, and as long as this gap remained unfilled by the logic of cause and effect, there could be no direct connection between the two sides. Schumpeter took the view that the capitalist nations were not so blind that this disjuncture was filled up by the emotion of jingoism.

First of all, the workers always remained vigorously anti-imperialist. At the same time the capitalist side preferred the steady continuation of good business to getting rich quick through war. For that reason capitalism was overall by nature anti-imperialist. The worsening of capitalist conflict in this period was due not to capitalism itself, but to deeply rooted and long-standing rivalries. Each country sought to establish a dominant position by overcoming their competitors in war, just as they had done since ancient times. Military victory not only enabled the arbitrary plundering of the property of the defeated, but also had the advantage of enslaving prisoners of war, meaning that war was something that made a profit. What caused the greatest frenzy, however, were the ceremonies with which victorious soldiers were greeted on their return from the battlefield. Schumpeter opposed the view of the Marxist economists that imperialist wars resulted from economic causes, arguing instead that even the most recent wars were not that rational in origin. Modern peoples rather resolved on war on the basis of their sense of justice, or other sense of moral obligation, their sense of mission that they had to put these values into practice. Behind this there was the ultimate desire to glorify their own people. This is apparent from the fact that in resolving to go to war the thing to which modern capitalist countries pay most attention is whether or not they have on their side sufficient moral reasons to persuade the majority of the people to back them.

Schumpeter's logic is diametrically opposed to that of the Marxists – the argument that the substructure always determines the superstructure. As opposed to the Marxist economists' view that imperialism is an issue for broad economics, for Schumpeter it was not just an issue for economics, but something to be regarded as an interdisciplinary issue for economics and the sociology of nationalism – coming within the remit of what I have called a very broad, or comprehensive, economics. Up until 1918 Schumpeter had mainly operated within the field of pure economics, and had continued to argue (particularly in his major work of 1908 and his treatise on the theory of distribution of 1916) that pure economics could in itself be sufficiently perfected to provide an explanation of economic problems. In the sense that he believed in the absolute supremacy of pure economic theory, Schumpeter could be said to have been up until then strongly 'Marxist'. For Schumpeter to claim in 1919 that imperialist economic conflicts must be understood as a problem for comprehensive economics not only showed him to be astute, but also marked a major change in his thinking – from the pure economics line to a broader social science one.

Now if we were to consider 'the unlimited and untargeted desire for aggrandisement on the part of a people or a nation', which Schumpeter considered to be the basic motive force behind imperialist aggression, and to call it instead a people's or nation's consciousness of power, Schumpeter's theory of imperialism can be rewritten along the lines of a Takata-type power theory. Takata, who had originally started off as a sociologist, argued for the significance of power in both sociology and economics, but his 'power theory' aimed at establishing a kind of economic disequilibrium theory by introducing elements of power into that type of economics which had taken the idea of general equilibrium theory into account.

Takata, too, however, frequently wrote about imperialism and issues of race. In *Sekai Shakai Ron* (*On World Society*) (1947), his last major work of sociology, he compared the advance of the overseas Chinese into Southeast Asia with the colonial advance of the imperialist nations, pointing out that whereas the Chinese had not received the protection of state power, the advance of the capitalist nations had been accompanied by state intervention or support. Seen from the perspective of which advance had been the more effective, there was no logical imperative why the capitalist nations should have taken the latter form of advance, and for that reason it was not inevitable that the capitalist nations would come into conflict with each other in an attempt to seize control of foreign markets. Takata, however, saw that advancing enterprises supported by state power were likely to be able to secure profits over and above those which they would normally expect to obtain. Moreover, he believed that if they were satisfied just with obtaining normal profits from exchange, then state support was unnecessary. Takata's views in this sort of situation were equivalent to those of Schumpeter, who argued that capitalism was not by nature imperialistic.

Takata concluded in addition (pp. 194–5) that:

> imperialism is not the outcome of capitalism. It bears no relationship to the rise and decline of capitalism, and is established out of the desire for self aggrandisement on the part of each nation and each people. It is just that the imperialism that has appeared during the era of capitalism bears a form specific to a capitalist era. It seeks neither slaves, nor tribute, merely the exchange, purchase and sale of goods in conformity with a particular pattern... The principle of the open door (free competition) is respected... However, since those capitalist nations which are in the position of controlling colonies are able to use the political strength given them by their actual power to secure favourable bargains, they can secure through political means special rights and interests, and also often award special protection to the enterprises of the home country. The result is that these enterprises are likely to be able to

> obtain some kind of excessive profits. This is what some scholars call 'monopoly profits'.

Thus in regarding the demand for self aggrandisement on the part of the nation or the people (the will for power) as the basic motivating force behind imperialism, Takata was a complete Schumpeterian. At the same time, in seeing that the capitalist nations made use of the power which their overwhelming position gave them, manipulated that power over exchange with their colonies or spheres of interest, and applied pressure to equal and free exchange, Takata was consistent in his standpoint of a power theory of economics – i.e. bringing to economic analysis a second approximation by incorporating the factor of power with the aim of rendering more realistic the explanations reached by pure economics. Seen from this perspective, Takata's theory of imperialism was broad economics, but had not become the very broad economics attained by Schumpeter. What, then, are the differences between the two?

It must be emphasised that in the title of Schumpeter's 1919 work (1) imperialism is not singular but plural, and (2) he deals with the sociology rather than the economics of such imperialisms. The second of these two statements shows that Schumpeter was trying to discuss a problem normally dealt with as being beyond the discipline of economics, that is not as a problem in broad economics, but as part of what I have called very broad economics. In relation to (1), out of all the multiple types of imperialism, what Schumpeter calls 'imperialism in the modern absolute monarchy' is worthy of our attention. By contrast, Takata's argument should probably be called 'the economics of imperialism'. His imperialism is not that of the Marxists, but is the application of Takata's own concepts to the analysis of the same imperialist economic phenomena discussed by the Marxists.

Let us now apply these concepts to the observation of Japan's imperialist war of 1931–45. First of all, the then emperor of Japan was an absolute monarch. This is shown through his possessing the sole prerogative of the right of supreme command of the armed forces and control over foreign policy. There existed in Japan at this time a legislature, but unlike in England it was unable to hold the powers of the monarch in check, being there solely to support the monarch. The Upper House (House of Peers) in particular acted to curb freedom of thought and to stir up ultranationalism. In addition all Japanese males had the duty of conscription, meaning that they could always be mobilised into the service of the emperor. Japan was in the situation of which Schumpeter wrote, where 'the sovereign is able to regard state and people as his private property'. At the same time, seen through the eyes of the military, Japan was a warrior nation, in which all the people were soldiers, and the aggression contrived by the military developed into a popular imperialism which ultimately received the support of the people as a whole.

However, the military did not pursue their aggression in accordance with any consistent plan. There was no direct relationship between the invasion of Northeast China (Manchuria) in 1931, the Shanghai incident of 1932, or the North China incident of 1937. Incidents of random aggression erupting totally unexpectedly were sparked off by different groups, and the elite were compelled to give approval subsequent to the event, gradually drawing the imperial army further into war with China. After the war the Emperor left a memorandum on 'Why we came to undertake this kind of war',[2] but despite this we still do not have a clear and persuasive reason. All we have is the emperor's statement that he felt himself to be in personal danger in the failed coup of 1936, and that if he had refused in 1941 to sanction war against Britain and the United States, contrary to the prevailing jingoism, he would probably have been killed. Similar statements come from the records made by General Tojo. This corresponds well with Schumpeter's statement that 'the ruling class was always inclined to declare that the country was in danger, when it was really only class interests that were threatened'.[3] The emperor feared conflict within the court itself, and sanctioned advance into war to avert such conflict. Japan's imperialism was what Schumpeter has called the imperialism of an absolute monarchy; it was at the same time the imperialism of a warrior nation, and the people's imperialism. It was not, therefore, what the Marxists have termed 'imperialism'.

The study of this kind of pseudo- or quasi-imperialism does not lie within the province of broad economics, but must for the most part be the subject of joint research in sociology and economics – i.e. falling within very broad economics. In fact, the circumstances of Japan's advance into Korea,[4] Manchuria and China were very different from those described in the 'theory of imperialism'. While the army carried out the invasion, the business world did not advance. The military fostered the so-called 'new' *zaibatsu*, stationing them in Korea and Manchuria. In the case of China, the Japanese government compelled business to advance into China by creating what were known as national policy companies, funding companies half through investment by the state and half through the private sector.

III

The theories of imperialism espoused by the Marxists, as shown by that of Lenin,[5] argue that 'a complete territorial division of the world between the major capitalist powers' is a precondition for imperialism and seek to analyse the economic conflict between the capitalist powers during such a period. Lenin argued that the imperialist era came after the last two decades of the nineteenth century, with the necessary acquisition of colonies virtually completed in the case of Britain by 1880 – a time when the doctrine of free trade was still dominant. France and Germany sought vigorously to acquire colonies during the last twenty years of the nineteenth century, and this can be seen both as fulfilling a delayed 'condition' and as a first step towards a redistribution of the world's territory. The aggressive wars undertaken by Japan, Germany and Italy in the years after 1918 were clearly wars aimed at territorial redistribution. I have previously referred to these countries as 'late imperialists', to distinguish them from the early imperialist nations which were already completing their territorial acquisition during the era of free trade.[6]

At the risk of digressing, I would like to say something about Japan's role in the Second World War. The Second World War was essentially a challenge mounted by the late imperialists to the early imperialist nations over the distribution of territory. Despite this, there are many Japanese today who believe that 'it is because the Japanese fought Britain, the United States and Holland that the countries of the East were freed from the domination of the white races'. This, however, is no more than a selfish distortion on Japan's part. Sixty years stretch between 1880, regarded as marking the completion of the early allocation of colonies, and 1941, when Japan declared war on Britain, Holland and the United States. During that time independence movements continued to operate in the various colonies, with many nationalists and communists being imprisoned. Because when the Japanese armies arrived they released these activists from prison, there was initially a strong sense of gratitude towards the Japanese as an army of liberation. They soon discovered, however, that the Japanese army was far more brutal than the early imperialist nations; they began to understand that the Japanese army had not come to liberate them, but to compel the countries to remain colonies, this time under Japanese rule. Since the situation in each of the countries exposed to the aggression of the Japanese army was slightly different, we must be careful about applying a uniform argument, but it is fair to say that in each case the advocates of independence and the members of the communist party fought side by side with their previous rulers against the Japanese. Then after the defeat of Japan, they achieved independence from those rulers. They had in fact won a twofold war of independence, and to claim that they were liberated by Japan, or that Japan had cooperated in their liberation, is to engage in an arrogant rewriting of history.

Whatever the case, Marxist theories of imperialism state that the division or redivision of territory is a given condition. Their object of analysis is how economic competition is carried on subject to this given condition. However, even though this may lead to a war, it will be an economic struggle, not a military conflict aimed at acquiring territory. Marxists take the view that military conflict something already established as a precondition for the economic war. For that reason Marxist theories of imperialism deal with problems totally internal to economics: just like the question of monopoly, it is part of the stage theory of the economics of capitalism. This was emphasised by one of the academic Marxist factions in Japan led by Kozo Uno. This faction sought to explore how the logic of *Das Kapital*, the fundamental text of Marxist economics, worked at this new stage.

By contrast, the theories of imperialism put forward by Takata and in particular by Schumpeter, were far more wide-ranging, with neither regarding imperialist aggression (i.e. the division and redivision of colonies) as a given condition. Due to Schumpeter's work being written in 1919, a rather delicate point in time, he did not discuss the aggressive attempts by Japan, Italy and Germany to secure redistribution which began shortly afterwards, but his theory of imperialism did not deal with such aggression as a given condition, in fact he treated it as a substantive part of the subject. As the analysis of Japanese aggression above demonstrates, this kind of aggression is less a part of economics than of nationalism and jingoism, hence it cannot be repeated too often that Schumpeter's theory of imperialism is essentially interdisciplinary, embracing both sociology and economics.

While, as I have said above, the emperor in Japan at that time was an absolute monarch, there was in the background a kind of military despotism. The combined forces of the military and the nobility constituted a political elite presided over by the emperor, and industry was made to serve the policies which this elite established. There was no question of the reverse – i.e. politics serving industry. In the case of Germany, the Nazis played the same role as the combined forces of the Japanese military authorities and the emperor. Such a relationship is exactly the opposite of Marx's substructure–superstructure relationship; the power relationship is reversed. Under these circumstances the law of costs cannot be fulfilled, and the imperialist nations exhaust not just economic measures, but other measures as well in their attempts to eliminate the confrontational measures adopted by other countries. Not surprisingly, the imperialist economic struggle becomes even more violent than envisaged by Marxism. To use Schumpeter's words (1991, p. 209):

> Whoever seeks to understand Europe must not overlook the fact that even today its life, its ideology, its politics are greatly under the influence of the feudal 'substance', that while the bourgeoisie can assert its interests everywhere, it 'rules' only in exceptional circumstances, and then only briefly.

This depiction bears a marked resemblance to that in Takata's power theory.

Having stressed in 1916 a pure economics theory of distribution in which any second approximation based on a theory of power was regarded as insignificant, Schumpeter had by 1919 produced a theory of imperialism which emphasised that movements within society were strongly influenced by the nature of the desire for power. The distance between his views and those of Takata had become very narrow indeed. At this stage the differneces between them essentially lay in Takata's belief that power was a secondary element in the perfection of economics, while Schumpeter regarded economics (i.e. pure economics) as one element in interdisciplinary study to be synthesised with sociology, for which the desire for power served as a setting. For Schumpeter it was sociology, and not economics, that should concern itself with power. To use my own vocabulary again, economics was thus expanded from broad economics into very broad economics. Schumpeter did come into contact with Max Weber, the pioneer of the very broad economics, and I am inclined to think that he had studied deeply Weber's research relating to the influence of religion on the ethos of businessmen, and its ability to become a fundamental element in economic development.

In 1942 Schumpeter published one of his most famous works, *Capitalism, Socialism and Democracy*, which took exactly the opposite line to that laid down in another of his best known writings, *Theorie der Wirtschaftlichen Entwicklung* (*The Theory of Economic Development*) (1912), indeed they almost seem to have taken the form of mirror images of each other. In this latter work Schumpeter highlighted the role of innovation – that is the pursuit of new combinations – as a factor in economic development, arguing that as economic development continued, the possibilities for innovation gradually diminished, making economic success more and more difficult. The economic world would be frustrated by a situation where a lot of innovative work would bring few rewards, resulting in more and more talented young people leaving business. It was not just in the business world that innovation was necessary; it was imperative for other sectors as well to experience renovation and reform. One notable example of a new combination in a field outside industry came between 1940 and 1950, when the young people of Britain enthusiastically committed their efforts to the building of the welfare state. Advanced countries thus turn away from capitalism, producing a shift towards socialism. This kind of substitution of socialism for capitalism does not result from the stagnation of capitalism of the kind predicted by Marx – the bipolar division between the rich and poor classes – but rather from a non-violent turn of the wheels – a U-turn.

This kind of argument for a dynamic system is not something to be discussed within the narrow perspective of economics, but needs to be advanced by collaborative research between economics and cognate disciplines, something which Schumpeter tried to do in his own works. Even so, it is easy for substantial mistakes to be made. In the case of Schumpeter, his estimate of the American population was totally wrong because he considerably underestimated the future population of the United States. This error was based on an underestimation of the effects of the Second World War and an inability to grasp accurately the movements of population to the United States that were to happen after the war. Where research in comprehensive economics is attempted, since the fields of related study are so great, it is often possible for things to be overlooked, and if there are more than a few major omissions of this kind, the research ends up as being just the personal view of a single, complacent researcher.

One major misreading on Schumpeter's part related to an inability to foresee the appearance of a Mrs Thatcher.[7] According to Schumpeter's scenario, by 1979, when Mrs Thatcher came to power in Britain, the country should already have virtually completed its transition from capitalism to socialism. By that time, however, the evils of socialism had become conspicuous, necessitating the appearance of reformists in both camps. Had such a reformer appeared within the Labour Party, socialism might well have been modified, allowing it to continue its previous advance. However, since the appearance of any such reformer within the Labour Party would have been regarded as a form of internal party treachery, it was likely to be possible only if the party were to be driven into a corner and find itself excluded from power over a period of years. Thus if a reformer was to appear, it had to be from within the ranks of the Conservative Party.

So Mrs Thatcher came to power, and the demolition of the welfare state proved far easier than its creation, if there was no alternative to the welfare state to be implemented in its place. This was the start of the Prime Minister's demolition activity, and the economy went into a U-turn. Innovation was highly regarded, entrepreneurs starting up new private enterprises were respected and given favourable treatment. Labour unions were subjected to unequivocal criticism, and management were given a barrage of protective powers by the state. The wheels began to go into reverse, and this period started to demonstrate the kind of movement which Schumpeter had recounted in his 1912 book.

It is of significance that Schumpeter was unable to predict this kind of reversal. Up to that time theories of system change had been typified by that of Marx – a pure economics theory of system change, with no comprehensive economics discussion of the problem as the one found in Schumpeter – but Marx's view had been that the stagnation of capitalism would lead to the eruption of violence and a transformation to socialism. It is likely that Schumpeter was influenced by such Marxist ideas, and he too believed that the change in the system would be one-directional, rather than a 'both-ways' type allowing a U-turn. However, he also emphasised that his change of system would be peaceful, and not violent, occurring within the framework of democracy, and for that reason it was possible for a reversal in any direction whatsoever to occur merely with a change of government. It shows a significant theoretical failing on Schumpeter's part that he was unable to predict the appearance of someone like Mrs Thatcher.

During Mrs Thatcher's thirteen years in power, the Labour Party also came to realise that it would be impossible to recover the route which they had taken in the past. During this time the party leadership passed from Foot, to Kinnock, Smith and Blair, and the line connecting them clearly tilts towards the right. The party can be said to have completed its preparations for the recovery of power from the Conservative Party before the 1997 general election. It is in fact true that a certain proximity between the two parties makes any change in direction easy. Seen in this way, it must be regarded as quite reasonable that

Britain again took a U-turn, the system repeatedly oscillating between capitalism and socialism.

Now if we assume that there is a cycle to system change, then is the amplitude of that cycle likely to diminish, or to expand over time? We have very little experience up until now from which to make a judgement, and we must be extremely careful about doing so, but if we compare the distance between Callaghan and Thatcher at the time of the first U-turn with that between Major and Blair at the time of the second which has just occurred, the second gap is far narrower. This means that while there may be a further U-turn, it is unlikely to yield such radical change. This would lead us to suggest that the amplitude of the cycle is likely to weaken over time. As the amplitude eventually contracts towards zero, the final result will be the system settling down in a 'form which is a hybrid of capitalism and socialism'. Such a conclusion is entirely likely and appropriate as long as people are rational enough to learn from past experience.

During the Cold War there was put forward what was known as the 'convergency conjecture', which argued that the opposing capitalist and socialist nations would learn from each other, leading to countries in both camps converging on an intermediate form – a hybrid form.[8] This assertion was not made on the basis of rigorous observation and proof, it was no more than the product of wishful thinking. In fact, because the socialist camp was wiped out through a sudden collapse (part violent and part peaceful) the convergency thesis ended up as no more than a daydream. However, in order for this kind of thesis to be realised, neither capitalist nor socialist nations must be pure and unadulterated adherents of capitalism or socialism, but we must understand that they will accept into their system elements of the opposing system, expanding and contracting the relative importance of those elements, with each country going through its own capitalist and socialist periods, and oscillating between them. Over the long term, the amplitude of the swing will contract towards zero, and each country is likely to home in on its own particular hybrid of capitalism and socialism. Then, assuming that each country can learn from the others, any country which regards as preferable the hybrid reached by another can itself move towards it, and by that means the mixed systems of each country will ultimately converge on a single, common hybrid system.

If the convergence theory is to hold at all, convergence is likely to be realised in the manner described above. This is nothing more than a form of speculation, but if the idea should prove to be worthy of serious observation, it is a major issue which lies outside the framework of broad economics, although one in which economics must have a strong interest. I have defined the study of this kind of question as very broad economics, or comprehensive economics. Weber's research on the Protestant ethic and its relation to the spirit of capitalism, mentioned above, as well as the question of Confucian morality and the different forms of Asian capitalism, fall within the remit of comprehensive economics. The question of environmental constraints on economic development is likely to be one which will be regarded as of increasing importance in the future. From the perspective of its actual importance, the marginal importance of comprehensive economics is likely to grow academically in the future, while the marginal value of pure economics will decrease. As Ragnar Frisch, one of the most important founders of the Econometric Society, admirably put it in his speech at the first world conference of the Society in 1965, 'the providing of economic theory with a greater mathematical armoury is nothing more than a form of intellectual entertainment'. As a mathematical economist, I find such observations painful, but from the perspective of its importance to society, mathematical economists need to take up the challenge of opening up and shedding light on the issues of comprehensive economics.

IV

Globalisation is one problem that comes within this category. Since the Second World War technologies with a global impact have been developed, particularly in areas such as weaponry, transport and communications. At the same time the countries of Europe have strengthened their resolve not to fight with each other again, and have moved towards greater economic cooperation. Taking account of Keynes' predictions at the end of the First World War that any peace treaty whereby the victors punished the losers might well mean that Europe would again find itself at war, the settlement in 1945 was along the lines set out in Keynes' *Economic Consequences of the Peace*. The Coal and Steel Union proposed by him was established after the Second World War in Luxembourg, developing later into the EEC. This subsequently became more comprehensive, and completed the work of building of a single market for the whole of Western Europe, then growing into the EU which has its aim of implementing equal standards in a range of social and cultural conditions, including regarding the treatment of workers, throughout the same area. This in turn has given rise to hopes and suspicions regarding the possible development and dissolution of the EU in favour of a United States of Europe.

I adhere to the materialist view of the history of states, which argues that the scale of the state is determined in accordance with the existing technology. It was the railway that enabled America and Canada to become giant nations stretching from the Pacific to the Atlantic; the same was true of Russia's expansion from the Baltic to the Japan Sea. Britain was able to build a massive empire covering the seven seas thanks to the invention of the steamship. However, while the scale of the state may be determined in accordance with technology, where it has expanded improperly extensively, it may become extremely difficult to sustain, and the country may end up by becoming divided.

After the Second World War Britain sought to form a sterling area based on her 'federation' (the Commonwealth) in competition with the EEC. One of the reasons why this strategy did not succeed was because links were weaker in the area connected by steamship than in areas brought together by railways and cars; Britain was forced to yield to the dominant force of cars and ferries, abandon the sterling area and join the EEC. The British Empire, like the Roman Empire before it, possessed the military, transport and travel technology to make it possible, but they were far weaker so that protection, unification and maintenance of its existence were difficult. States which have become in this way overextended break up to adapt to technological imperatives. For a while friendly relations continue to exist between the former home country and the territories and colonies, just as in the period of feudal control, but before long they become totally independent, ending up as separate countries able to take advantage of more powerful technologies.

The period since 1945, which has witnessed this kind of historical development, has been one of tragedy for Britain. This was due to the fact that, notwithstanding Britain's position as the uncontested victor within Europe, she found herself a late partner in the EEC, whose leading members were the defeated Germany, the quasi-victor France, and the pseudo-victor Italy. This situation dealt a blow to Britain's nationalist pride; moreover those other countries which, though far away, had formerly been part of the empire, which still spoke the same language, and which had, moreover fought as Britain's allies during the war, were prospering as members of a loose union, the Commonwealth. Britain's tardiness in responding to the changed situation is understandable.

However, new forms of transport (the jet and the car) tend to bring not just profits, but new friends as well. The EEC was an association – *Gesellschaft* – aimed at economic profit, but economic negotiations lead to a deeper mutual understanding, and as friendship develops this eventually gives birth to a new 'mixed blood' generation. Although it is often said that it becomes harder and harder to sustain community – *Gemeinschaft* – and that communities eventually turn into *Gesellschaft*, I believe that we can have the opposite phenomenon, namely a society formed purely as a *Gesellschaft* engaging more and more over time in mutual support and assistance by means of communal internal activities. Through colleagues, people come to know their countries. This means that we get the appearance of a tendency for *Gemeinschaft* to develop out of *Gesellschaft* in parallel with the opposite trend. It may take time, and the path will be a meandering one, but I believe that it is not unrealistic to envisage the future history of the EU as that of a development into a United States of Europe (USE). A time will come when new technologies in defence, transport, travel and communications (technologies which bear no comparison to those of the prewar years) make a United States of Europe not just possible, but even necessary. This is the next period of our era.

The nation states of the nineteenth and twentieth centuries are thus likely to be replaced by a superstate. However, at the start the peoples of each nation state within the superstate will continue to have strong mutual feelings of unity, while the USE as a whole will continue to be something of a 'multicoloured' entity. Nor will economic relations be uniform across the region. With trading customs differing according to the nation state, the rapid unification of such practices cannot be determined by economic laws, rather political power relations are likely to play an extremely important role in this process. A time will come when the economic development of the participant nation states will be strongly dependent on their influences through the government and legislature of the USE. As Tugan-Baranovskii once remarked, and just as Takata recognised the same thing for the feudal period, the distribution of income and produce will not be determined by economic theory, according to terms like marginal utility and marginal productivity; this will be an era when political clout will reign supreme. Unfortunately within the USE politically strong nation states will tend to prosper economically, while the second-rank states will be less well off and the USE will end up becoming a two-tier system economically as well. A time is coming when economies are determined by politics, social forces and cultural prestige (i.e. the superstructure), and not the other way around.

We cannot know how long such a period will last, but providing the USE has a democratically operating legislature, politics are likely to become before long rather more rational, leading to a deeper mutual understanding of each others' cultures by the various states. When this happens the political distortion of economic interests will become very difficult. We will have the kind of period depicted by Böhm-Bawerk in his 'Macht oder ökonomisches Gesetz'. Questions of distribution in the USE will be determined by the laws of economics, according to the principles laid down by Schumpeter and, as Takata emphasised, the influence of the superstructure will come to be no more than secondary.

Until this final stage is reached, until we have moved from the time of Tugan-Baranovskii to that of Böhm-Bawerk, the various disciplines of the superstructure will be just as essential for our research as economic theory. This means that the study of comprehensive economics is imperative for at least the next century or more, until the EU has reached the stage of a well established USE.

We must not just stop there, however. The new technologies which Western Europe is having to confront are also facing the other countries of the world. If my materialist historical theory of the state is correct, this raises the question of whether or not economic communities are bound to be formed in other regions as well. Many of these regions – for example, the northeast Asian area consisting of China, North and South Korea, Taiwan, Okinawa and Japan – have reached a stage of economic development to be able to plan such an economic community. In cultural terms as well, these countries possess a homogeneity similar to that of Western Europe. There exists between them, however, feelings of mistrust engendered by Japan's aggressive acts of the past and China's communism, and the desire to form such a community is lacking; there does not in any of these countries exist the political passion and force to break out of this stalemate.

However, if this situation persists, they will end up being unable to reap the economic benefits brought by the new technology. The result of this is likely to be the opening up of a gap between these countries and those which have formed a community. When the countries of northeast Asia can no longer tolerate the existence of such an obvious gap they, too, are likely to form an Asian Economic Community (AEC). When this happens the AEC will begin to take on a life of its own; it, too, could soon develop into an Asian Union, and then into a

United States of Northeast Asia (USNA). We may be sure that similar trends will appear in other regions of the globe. We are likely to move into an age in which the world is divided into a number of large zones; the United Nations will cease to have as its basic unit of operation the nation state, as at present, and will shift towards membership of wide-ranging economic communities or extensive federations.

This kind of view of world society is rather different from that which Takata conceived in 1947. The key difference is that Takata's world society is one which is moving decisively from *Gemeinschaft* to *Gesellschaft*, a society marked by an extreme *Gesellschaft* character. In his world, we have profit-seeking activity across countries, with no regard for national boundaries, activity very much in the mould of pure economics. Any world society which is going to permit this sort of activity must possess an authority which will be protective of such activity, or which will at least regulate it, and here Takata put his hopes in the United Nations. At the same time he took the view that such systems as imperialism and collectivism were likely to impede globalisation. In the case of the former, however, he regarded the heterogeneity of individuals as increasing as globalisation progressed, whereas he saw groups as becoming more homogeneous. As groups become more homogeneous, the binding power of individual groups will weaken. The prerequisite for the establishment of world society, namely the relaxation of the intermediate unions – at this time symbolised by states or nations – will thus be met. He believed, therefore, that globalisation would not intensify imperialism.

Takata was fierce in his judgement of collectivism. Although he was strong in his praise of Marx's enthusiasm in the Communist Party Manifesto for the achievement through communism of equality throughout the world, we must say that if we assume that the above-mentioned convergency hypothesis – something which had yet to be articulated at the time Takata was writing *Sekai Shakai Ron* – is correct, it is not conceivable that any extreme form of collectivism should last for long in the world. At that time, however, the United Nations had only just come into existence, while the movement for European unification had hardly got on the rails. Takata's thinking concerning what happens to sovereignty when faced by the strengthening and advance of integration – the question of the transfer of sovereignty from the nation to the integrated unit – was that no country possesses sovereignty in the sense of 'the supreme power of autonomy'. Such a thing is no more than a fiction reflecting the collective demands for and the needs of a nation state. State power cannot be said to have total autonomy in relation to a large number of internal groupings, since it finds itself restrained by the wishes of churches, labour unions, political parties or the organs of public opinion, and is forced to shift direction accordingly. In the same way as the state possesses no sovereignty, no federation of states can possess sovereignty, and Takata took the view that such federations are one more grouping which operate side by side with, and come into conflict with, nation states.

Under these circumstances states fall into three categories: the regional state (substate), the nation state and the federation of states, and state functions are divided between these three organisations. Common sense would suggest that there will be some sort of hierarchy among these three organisations, with the sovereignty of the nation state being transferred to the federation of states. But Takata argues in the following way: There is no such hierarchy whatsoever, since each organisation is restricted to a different jurisdiction. In each of the three organisations it is individuals who are members, and this is ultimately true even in the case of federations of states. The three organisations are distributed different powers and different functions. One group (society) is not an element in another group. He, therefore, concluded that those groups regarded as having a lower position (in relation to groups formulating and implementing a collective will) were considered as if they were members of a group of a higher position.

Takata argued that if associations of agents (individuals or organisations) become more involved, over a long period, in pursuit of economic interest there will develop a thorough mutual understanding between the individuals (or organisations) who have been involved. Although he did not argue this, this may well lead to the formation of a community between them. This is true for international associations, too. World society is, in fact, more prone to community than Takata believed. Moreover technology has grown by leaps and bounds, and international relations have become closer as a result of that technology. However, technology brings not just advantages, but disadvantages as well; the disadvantages brought by massive technologies are even capable of destroying the globe. This means that we have to have an earth many times greater than the present one if we are to engage in the unlimited pursuit of profits; and since that is clearly impossible, the people of the earth therefore have no choice but to seek mutual understanding and cooperation in order to protect our globe from these disadvantages.

Theories relating to communal society are no more straightforward than those relating to a profit-oriented society. That is because such societies are not organised according to rational objectives, with clearly defined goals. For a world government, or a United Nations where the will of world society as a whole is decided, a balance has to be struck between the desires of the representatives of many regional interests, and theories explaining how such a balance is made are not so simple as the theory of the market. The theory of pure economics and the theory of communal society belong to totally different disciplines, and any attempt to understand world society through bringing these two theories together, comprehensive economics in that sense, is completely multidisciplinary. The fusion of different disciplines to create a new original discipline of higher standards is something that lies more in the field of composite artistic endeavour than of scientific activity, and imposes a great burden on the abilities and senses of the scholar who becomes party to such work. However, that is no reason to entrust such work solely to a scholar's intuition; the methodology of comprehensive economics must be clarified to a certain extent beforehand.

V

Those disciplines which must play the principal role in the new economics are economics and sociology. There used to be considerable interchange between these two; since in the early twentieth century there were very few universities that put on lectures in sociology, even many of the famous sociologists lectured in economics at their universities. Ferdinand Tönnies, who taught at Kiel University, for example, delivered his lectures as economics lectures. Takata, too, gave economics lectures at Tokyo Commercial University (now Hitotsubashi) and elsewhere. In Takata's case, he attempted a fusion of economics and sociology through creating a second approximation by means of power, but in Tönnies' case sociology and economics merely operated side by side, exercising virtually no influence on each other.

Tönnies' major work was *Gemeinschaft und Gesellschaft: Grundbegriffe der reinen Soziologie* (1887), in which the two core chapters were Chapters 1 and 2 of Part I, entitled 'Theory of *Gemeinschaft*' and 'Theory of *Gesellschaft*'. The first of these provided a theory of society dealing with such aspects as kinship, neighbourhood, friendship and family, the village and the city. While the second claimed to be a theory of *Gesellschaft*, it was essentially economics (in Tönnies' case, basically Marx's economics). These two theories were merely set out in parallel, with virtually no analysis of any mutual relationship. This was due to

Tönnies' belief that *Gemeinschaft* and *Gesellschaft* were two pure, opposing types; there was no element of the latter in the former, and vice versa. Tönnies' took the view that society was developing away from *Gemeinschaft* in the direction of *Gesellschaft*. For him, there was no concept of the reverse happening – namely, no concept that the *Gesellschaft*, which was established as a mechanical body, might also, if given enough time, become the forum for an essentially organic life, becoming, in effect, a *Gemeinschaft*. For that reason Tönnies' world society, like that of Takata, became like the thoroughfare of a large city, in which people are driven by their own self-interest, where they hustle and bustle in a disorderly fashion, always with a shrewd eye to the main chance.

While a world society remains but a distant dream, people may well regard it in this light, but as a world society becomes a more realistic prospect, people will begin to talk about feelings of superiority, inferiority and dignity on the part of particular groups within that society, the concepts of service to world society, feelings of loyalty towards it, and the need to protect it and make sacrifices for it. People will come to regard world society as a kind of great community. The UFO phenomenon demonstrates that people have already begun to think of the world as a *Gemeinschaft*, since people have already become more aware of worlds outside their own, and want to consider how best to protect their own world in relation to these others. It was to be expected that Takata, who had lived through two world wars, should take a different view of world society than Tönnies, who was writing before 1914, but even so the broad similarity of Takata's view to that of Tönnies' resulted from the fact that 'community' arrangements on any world scale in their times remained weak, and that the existing theories of community propounded by sociologists were essentially descriptive, and not analytically penetrating.

By comparison, economists such as Pareto and Schumpeter, who took an interest in sociology, made a major contribution in the direction of fusing the two disciplines. Pareto in particular paid considerable attention to what he saw as the poverty of theories of community, and gave a great deal of thought to how best to establish such a theory. His methodology was distinctly idiosyncratic, and his process of thought was different from those of other sociologists; it was also very different from the methodology of economics. Pareto argued that people's social actions are not necessarily rational, but driven by emotion and impulse, and sometimes even self-destructive. (In this respect, he differed from Max Weber who was mainly concerned with rational aspects of human beings' social behaviour.) For that reason the line of thought of the kind used in economics, which lays down axiomatic ways of thinking, could not be adopted for sociology. He consequently devised the theory which will be outlined below, but his grand methodology generated very little in the way of concrete analysis – except the theory of circulation of elites which will be mentioned below. Schumpeter's theory of system change was the one thing suggesting that grand, and utterly dazzling questions of comprehensive economics could be put in a form that tacitly indicated a reliance on Pareto's methodology.

Before outlining Pareto's methodology, we need to say something about Marx. Marx moved from philosophy into economics, and showed interest in topics of what I call comprehensive economics, but since it was economics that he made the focus of his own studies, and because he also took a materialist view of history, he did not seek to fuse economics with sociology which was essentially the study of the superstructure. For him, the various social phenomena were basically reflections of economic phenomena, but not vice versa and there was consequently no need for him to examine whether economics, as the study of these economic phenomena, might be influenced by sociology or not. For him, there was no need for any such fusion. In that sense, Marx retained the purism of economics.

It is somewhat ironic that some economists of the Chicago School are as purist as Marx was on this point. Such economists take the view that issues normally considered to lie within the province of disciplines other than standard economics – such as questions of choice regarding things like marriage, numbers of children, their educational progress, as well as divorce, or whether or not to engage in criminal activity – are things that can be explained by the application of the principle of utility maximisation, and belong, in effect, to the sphere of economics. This is, of course, an incredible extension of the territory. However these questions have to be looked at from a variety of perspectives, as Schumpeter did in the case of imperialism. Just as the Marxists saw imperialism as a manifestation of the principle of profit maximisation at a particular stage of capitalist development, so, too, the Chicago School can only partially see social problems such as family issues and racial discrimination from the perspective of utility maximisation. This monism on the part of both Marxists and the Chicago School will never lead to multidisciplinary research on issues between economics and other disciplines. The Marxist School separates sociology and other disciplines of the superstructure from economics, arguing that as the superstructure is a reflection of the substructure, i.e. economics – reflection is, of course, a very vague term – there is no need to discuss them when the substructure is made clear. By contrast, economists of the Chicago School approach it from a standpoint of the imperialism of economics, in the sense that they advance the study of substructure into the areas of the study of superstructure, by researching it as economics. In this respect, the Chicago School are more aggressive than the Marxists. In any case it is true that they both belong to the 'far right wing' of pure economics.

By contrast, Pareto, Schumpeter and Takata all retreated from a materialist view of history. There are, of course, cases where a historical materialist explanation is valid, but it cannot be denied that in other cases different lines of thought might be more accurate. It is a mistake to assume in all cases that the substructure always determines the superstructure, indeed empirical observation suggests that the reverse is often the case. Subtle shifts in people's sentiments can influence the state of the superstructure, and sociology has therefore to start from the analysis of sentiments or mind. By contrast, economic decisons are based on cold calculation, with sentiment impinging on economics only as an indirect influence from society. Any rejection of the universal applicability of the concept of materialism necessitates a synthesis of economics and sociology.

Pareto cited six basic factors (residues) to explain shifts in people's sentiments.[9] Of these, the most important were the first residue, termed 'the instinct for combination', and the second, 'the prevalence of aggregation'. He assumed that people's basic instinct was to get ahead of others by seeking for new combinations, albeit through an objectless process of trial and error. Schumpeter's entrepreneurs were individuals well supplied with this first residue. People of this kind were full of a progressive spirit. At the same time a certain mixture of sentiments existed in people's minds, and established a kind of reality. Many of the things which became social factors were of this type. Various sentiments associated with religion, the family, the state, peoples and social classes – including feelings of ancestor worship, nationalism and socialism – were mixtures of sentiments due to the second kind of residue. Such sentiments were essentially ideological, having no corresponding actuality, and had to be regarded as 'religious' sentiments in the broadest sense of the word. Whereas the first residue was the search for new combinations, individuals who were rich in the second residue tended to be conservative, sticking to existing combinations and existing concepts.

Through observing which of these residues was dominant under what kind of circumstances, Pareto explained what he termed 'the circulation of elites'.[10] Schumpeter's system change from capitalism to socialism is an outstanding application of this kind of residue theory. As we shall soon come to understand, the entrepreneur-led society which is capitalism marks an era when the first of these residues flourishes, while socialism, a structure aiming at the bringing together of many feelings of the people, is an era which, ironically, is dominated by the second, conservative residue. One of the last public statements by Michael Foot – who was, incidentally, a dog lover – before retiring as leader of the Labour Party following its defeat by Mrs Thatcher, was 'Now is the time of the cat, but the time of the dog is bound to come', a statement that must put him straight into the Pareto–Schumpeter school. At that time the first residue was stronger than the second, but in the years after 1918 the opposite was true, and this opposite relationship was gradually strengthened in the years during and after the Great Depression.

The concept of power identified by Takata does not appear explicitly in the analysis of residue undertaken by Pareto. However, power is taken account of as a result of an aggregation of sentiments, and since Pareto would probably have regarded the labour movement as a kind of religious movement, power can be categorised as belonging to the second category of residue. In fact, he did regard the sentiments tying together social groups, such as castes or sects (and hence Takata's concept of power as well) as belonging to the second residue. The final typology of residue was sexual residue. Some of Schumpeter's imperialism – those which can be categorised along with the Japanese imperialism I have already mentioned – can be said to be closely tied in with the people's 'sexual' impulses. This is because if the urge is so compelling that it surges forward and works itself out, the desire is then allayed. Power, too, belongs to the second residue, but the desire for power – i.e. its promotion and its exercise – must be regarded as belonging to the sixth residue, sex.

Viewed in this way, it is possible to elaborate Takata's power economics by introducing Pareto's residue theory into it. Without such an elaboration, power economics could be no more than a discussion of a second approximation to post-equilibrium theory, something which Takata himself attempted on numerous occasions. That is in itself important, but without some kind of theory of movement of sentiments, not necessarily Pareto's one, it is impossible to obtain a deep and conclusive explanation of the rises and falls of nations in a period in which the decisions and desires of the governments of the EU and other large regional economic communities are curbing the economies of the member nation states, and the relative powers of the different regional economies exercise a major influence on the world economy. The problems of this era must be analysed not through economics, or even broad economics, but by means of a very broad economics – a comprehensive economics that embraces economics, sociology and other fields of study in order to make it truly interdisciplinary.

* * *

With the scope of economics having to deal with more and more complex problems in the future, I consider that broad economics and far broader one will become very significant academic subjects. Under such circumstances I reckon that we should return to the problem of 'Macht oder ökonomisches Gesetz' originally proposed by Böhm-Bawerk. Then the present volume has been edited as follows. Part I contains an English translation of Schumpeter's very pro-Böhm-Bawerkian article on distribution (1907). Part II is a selection from various Takata's works (1937, 1940, 1941, 1955) quering that point of view. Its Section I contains Essay 7 of Takata (1941); Section II gathers chapter 3, chapter 4, excluding pp. 50–9, and chapter 5 of Takata (1955); Section III chapters 1 and 2 of Takata (1937); Section IV a part of chapter 3 of Takata (1940); finally Section V chapter 4, pp. 50–9, and chapters 5 and 6 of Takata (1955).

It is interesting to see that Schumpeter has kept his original position through his life and created a new area of 'far broader' economics outside of his original territory of pure economics. He has become more well-known as a far broader economist than a pure theorist. It is further noted that, after Takata's works on power contained in this volume had been completed, Preiser's paper (1949) of a similer nature was published. Although sections II and V of Part II of this volume that were written after Preiser, Takata yet did not mention his 1949 paper, probably because it was the aim of Takata to discuss Keynes from the power theoretic point of view, whilst Preiser ignored Keynes and remained in the Böhm-Bawerk framework.

Finally, at the time when Schumpeter and Takata wrote the papers contained in this volume, not only they but also many others did not give details of references and citations. It was impossible for me to make the Bibliography section complete.

Part I
The Fundamental Principle of Distribution Theory

I Preliminary Remark

It is quite a long time now since the last great controversy over questions of theoretical economics. In Germany there was never a great deal of discussion in this area and even the occasional arguments (especially in book reviews) do not amount to anything. Any theoretical work that is going on does so for the most part behind a kind of curtain which hides it not just from public view but even from the rest of the academic community. And yet for all that there is still a widespread feeling that we have had more discussion of theoretical questions than is really healthy or useful. Those who are familiar with the social psychology of academic life will not be surprised by such a contradiction; they will be inclined to see in this reaction a paradoxical consequence of the rarity and perfectly comprehensible unpopularity of such debates. It means that the first words in any theoretical discussion, however modest – and the present work is modest indeed – always have to be words of justification, introduction or even apology. This is all the more so if an author wants (as I do) to avoid the suspicion that he overrates economic theory or the current practice of it and wishes to stress the fact that he himself is participating in the discussion of the theoretical questions of the day only reluctantly and out of a feeling of necessity.

To come straight to the point: it is an inescapable fact that in addition to other tools, many of which are more important, the solution to a great number of social-science problems will customarily require the employment of the analytical tools of economic theory.[1] If the answers given to a variety of questions often fail to meet the simplest requirements it is to some extent (though not perhaps primarily) because the great majority of economists have failed to master this tool. Almost no-one really deals with a problem comprehensively – instead, problems are smothered in 'facts' or turned into sociological issues. To take just one example: to the extent that it is not purely historical, the Webbs' work with its far-reaching conclusions is over a very large area obviously based on unacknowledged analytical assumptions and because of the partial inadequacies in these assumptions the treatment is completely worthless over this whole area. Old problems whose monotonous persistence usually arouses a smile – such as for example the problem of interest – thus remain perpetually unresolved, even though their solution is absolutely essential to an understanding of the economic structure of (for example) capitalist society. The sort of judgements that are passed on such problems are quite grossly unsatisfactory; the solution must be to give the issues a thorough airing.

There is nothing new about all this but I want to focus on the general current situation – especially in Germany. Not very long ago theorists were keen to suggest that externally economic theory was trying to put itself in the right relationship to its sister disciplines while internally it was gradually managing to reach a uniform standpoint on basics such as would be a precondition for further progress in the only really important individual questions. It seemed as if light was beginning to dawn amid the tangle of contradictions, and the shape of the terrain was gradually becoming visible and assuming broadly the same shape for everyone. I do not think this was a case of mere self-deception, but an accurate picture of the way things were going. It is not however the way things look just at the moment, when the path ahead seems to be shrouded in mist and we are all too likely to lose our way. In England many people think more highly nowadays of Hobson than of Marshall, in America quite a lot rate Veblen above Clark, in Italy Jannaccone or Loria are often a bigger success than Pareto, and so it goes on. Many of the hopes for unity and progress that might have been nourished ten years ago have been dashed.

The situation is particularly extraordinary in Germany. Although you will not find it stated in their theoretical observations, the great majority of German economists are actually not quite so opposed to theory as they were twenty years ago. It is true that we are only now seeing the effects of the dictatorship of those 'opposed in principle'. In their day there were still a great number of survivors from the preceding era who had preserved a stock of theoretical knowledge and theoretical interests (mostly of a classic or Rodbertist or similar hue) while today the complete breakdown in theoretical 'training' – which can never be replaced by anything else at a later stage even if a person does manage to acquire a certain positive respect for theory 'in principle' – is becoming crystal clear. In the absence of any informed criticism and in the presence of an implicit (though completely Platonic) receptiveness to theory, a theoretical literature is now growing up in this previously abandoned field, but although the literature includes many undoubted examples of talent, it also perpetuates the most horrendous errors. It offers no defence against a massive invasion of the most elementary errors, errors pure and simple that cannot be defended from any 'standpoint' whatever, errors that remain unnoticed and uncorrected. The most antiquated and more or less prescientific views can be rehashed quite brazenly. The sort of basic misunderstandings that so often accompany the initial study of a theory are being given the status of serious and indeed crucial 'objections', and this is all happening quite peacefully. People's judgement is so uncertain that many are very careful to treat every theoretical work sympathetically and accord each author a certain degree of respect, without any personal desire to become more closely acquainted with the individual works and without even being capable of doing so (for theoretical understanding can only be acquired by dint of hard work). These remarks are not motivated by any personal animosity, especially since such deficiencies are balanced by so many distinguished activities in other areas, and furthermore even the worst offenders in this area must usually be credited with excellent intentions and with an abundance of talent. But when the area does come up for discussion the focus is usually on methodological questions or a sociological aspect or a practical result or a general standpoint – never on the real central issue.

It is essential to be aware of this situation if we are to understand where economic theory is currently at, and it is a situation that makes discussion very difficult. On the one hand there has to be wearisome repetition of many trivial points, while on the other all the more demanding arguments may seem very unconvincing to readers who are not generally familiar with the terrain.

II The Economics and Sociology of Distribution

The knots in the threads of theoretical thinking that cause the most confusion are to be found in distribution theory. There is an assumption today among a whole group of writers from various countries about marginal utility theory – I use this term for the theory held by most present-day theoreticians even though it is in frequent use only by a small group of them, on the grounds that it does at least represent the nucleus of this theory. The assumption is that this theory does give an accurate account of the foundations of value and price formation[1] and that it does give an adequate account of the world of consumption goods, but that it fails to cope with the problem of distribution. I shall begin with a discussion of this assumption. As a starting-point it offers the great advantage that it frees the discussion from a large number of methodological and factual preliminaries, because it assumes an understanding and recognition both of the essence of economic theory generally and of the foundations of the marginal utility theory in particular. Taking as an illustration the problem of wages I then want to ask whether in fact the explanatory principle offered by the theory of marginal utility can indeed adequately account for as much of the social process of distribution or income formation as can generally be explained by a purely economic theory.

The assumption I have outlined is often stated baldly as an assertion, though at other times it may just crop up as a vague proposition or lurk at the implicit level. In many writers it appears in connection with other elements, for example with a fundamentally anti-theoretical position or with an overwhelming interest in individual concrete questions. It is to be encountered in its purest form in a recent work by Tugan-Baranovskii,[2] and where I engage in polemic it is this work I shall be focusing on. The choice of this particular writer is justified by the following factors: his reputation and his work, his adoption of a position that evokes a great deal of sympathy at the present time, and the belief he shares with almost all theoreticians that debate can be fruitful. Although he repeatedly refers to a special 'method' which he is applying to the problem of distribution while accepting the marginal utility theory for the world of consumption goods, his thesis that it is not value and price laws that are determinate for distribution but social relations of power involves no special method in the logical sense. While the prevailing theory denies the possibility of wage increases through juridical measures or organised action by the workers, his own theory proves it to be a fact, and his thorough treatment of the subject offers a welcome practical focus for the discussion which I now wish to engage in.[3]

First of all I shall formulate the essence of the marginal utility and marginal productivity theories[4] in their original form and in the form of the so-called equilibrium theory (Pareto) that depends on it, perfects it and generalises it *par excellence*. In principle and on a further level of abstraction that considers only the basic form of the economy, what I shall be saying applies to all imaginable forms of social organisation, but I shall limit myself to the narrower problem of the 'free market economy' characterised by private property, etc.

First of all, the pure economic object of knowledge that we abstract from the actual object of the economic process for our purposes is strictly uniform.[5] What we see here is one and only one activity, whose distinguishable elements have an indissoluble connection; they are involved in an exchange that is indissoluble in principle, and it may at the most occasionally be ignored in the individual case in a first approximation. These elements determine one another mutually and unambiguously,[6] and their effect on each other may be described in terms of just one single principle. These elements are quantities of goods or individual psychic[7] amounts of value, and in general it is only a question of expediency whether we lay the emphasis terminologically on one or the other[8] – whether we define our system of elements as a system of quanta of goods or as a system of individual psychic amounts of value; it comes to the same thing in the end. This uniformity does not prevent the theory from resolving a vast number of highly diverse problems. The questioner's concrete interest constitutes the special problem which the theoretician always seeks to answer in the same way, always pursuing what is ultimately the same line of thought – that would be valid for all other pure economic problems – only each time in another guise.[9] For all its uniformity this theory is susceptible of endless variations through the introduction of particular facts – special conditions – and it is precisely by means of the introduction of particular facts that most of its results of 'practical' interest are obtained.

Just as all the quantities of goods and all the valuations that there are at a given time in an economy or in the minds of economic subjects are so to speak adjusted to one another, or suited to one another, or form a system that can be compared with a mechanical, an organised or an organic system depending on one's viewpoint,[10] so the successive situations of the world of goods or valuations fit with and are adjusted to one another; and insofar as the theory is not affected by alien factors, each is determined by the one that goes before it just as it determines the one that follows: and the governing principle is the same as the one that governs the interactions of the elements at each moment. This flow of the economy has no identifiable temporal limits and we can only grasp it by picking out a piece of it equivalent to the duration of a technical production process, a purely formal accounting period, the lifetime of a company, or some shorter or longer 'economic period' sufficient for the factors under discussion to have their effect. Such periods we then schematise in a suitable manner.[11] In each economic period of this kind there is production and consumption and a cycle of economic life is completed. Using a concept familiar since Quesnay we can interpret what happens over such an economic period as the production and 'distribution' of a 'social product'. This does not mean we can connect it with the idea of consciously planned combination by economic subjects, for it is only individual economic plans that have psychic reality and even these only partially, since a very large proportion – perhaps the greater part – of all economic activities function on the basis of impulses or customs.[12] But through the interplay of all the individual demands and supplies a whole results whose outline definitely gives to the observer the impression of being purposeful; it is called an economic plan and can be regarded as the equivalent of the conscious economic plans that are drawn up by the 'Minister of Production' in a Socialist state. But we cannot go on to make a connection with the idea of a stock of goods, for what we actually find is an arbitrarily detached piece of a constantly flowing and constantly renewed stream of goods – which could moreover equally be defined as a stream of valuations or need satisfactions.[13]

As the last remark indicates, the social product consists of the material and immaterial consumption goods that are consumed in a given economic period. To the extent that the consumption or production goods produced in one period are passed on to the following period, in a stationary economy the same amount and in a non-stationary economy nearly the same amount of goods are being passed on. To the extent that production goods mature into consumption goods within one economic period – otherwise produced means of production belong to the category of 'passed on' goods referred to above – they cannot be distinguished from consumption goods. Thus we can understand the paradox that the whole social product consists purely of consumption goods, so that apart from external loans, etc. the consumption stock of an economic period normally represents the overall result of all the national production forces, and yet there are always other products of these productive forces present as well.[14] The case of consumption goods that remain in existence beyond a particular economic period does not need special discussion.

Just as this social product, this stock of consumption, this national dividend (Marshall) is the net result of all the different kinds and qualities of personal activities, raw materials and natural power, and produced means of production or (since the third category may be 'resolved' from the point of view of economics into the first two) is ultimately the net result of all the 'work' and all the 'land', so the social product is the source of all the yields produced in the economic arena, and they completely exhaust it.[15]

This is clear enough, and the best way of proceeding is generally thought to be to separate the two sides of the process – production and distribution – and constitute them as particular phenomena and problems; to view the former as more under technical–economic influence and the latter as more subject to the sociological–historical factor; to formulate specific 'laws' for each; and only then or later to bring in the most essential connections between them. The understanding is that the place to start is with production, because something must first of all be there before it can be 'distributed', and after that to move to a consideration of the social product to be distributed. This accords with the old subject division in pure theory – 'circulation' being only a mechanism binding production to distribution, and the chapter on 'consumption' a dumping-ground for miscellaneous items. It also accords particularly well with the position of those authors who give 'social relations of power' the crucial role in the distribution problem.[16]

This approach is deficient in every sense. For in reality 'distribution' clearly decides what is produced and how it is produced, since the income and demand capacity of the economic subject depend on it. At the same time it is equally obvious that relations of production govern 'distribution', for they decide with what claims the individual can approach the social product.[17] Finally, it is clear that production comes as much under the influence of social regulation as distribution and distribution comes as much under the influence of technical natural laws and economic necessities as production. Although of course they both govern the whole of economic life, the specifically technical factor and the specifically sociological factor are moreover alike alien to the economic factor, and it is the erroneous confusion of the former with the economic essence of production and of the latter with the economic essence of distribution that impedes insight into the interrelation of all the elements of the economic process on exactly the same level; it also prevents us from grasping the fundamental idea of the market economy and of income formation in the market economy and explains that quest for special explanatory grounds for each individual phenomenon (e.g. each income sector) which led to the botch-up of the old theory by completely missing the link between individual appearances.

By contrast it has been a real advance to recognise that the fulfilment of the productive role – in the economic sense – of each element of productive power achieves *uno actu* the return that is in the market economy the foundation of its master's income formation. Production and distribution are not two distinguishable separate activities that somehow affect one another, but two aspects of one single activity matching each other step for step.[18] Each productive activity is simultaneously a distributive activity, each distributive act is a link in the chain of the production process. We cannot grasp them as independent in principle of one another, – for what can be grasped as separate belongs to technology or sociology – and nothing in them is comprehensible apart from the whole of the economic process. Of course we can – and occasionally must – pick out one element and regard the others as constant. In order to make a start somewhere,[19] we can begin by constructing a market for consumption goods which consumers with a given fixed income enter to buy their consumption goods from the entrepreneur – but to this 'market' as a necessary extension belongs another, in which the same consumers offer their 'productive activities' to the same entrepreneurs for the same sums of money, which are now in the hand of the latter, and a full understanding of what goes on in one of these fictitious markets always requires that attention be paid to what goes on in the other. For particular purposes – and especially in order to answer concrete questions – we can and must isolate individual elements, e.g. certain particular kinds of consumption goods, and regard all others as 'given', but here too there is a simplifying fiction.

In itself then the kernel of the theory is only a system of relations between completely colourless quantities of goods or valuations; within the system there are in principle no differences, nor is there any particular distinguishable distribution problem, and if the system is analysed into separate parts or put to the service of a particular complex of questions, it can only be for didactic or other practical reasons, and the specifically theoretical train of thought is gone through each time, though in a different guise. As I have already observed, recent work on economics has distilled out of the old series of economic question-complexes a fundamental matter common to them all, a matter which is 'purely economic' *par excellence*, with everything else clearly having a technological, sociological, etc. character. I say 'clearly' because it really ought not to be difficult to see, e.g. that (especially) the phenomenon of waged work and its origins, its effects, its cultural meaning and significance confronts us with sociological problems; and taken overall it is something very different from the phenomenon of labour value, this latter being only one manifestation of a much more general phenomenon that calls for a uniform theory.

I do not wish the reader to think that I want to limit economics to the discussion of this basic economic matter. On the contrary, though such discussion is very necessary the only really direct insight it gives us is into the essence of pure economic connections, and it only really begins to be fruitful when applied to problems raised from outside economics. It yields most of its results only when its general data are concretised in terms of particular conditions – e.g. of wage formation – and only when the mechanism of its thinking can be grasped as it were in some kind of technical or sociological factual material. The separating out is necessary only in the interests of a better elaboration of a methodologically autonomous factor – which for an individual investigation may be combined as required or desirable with others. It is important to realise this because theorists and opponents of the theory are for ever misjudging this situation; the former regard, e.g., incomes as 'manifestations of value' and consider that the basic problem of the distribution process has generally been resolved, while the latter again regard such a view as an error of principle; also because objections against the theory as such may be based on mistakes in concrete data that have been included in the theory.

I am all too aware how dangerous it is in this area, where there is simply no place for a specifically analytical interest as far as the specialists are concerned, to say things that would be disapproved of even by most of the authors whose views I want to defend, things which are usually dismissed with some banal old remark about 'theoretical frivolity'. But the truth is that what are dismissed as 'refinements' have purely practical implications too, for the confusion they tackle turns out in fact to be the most fruitful source of misunderstandings and controversies in the area of distribution theory itself. It is because

I believe these that misunderstandings and controversies can be resolved by the application of the necessary logical rigour that I have made the above remarks, pedantic though they may have seemed; and I would now like to apply what I have said to the question of the social relations of power as the determining basis for income formation (particularly as discussed by Tugan-Baranovskii) and more generally to the group of questions in relation to which expressions like 'economic' or 'historico-legal' categories and the like can be used.

Most authors who are in practice in agreement with the viewpoint put forward here would state as the starting-point of marginal productivity theory that income in general and wages in particular 'are' value and price phenomena. But it would not be difficult to obtain their agreement to two concessions which would link their view epistemologically with the one expounded here. They would all admit in the first place that their theory explains only the essence and the law of income levels and not actual concrete income levels – which depend on variable data that always need to be studied in an 'empirical – realist' way; nor does it explain the particularities in the formation of the distinguishable individual kinds of wage – for these depend on particular further facts to be established by particular 'empirical – realist' investigations and which are to be inserted into theory on the occasion of 'practical applications'. This would seem self-evident to them all, and none would have any problem with the statement by B.K. Diehl for example (stated as an objection) 'that wages theories without empirical – realist foundations and based only on the logical consequences of certain 'general – human' utility debates cannot achieve their goal'[20], if this goal is the explanation not of the essence of things but of the concrete formation of things. In the second place they would all unhesitatingly accept that their theory clearly does not explain all the 'aspects' and relations of the distribution process. For example it clearly does not explain the emergence of the system of waged work or its cultural consequences and presuppositions, or the extent to which that system either develops or is blocked by ethical, legal, etc. limitations, or the way it is maintained from the organisational point of view, or a great deal of other related matters. From here it is no great distance to the view that for economic theory – or for the chapter of a wider economic theory which these authors are the ones to cover – incomes in general are to be considered as value and price phenomena.

This starting-point is far from being peculiar to marginal productivity theory. What is peculiar to that theory is only that by means of a particular analysis it was put into a position to explain the essence and the law of values and prices on the basis of the productive role of individual means of production, from the prices of which incomes are put together, and to deduce that essence and law from the law of marginal utility. The fact that constitutes this starting-point has in fact never been denied and can never be denied, even by those who consider that the conclusions drawn from it by marginal utility theory are mistaken. For example Tugan-Baranovskii, to whom this last remark applies, not only acknowledges the obvious fact that income formation takes place in the outward form of price formation, but concedes to 'productivity'[21] at very many points an influence on income formation, and indeed the existence of some kind of connection between the two is implicitly accepted even by authors who do everything to tear them apart or at least avoid giving the connection any emphasis, as for example the representatives of the most primitive kind of wage fund theory.[22] The only debatable thing here is the assertion that incomes are the prices of 'productive activities', and the truth is that resistance to this assumption has all along been the result of incompetence rather than sheer bloody-mindedness. In the context of the general standpoint of the classical economists there was no fundamental reason in principle why such a basic idea should have been ignored – it had been stated by Say and by others before him: it was simply that no-one could see how to build anything on it. It is quite false to argue that the classical economists fully recognised the significance of the utility value factor but did not bother to say so because they thought it self-evident; and it is equally false to argue that the principle of incomes being the prices of productive activities is irrefutable but has been ignored simply because it is so self-evident and banal. There is a parallel here with the argument that is always being put forward in the value discussions of the 'classical school' – that utility value cannot be crucial for 'market value' because things of very great utility value often have little or no market value; the appeal to this argument merely demonstrates that its advocates have no idea how to tackle the subject. A quite similar argument is put forward against the productivity idea – namely that all production factors are necessary for production and so there cannot be any distinguishable product of the individual production factor; but again, the use of this argument merely demonstrates that its proponents have completely missed the point about the marginal utility theory. The marginal utility theory actually contains the answer to the objections concealed in both arguments – objcctions reducible in the last analysis to a single one.

Now since these objections have in fact been answered, it would be a misunderstanding of the whole situation if we were to regard the classical viewpoints as equally valid rivals of the marginal productivity theory, rivals that were preferred to it by their authors in a free vote on several options, rivals that were equally valid from the theoretical viewpoint. If today we are going to reject the productivity idea in the particular form that involves basing income formation on price theory and hence on the law of marginal utility, we cannot just baldly deny it. We have to offer specific reasons for doubting the structure of the theory or else show that other factors than those involved in it explain the essence and the law of incomes. The most important of these other factors are 'the social relations of power'.[23]

Now it is clear from the outset that this expression, properly understood,[24] has much more to say and much profounder things to say not only about 'distribution' but generally about all economic phenomena than can be yielded by our reference to the value and price mechanism, whose circle of reference is so narrow as to exclude virtually all the great facts of the destiny of peoples. The social relations of power – again, in the best and richest sense of this much abused slogan – are the dyestuff with which the panorama of history is coloured. And if we wanted to adopt the artist's approach and sketch out just the leading features of this panorama so as to stamp them on the mind of the observer, then 'power' and 'sexual egoism' would ultimately be just the job. In its initial phase every science tries to do this kind of thing. For the discovery of the multiplicity of objects of knowledge is fundamentally a very bitter pill and people are not keen to swallow it, nor do they do so immediately: – the object of knowledge is pale and shadowy and it is much more attractive to absorb oneself in the fullness of life. But if we reach the point where objects of knowledge become distinguishable, then we have to face up to the necessity of treating each one in isolation if we want to push on any further. What this means in practice here is that while the classical economists, for all the abstractness with which they are reproached, still sought to encapsulate in their theory a picture of the social classes and their struggles based on the struggles of their own time, we for our part no longer pursue such an aim within the framework of theory – or if we do it renders our work worthless. In particular we need to be clear what aspect of the distribution problem is to be dealt with and what we expect from a theory of distribution. It is obviously not going to provide any sort of practical remedy, nor of course can a general theory directly generate any kind of historical account or even a simple concrete situation-picture. But in this connection few people want to face up to the fact that we cannot accept any social psychology and especially not any sociology of 'distribution' *uno actu* with the economics of distribution. The *uno actu* qualification is crucial of course: the theories of social psychology and the theories of sociology are necessary: of course we need different theories about the formation of social classes and about the essence and driving forces of forms of social organisation. Their conclusions are of course related – as data – to the area of 'economic' problems, the range of problems that we have always preferred that name for even though the economic factor also governs wide areas that lie outside of it. Economics is concerned with showing how the process of daily economic life and its special phenomena are to be explained within given or all forms of organisation. This is all that economic theorists want to do and no-one can be reproached on the grounds that when dealing with one problem, he fails to resolve another one at the same time that is so complex as to make particular treatment necessary. These are self-evident truths indeed, but if such obvious truths are persistently ignored the result is endless confusion.

There is however an entirely different question to be asked as to whether economics has enough autonomy *vis-à-vis* sociology – or, more particularly, whether the distribution problem has enough autonomy *vis-à-vis* power relations in general – to enable it to be studied in isolation: i.e. – do the social relations of power countermand 'value and price laws' and somehow determine the 'distribution of return on production' directly? Only if we answer this question in the negative do we find ourselves in conflict with the commonly-held opinion as represented here by Tugan-Baranovskii. I have already observed that the question is not a methodological one but a matter simply of the rightness or wrongness of a particular material claim. I emphasise this point because to portray a question as methodological makes it easier to dismiss the argument of the opponent from the start – something which easily takes debates in economics right away from the problem at issue (though this is certainly not the way Tugan-Baranovskii proceeds).

In the first place: If the forms of organisation of the economy cannot be explained with reference to 'economic' theory but only in 'sociological' terms, i.e. by facts generally designated as the 'social relations of power' – in which the economic factor does of course play a part, only a very different part from the one ascribed to it by theory with its value and price mechanism; and if moreover there is for each of these forms of organisation a particular corresponding form of economy –

what scope is left for a theory that 'ignores all that'? The answer is simple: it does not ignore all that, it includes what it sees as the real characteristics of each form of organisation among its presuppositions, in order to investigate the course of the economic process in each of them. The particular nature of its task, by contrast with the task of explaining the emergence of forms of organisation and their characteristics, etc., depends on the fact that the course of the economic process is not itself directly explained by the explanation of the emergence and the characteristics of forms of organisation; rather it is a matter of showing how economic life develops within each form of organisation. In other words each form of organisation has its economic consequences, but none decides sovereignly of itself about these consequences, which depend much more on other groups of causes such as milieu, technology, etc. Among these other groups of causes there are also certain fundamental facts of the requirements of living and economic behaviour and it is these that 'economic theory' investigates. It would be as reasonable to suppose that economies are governed by climate, for example, as it would be to suppose that they are governed by 'relations of power'. Each is correct in the same sense and each is inadequate in the same sense: relations of power 'dictate', but how these dictats operate depends on many factors other than relations of power. There are other 'data' for the study of each of the distinguishable complexes of causes and there is a particular methodologically autonomous theory for each. Now when economic theory studies the course of the economy in the different types of forms of organisation, it emerges in fact that certain fundamental laws are valid for all. What they are and what their consequences are cannot be stated generally but only from the standpoint of the whole structure of each theoretical system and the particular content of each theoretical principle. It should however be noted that differences in economic terminology, forms of law, etc., peculiar to the different forms of organisation do not intrinsically entail different explanations of the economic phenomenon that they conceal: things may look very different from the outside in terms of their economic nature but yet remain 'still the same', i.e. they may be traced back in the last analysis to the same explanatory principles. In particular income formation in the price war is surely a phenomenon that is found only in the market economy. But the question whether its categories – wages, rent, interest, etc. – are 'economic' or 'historico–legal' is settled in favour of the latter alternative only in a very superficial sense, namely in the sense that they exist only in a market economy as categories of private law and only in this sort of economy does private law protect the private connection of rent, wages, interest, etc. precisely to the advantage of the persons who have control over the relevant means of production in this form of legal order. Nothing is learned here about the broader question of the essence of this income sector, and we can still clearly demonstrate that it is to be explained on the basis of a principle that is valid for other forms of organisation too – even if with other concrete consequences and in another guise. As Böhm-Bawerk emphasised in the article quoted [1914], therein lies the meaning and the justification of what Clark called 'functional' by contrast with 'personal' distribution and the difference between the essence of the return on a production factor and the obtaining of this return by given persons. Therefore theory habitually refers to the 'productive activities' of productive factors and not to the productive activities of the possessors of these factors. If Adam Smith had grasped this distinction he would never have been able to say that where the worker has no employer on whom he depends, and there is absolutely no subjection of the worker to different persons, any return is work income; and he would have recognised that there is a sense in which there can be 'distribution' of the whole return to different 'income sectors' even in the economy of a Robinson Crusoe – namely in the sense that here too a valuation of the means of production is formed which is ultimately analogous to those on which income formation rests in the market economy. If Tugan-Baranovskii had accepted this distinction, which may be linked to any sociological or political viewpoint, his analysis would really have swept all before it.

All this may be illustrated by the example of ground rent. 'Pure' or 'economic' ground rent has no basis in any work activity or in any other different activity on the part of the landowner. If we explain it in the manner of the marginal productivity theory as determined by the 'marginal product' of the soil, we have not done anything at all to show proof of any 'productivity' on the part of the landowners. It is perfectly obvious that in a Communist community ground rent would not be the perquisite of any particular group of persons. Yet there is good reason to regard it as a pure economic category in terms of its economic essence. For even in a Communist community the return corresponding to it would exist, and though from another standpoint it may be said to be 'created by' work, the leadership of such a community must be clear that on control over the individual land element depends that element of return which in the market economy would form ground rent, and on control of all of the land would depend the whole social return on productivity. They must also be clear that in respect of the goals of economic behaviour the same thing would apply to that as to the the production factor of work, which would be on the same lines as the production factor of land, for there would obviously be no sense in ignoring the marginal productive significance of land and thereby the fact that it is an economic and not a free good. In the modern social order these elements of return fall to the landowner, while in a socialist order they would be available for all – but the economic essence of the thing would clearly be the same in both cases.

Now it is interesting that Tugan-Baranovskii recognises this up to a point, even if it is from the standpoint of the Ricardian theory of ground rent that he puts forward.[25] He explains ground rents on the basis of differences in natural conditions in agricultural production and expressly states that there is no direct connection between their level and the social relations of power since they can only be influenced indirectly by the latter through a change in the conditions of agricultural production. This standpoint is identical to that of all other theorists. And I note the extent of our agreement with all the more pleasure in that the opposite was to be expected from the outset for the case of ground rent, the obtaining of which is the consequence of a property position that no doubt partly rests on 'relations of power'. If ground rent is a creation of relations of power only indirectly and in something other than a purely economic sense, if Tugan-Baranovskii – in opposition to a long series of authors of similar tendency – can describe the role that relations of power play in it so appositely, and indeed recognise so clearly that a simple reference to the 'power factor' achieves virtually nothing to the point and that the economic explanation can arise only from economic factors – must the same result not be obtained *a fortiori* with other kinds of income? To the extent that Ricardo's thought seeks to be a special explanation of ground rent, it suffers from the very great weakness that it may be applied word for word to other production factors as well as to land, for the special case of which Ricardo only actually stated what is in fact valid generally. And Tugan-Baranovskii's argument about the merely indirect influence of power relations is just as much right for the former as for the latter, even though he limits himself to the case of the latter, in which the facts 'of external nature' appear as specially imperious: but the facts of external nature never explain a price phenomenon on their own, quite apart from the fact that the technical necessities of production do not make themselves felt solely in agricultural production.[26] The arguments that Tugan-Baranovskii puts forward against the purely economic explanation of wages and interest would if successful be equally damaging to the pure economic explanation of ground rent – and indeed more so.

I will consider the especially suitable example of interest on capital in order to emphasise a few particularly relevant points. First of all we see that the question whether we are dealing here with an economic or historico – legal category, with a creation of 'economic necessity'[27] or a 'dictat of social power', understood in their customary sense, requires a different answer depending on which interest theory is preferred. The only sure thing is that interest – like ground rent – would exist in the form of sums paid to private possessors of capital or as a type of income accruing to them in the economic process only in a market economy[28] and that, if we want to apply the word 'interest' only to the obtaining of this private interest, it is a historico – legal category: since no-one has denied this – and we must distinguish between it and the assertion that its abolition would have certain 'damaging' consequences – the theorist who speaks of 'interest in the socialist state' can of course only mean that what in the market economy is devoted to interest income for the capitalists, would in the socialist state be present as an amount of profit. This is correct whether we follow the so-called productivity theory[29] of interest or the abstinence theory or the speculation theory: there would be a surplus value of the produced means of production and potentially of the consumption good over and above the value of the work actually contained in it in the socialist state too, and this surplus – the fact that the production managers of the socialist state value the produced means of production correspondingly higher – would be based on the knowledge that more depends on the possession of these goods than what corresponds to the investment of labour in them. This would be highly relevant for the conduct and book-keeping of the socialist society and at the same time would lead to the establishment of an income element accruing to society – going of course to the 'workers' but not as workers – even though this would not necessarily be evident as such in relation to the individual comrade. Interest would thus be an economic category and to recognise that it is the same in all forms of organisation would be important not only for our understanding of the world of the economic but also for practical reasons. However, if my theory of interest were to be accepted,[30] the situation would be different. The return which in the capitalist economic process is interest would still be present in the socialist process and would need explanation – since the explanation that it is present because it has been produced gets us nowhere[31] –

but this explanation would be found in that greater overall value which is for the employer's profit[32] in the capitalist economy, for there would still be an element of this in the Communist community – though not a distinguishable element. In my opinion it would thus simply disappear as a category from the socialist state and its managers would not have any practical reason to be known as anything in particular. On this view then interest would be a historico–legal category.

This it would also be according to Marx's exploitation theory, though in another sense again: what is return on capital in the capitalist economy would in the socialist economy just remain as an indistinguishable part of the product of labour, from which it had eliminated the private ownership of the means of production. But Marx has something important to teach us here. Of course he is one of those who have put great emphasis on the power factor, and no-one could complain that he underrated or excluded it. But does he consider it sufficient to explain interest all on its own? No, he does not, and any attempt to construct something in the economic arena on the basis of a mere reference to 'power', and especially any attempt to explain surplus value – and so any attempt to make profit on capital arise directly through social relations of power – he clearly acknowledged to be flawed, and thereby he made a real advance in this area of thought, an advance which would unfortunately be rejected by many writers – including Tugan-Baranovskii and Diehl. In Marx surplus value derives from the mechanism of market value, and so from purely economic thought, and the same place is in principle allotted by him to the power factor as in the system of the marginal productivity theory: the place of an assumption, the content of which, though a starting-point, is not an element of much more methodical economic reasonings of quite another kind, and the discussion of which is a subject all by itself. However private ownership of the means of production may have arisen, however the power dictates that protect it are explained, the surplus value theory always remains the same and no sociological – 'power' or other – factors change anything as to its theoretical meaning, which can be discussed quite independently of them. If you read his bold condemnation of all earlier exploitation theories, which many people are now simply falling back on, you will again see how much further on he was than our time. There is ample further evidence of this fact elsewhere in his writings.

So then we have the result I have been aiming at: as generally understood, the broad question 'economic or historico–legal categories?' makes absolutely no sense. All income sectors and generally all the things with which theory has to do are at once both 'economic' and 'historico–legal', governed both by economic laws and by the social relations of power. This does not however mean that the two somehow stand alongside each other and that with the coordinated help of both we can get to an economic result. It means that each deals with a different range of problems, that their results are data for each other, that within each individual range of problems methodological autonomy is the rule and that we cannot resolve the specific problems of the one by an appeal to the other; on the contrary, such an appeal may totally confuse the issue and end up concealing the absence of a solution.

To the extent that the social power factor goes together with the factor of social organisation of economics, we might justifiably consider the controversy to be over and recognise as equally justified though in different senses the two apparently contradictory but nonetheless mutually compatible affirmations: (1) 'Economic life is the creation of social relations of power', and (2) 'Economic life is the creation of economic necessities'.

Up to a point this would take account of Stammler's view for example, of the standpoint of sociology and of that of economics as well. There would be no argument about general questions of principle or method but only about matters of detail – namely the question whether something that seems a capitalistic category in the capitalist economy might also turn out to be distinguishable in the communist economy. As we have seen, the answers would always be dependent on the actual content of the explanation of this capitalist 'something', and that in turn could be decided only by means of theory and within theory.

But for most of those who speak of relations of power within the economic sphere, and especially for Diehl and Tugan-Baranovskii, the influence of relations of power is far from exhausted in the formation of a form of organisation. For them the power factor comes out of its 'data role' to influence (directly and not simply through the formation of preconditions) the results of the economic process, in particular the market struggle and more specifically income formation. On this last point the power factor would not merely regulate in principle the conditions for the control of the means of production (or rather the way the social means of production is controlled) and create certain legal containers for the flow of the social return on production of which economic life would avail itself; it would also determine the results of 'distribution' – especially the relative level of incomes, not behind but alongside 'value and price laws' and potentially in their place. We are dealing with a slogan so often appealed to that it threatens to degenerate into a vague phrase inimical to any rigour in economic thought, but what I have said must express its meaning in essence, if it is actually to have a precise meaning and be available to oppose the prevailing theory.

Now it is quite clear that the social power factor can intervene directly in this way in the results of the economy, quite apart from the fact that individual valuations are 'socially conditioned' and in a way subjected to social influences which could ultimately be brought under the heading of 'the concept of power', so that one can certainly not simply conceive them as 'ultimate causes'. Examples of such a direct influence are tax arrangements intended to apply the tax yield to old age pensions for workers, statutory price and wage levels, etc. ... Moreover social and political relations of power exercise pressure on the conduct of individuals even where there is no legal regulation, so that for example they often prevent a monopolist from setting the price most advantageous to himself. The phenomenon of social prestige is very important here: if some servant girl from the country approaches her 'master' with such a feeling of subordination and such a fear of speaking that she does not for example dare to terminate her contract of service, it is clear that the fixing of wage levels cannot be a matter of the 'free play of economic forces'. All such (in practice of course often exceptionally important) cases have always been recognised by economics as facts, even though not every economist has used them as ballast for his theoretical studies. The role of theory is thus limited to the study of the economic meaning of processes – governed by relations of power but for that reason not yet explained in their essence – and to the consequences of such dictates of power, but the theoretical wage level then has only the same meaning as the law of gravity for a stone on a table. In the name of good scientific thinking we can renounce any investigation of arguments which manufacture 'objections' out of facts such as these.

There is nothing of any consequence here then, and the power factor would have to manifest itself in other ways if it were to be an element in theoretical thinking to 'exclude' which would be an 'error'. But this it does not do. The story of attempts to prove a direct influence like this is a story of horrendous errors of judgement. It is a matter for astonishment and discomfort that (for example) even a specialist with such strongly theoretical interests as Karl Diehl (e.g. p. 605) thinks he can contradict the marginal productivity theory of wages with the remark 'that the wages paid for identical work are at different levels depending on whether labour is organised or not'; and he continues: 'What is the issue here? From the purely economic point of view the work is identical, but the wages paid are different because of the differences in the social relations of power.' So is it a refutation of theory that if the supply of a good is monopolised it reaches a higher price than when it is supplied in free competition? Can a monopolistic or quasi-monopolistic price formation be beyond the grasp of theory, considering that theory's most fully-developed chapter is its teaching about monopolies? And does marginal productivity play no part in monopolistic price formation, when monopolistic price formation for consumption goods is based on the marginal utility law? I shall be returning to these questions later, but two things are already clear: firstly, that we do not need the power factor in the case under discussion, because theory is perfectly up to the task. Secondly, if theory were to be found wanting in this case, we could not supply the missing explanation by appealing to power relations. In fact we would be left with no explanation, for 'relations of power' have no contribution to make.

That we have no need of the power factor, however accessible and available it may seem to be, can be demonstrated best of all perhaps in Oppenheimer's system. In this system 'ownership by force' of land as a creation of relations of power has a crucially important role. In his mind 'relations of power' are the complete explanation of this ownership by force itself, but only economic theory explains its consequences, and in that area 'ownership by force' is an irrelevance. The fundamental issue is the fact of a monopoly of land. Granted that this fact exists – which however is not the case – then the pure economic theory of monopoly – and not the power factor – provides the explanation for what Oppenheimer would conclude from his ownership by force: this means we can say that he makes no more use of the power factor than any other theorist. Whether or not his own system is challengeable, it does nothing to encourage the use of the power factor in economic thought. That the same goes for Stolzmann – for his doctrine and his critique alike (leaving aside the fact that both are very erroneous in every point and neither can be maintained from any standpoint) – I have shown in another place.[33]

The most significant of the points at which many theorists grasp for the 'power factor' is in the theory of interest. The way most of them want to use it is first of all to show that interest as an independent source of income results from the direct impact of the power factor. But I have already noted that what is worth retaining in all these attempts was noted once and for all by Marx. Moreover he gave an exemplary demonstration of the meshing together of the power factor and the economic factors in his wage theory: first of all a masterly picture in glowing colours of the emergence of the army of workers (the most detailed research has been able to change very little in this) – and economic thought is thereby anchored in particular modern capitalist sociological data. But then this thought itself follows in its full methodological rigour: always adapted to the concrete social conditions of the time, but always mastering them theoretically, never simply appealing to them. As he put it: 'Force is the midwife for every old society that is pregnant with a new one, and it is itself an economic power.'

But this economic power was never for him the *deus ex machina* which had to do the work he himself could not do, and he was well aware of its precise place in the explanation of social being. If we had only grasped this model properly, Dühring for example would never have been able to conclude that the principles of economic theory were inadequate to cope with the distribution problem, on the grounds that the facts of men's social and community membership of an economic area as explained historically and politically are indispensable to an understanding of distribution, and that we must first eliminate 'ownership by force' before we can ascertain the 'natural laws' of the economy. Nor would Oppenheimer have been able to conclude that the principle that 'it is not economic relations between free men with equal rights but political relations between conquerors and subjects that have created social and economic classes' – correct as far as it goes – resolves some sort of economic problem. Nor would Lexis have been able to conclude that the source of the slave owner's profit is 'unmistakable' – i.e. that there are no questions to be raised about the basis of the emergence of his slave property, etc. Finally, Albrecht[34] would never have been able to criticise theory for getting so bogged down in the question of what part in the overall result of production the individual production factors bring to their owners, while saying nothing about why these particular persons are owners of these production factors: a 'weakness' in theory that only exists to the extent that mastery of production factors is to be explained by what theory views as non-economic factors, and a weakness which to that extent is very natural.

To grasp all this is to comprehend how totally unfounded is the view that the problem of income formation has a special position because of the supposed influence of the power factor, and how little is achieved by an appeal to this view. Moreover we can now appreciate that if it makes some general affirmation, any explanation of income formation which works with the power factor must (implicitly at least) contain theoretical thinking of a pure kind in addition to whatever assertion it contains about the sociological data of the distribution problem; any such explanation is thus verified by means of theory and there can be no deviation towards sociology. Finally we come to grasp the fact that we may not discuss the relationship between 'power' and economic law as a relationship involving parallel actions along the same lines, but only as the consecutive actions of different links in the chain of social causation; and although these do all influence one another in the overall connectedness of things, they are nonetheless autonomous from the methodological standpoint. If I may recur to an analogy which expresses the essence of the matter for the purposes of economic theory (though not for the purposes of a sociological overview): it is of course quite fair to say that the success of a player in a card game depends on luck, but only in a game of pure chance would this explanation of a concrete result be sufficient. Otherwise the influence of luck is confined to the distribution of the cards. Beyond that the result is to be explained by the player's actions; for each game such actions can be articulated in certain formal rules, and they alone decide which of the results that are generally possible within the given distribution of cards actually occurs. The relationship between dictates of power and economic law in economic life is the same as the relationship between the distribution of the cards and gambling technique in card-playing.

This has implicitly at least always been the view of all theorists, and it is not vulnerable to Tugan-Baranovskii's attack, so that in the capitalist economy incomes can continue to be understood as value and price phenomena in the only sense in which that could have ever generally been affirmed. This is particularly easy to demonstrate in respect of a man of Tugan-Baranovskii's fairness and insight, for it is perfectly simple to show that the barriers he erects between himself and theory (which he judges very generously and which he would be highly competent to extend) are very far from being insurmountable.

His starting-point is that in the distribution process there is not (as in the market for consumption goods) an encounter between undifferentiated masses of buyers and sellers, but an encounter between social classes whose relative power is so crucial that the distribution process falls right outside the group of facts which value and price theory can satisfactorily describe. But even if we admit that there exists a social class togetherness within the parties that encounter one another in the markets for productive activities – so that the concept of social class coincides with the result of the old classification of economic subjects into workers, landowners and capitalists – does it not correspond to the basic idea of the capitalist economic order essentially to abandon the individual to his own devices and to allocate to each person in the distribution process what he can grab in the price war, so must income formation not therefore be explicable either in terms of price theory or not at all?

In Tugan-Baranovskii the greater economic power of 'the owners' manifests itself in the only factor in which it can manifest itself – control of the means of production. In his thought this economic power appears to be both the cause of this control and also its consequence, but in fact the nature of power is very different in the two cases. As the cause of the control of the means of production it may consist in the possibility of establishing or maintaining oneself in ownership through physical force. As a consequence of the control over the means of production it is clearly something else – namely the possibility of making an income through the sale of 'uses' of those means. There is admittedly the further possibility that derives from this one of influence over law-giving, etc., but it hardly needs to be emphasised in relation to a theorist of the rank of Tugan-Baranovskii that this obviously cannot be any part of economic thinking; apart from that, ownership of the means of production does not bring with it any other power. The essence and extent of this power is of course completely dependent on the productive significance of the means of production in question, so that even from Tugan-Baranovskii's standpoint the explanation of ownership income should arise from this productive significance. This is true even if we acknowledge the reality of that first kind of power, which I will accept here even though the truth is that not all land ownership (still less all capital ownership) is actually explicable in these terms. Only if it is stated that capitalists and landowners do not acquire their income by selling the use of their means of production, but simply take it by force (so that they would not initially need to possess any sort of means of production) could we speak of power apart from and outside the productive meaning of the means of production, thus of power in the true sense as an element of the distribution process; otherwise power would only be the ground of explanation of certain data of this process. On this assumption Tugan-Baranovskii's way of looking at the problem would be fully in line with normal usage and he could only get to the solution by means of value and price theory.

However Tugan-Baranovskii clearly thinks that the social relations of power also enter directly into the process of income formation, which would invalidate the laws of value and price. He finds the entry point for their influence in the tactical position of the working class, an unfavourable one because of its needy position *vis-à-vis* another more powerful (i.e. richer) class; because of its exclusion from the existing means of production and thereby from further production potential, the working class is prevented from appearing as a partner with equal rights in the wage contract, but has to submit to the power of the capitalist, which then leads to the emergence of return on capital. This is based on the expectation that the worker is a poor devil who must more or less take what is given to him. In order to focus on what is the crucial issue for theoretical thinking, I shall not engage in any discussion of whether it is generally true to say that the workers are always in a weaker position in the exchange struggle. I will simply take that for granted, since to begin with it clearly does not mean that price laws are out of the reckoning – it only means that they involve the special condition that one of the parties in the exchange presents a particularly pressing offer and 'cannot hold out so long' as the other. There would be nothing odd about the labour market in this, for every market has its peculiarity, but that does not mean that general price laws are therefore inapplicable to it. Secondly, it is clear that the consequence of this peculiarity could be established only by way of the price theory, as is strikingly proved by Tugan-Baranovskii's own presentation. For the result that Tugan-Baranovskii deduces from it, namely exploitation and a necessary surplus in favour of the capitalists, would in fact inevitably follow from it only if the capitalists were organised monopolistically. That is however generally not the case, and it is all to the credit of our author that he rejects the abuse of monopoly thinking that has become so popular again today and limits the monopoly factor to the exceptional case where in a backward area a company really does have a monopoly position and thereby obtains a still greater surplus. Outside of this case however it is not really so self-evident that the unfavourable position of the worker always does guarantee a profit for the capitalist entrepreneur, and one of the most essential material objections against the teaching of the eminent Russian theorist is that he fails to provide proof of that assumption. The question will be tackled in what follows, but for the moment I only want to establish that no appeal to power relations can by itself alone prove this – or any other – economic consequence of such power relations. In particular it is the case that ownership won by force does not explain income obtained by force: explain ownership of the means of production in terms of violence to your heart's content, there still has to be a further explanation of how this violence and its consequence, i.e. this property, leads to an income. Our author admits this up to a point when he says that rates of profit are fixed by supply and demand (1913, p. 79), which in conjunction with his adherence in principle to the theory of imputation (1913, pp. 52–3) means much more than he is himself inclined to accept. In this respect it matters little that he counters the thesis that 'profit' is based on the specific productivity of the capital factor by claiming that profit is a category of distribution and 'hence' rests on social relations of power, or by saying that ownership is based on force, which means that if it is an income from ownership, 'profit' must be dependent on social relations of power. Thirdly it is clear that even if the social relations of power actually governed income formation directly, the marginal productivity theory would still have meaning: for it still represents the standard by which deviations caused by the power factor might be measured.

I must now tackle an argument of Tugan-Baranovskii's that is quite simply wrong. In his view the pure economic explanation of income formation also falls down in that workers and capitalists can compete only as inferiors and superiors and not on a level. The cotton magnate who finds the price of his product too low can start producing something else and begin purchasing what he himself previously produced, but the worker cannot: he cannot transform himself into a capitalist. Again I will take it that this is a valid assumption, and thus accept that there could not really be any question of real competition between labour and capital, and hence no question of any competition between workers and capitalists. But in the first place it can be shown that this circumstance is quite irrelevant since in every market buyers obviously compete only with buyers and sellers only with sellers, without this preventing the establishment of a perfectly fixed equilibrium state in the economic i.e. price-theoretical sense. The mobility of labour and capital between the individual sectors is moreover fully sufficient for the existence of both 'commercial' and 'industrial' competition in Cairnes' sense. In the second place, if this phenomenon was important, it would apply in just the same sense to capital and labour alike, with no real possibility of any advantage for the former: for capital too there is only mobility between the sectors, and capital cannot transform itself into living work nor take the position of the workers (if we ignore the possibility in Tugan-Baranovskii's sense of replacing work by capital). What Tugan-Baranovskii's cotton magnate does – namely go over to another sector – any worker can do too; and it leads to losses for the cotton magnate and for the worker alike. In the third place, the cotton magnate can certainly abandon his production if the price in the sector becomes unviable, but this operation only has sense if the viability is less than in other sectors of industry; capital can only avoid partially unfavourable conditions and not universally unfavourable ones. The capitalist cannot in general give up production without coming into precisely the same situation of need as the unemployed worker, so that the position of each party in this relation is absolutely the same.

Here we can again see that only price theory can decide whether the circumstance in question is relevant and what consequences it has, so that we are back to theoretical problems, perhaps even (under particular conditions) purely economic ones. Therefore it is pointless to try to explain 'profit' on the basis of 'force' and to attribute primarily to force the surplus value of capital from which marginal productivity theory somehow (there are many different views) derives 'profit'. Tugan-Baranovskii's thinking is simple. Labour produces, the 'force' of the owners takes from labour a part of the product, and the fact that this can happen gives the means of force (capital) its value. The argument fails when we know that the force spoken of here is not the social or physical force involved in the obtaining and keeping of control over the means of production but the position linked to its ownership. The only content this position has however is what is given it by the level of necessity of the means of production for production, and thus its productive role or its marginal productivity. Only the marginal utility theory fully explains the fact that the workers have this 'power' in principle even though sometimes one, sometimes the other party is the stronger in the exchange struggle. For the workers too have an indispensable means of production and while it is true that they are unable to produce without the help of the capitalists it is equally true that the capitalists cannot produce without their help. This power is thus only another name for the relative marginal significance of the material means of production and the circular nature of Tugan-Baranovskii's thinking would become crystal clear if this concept were substituted for the word 'force', which has only a transferred sense here.

In saying this I am not unaware that from the point of view of economics the situation would have the same essential features if the workers and the capitalists were the same persons – if for example capital was shared out among the workers. Such a society would of course look very different socially and sociologically from ours, but the principles of the economic understanding of things would be just the same. The 'workers' would have 'power' to 'exploit' one another according to the law of marginal productivity of the material means of production, just as they in fact 'exploit' one another already in the case of present-day society according to the marginal productivity of labour. Such exploitation would not be of a class nature and there would be no grounds for moral condemnation of it from Tugan-Baranovskii's standpoint, but the economic meaning and the economic cause of income formation would be the same; and the factor of force would play the same role in principle. Tugan-Baranovskii repeatedly states that in principle he distinguishes between large-scale and small-scale ownership of land and capital. From the sociological point of view he is right. Even from the economic point of view he would be right if he were thinking of the case where an individual's or an organisation's land and capital ownership is so massive that they have a monopoly or quasi-monopoly position. But this is not what he means, for he ascribes to each case of large-scale land and capital ownership – to the land and capital ownership which brings in income apart from work – a particular role in principle. But all land and capital ownership does this, and the worker-capitalists of our case would have income elements apart from work that would be explicable exactly as general income apart from work is in our social order. Tugan-Baranovskii of course understands the income of peasants and craftsmen as a single work income, and reproaches theory for neglecting this kind of income, and yet that is in fact just what theory does not do, for no theorist would deny the numerous special features of this income. In principle theory simply recognises that it is quite irrelevant from the economic viewpoint whether the craftsman combines his capital with his labour or lends his capital out and exploits his labour in a factory. In economic terms his situation is just like that of someone who is both a civil servant and the possessor of capital. What would be the point of calling the income of a man who has a salary of £10,000 and share dividends of another £10,000 per year a work income of £20,000? The two cases are vastly different in terms of development history and the sociology of income forms. What is to be gained by mixing up the sociological and the economic viewpoints? Furthermore we can quote Tugan-Baranovskii's own remarks as a contradiction of his own view. In his discussion of the 'labour theory' of 'profit' he puts forward as an argument against it the fact that profit varies with the amount of capital invested, but elsewhere he observes that the size of a peasant's income depends on the extent of his landed property!

Finally if we recognise the nature of the 'force' which is supposed to be the only real explanation of income formation, we can say that Tugan-Baranovskii's statement that profit depends on the productivity of labour and the relative power of the capitalist class is perfectly reconcilable with the marginal productivity theory. By the productivity of labour he understands physical productivity and therefore – because he ascribes overall productivity only to labour (which of course terminologically he is free to do) – simply the amount of the social product. Yet the relative power of the capitalist class is nothing but the expression of the relative importance of a marginal amount of capital – for that is the only content of the economic power of property over the economy and the weapon in which it is concretised – and so Tugan-Baranovskii's principle coincides with the principle of marginal productivity theory, which offers scope for many internal theoretical controversies and can lead to very different explanations of interest. 'Profit' in fact depends on the size of the social product and the relative marginal productivity of capital. Since our author clearly does not reject the theory of imputation, all the assumptions are thus in place for him to be claimed as a supporter of the marginal utility theory in the area of the distribution problem too. And that is perfectly natural, for it is certainly not necessary to overestimate the worth of the marginal utility theory to see that in this question the modern scientific situation speaks pressingly in its favour. We may try to direct scientific interest towards other questions, we may conceal the facts of the matter by stressing other factors or another terminology or by exaggerating related things – eventually we always come to the conclusion that we set out to combat. If we have acknowledged the shortcomings of the Marxian exploitation theory though, it would really be a bad way out to revert (as all authors do who appeal to the power factor in the economic thought process) to a pre-Marxian position; just because we cannot accept Marx's analysis it would be a terrible mistake to go back to a conception whose inadequacy was clearly seen by Marx. Nor is such a step essential for anyone to be able to make moral or other assessments of 'exploitation', for a moral condemnation of interest income may also be attached to marginal productivity theory.

III Foundations of the Wage Theory

From the standpoint of economic theory then, 'distribution processes' are thus only an artificially separated group of price problems that are where necessary picked out of the general system of mutually dependent quantities of goods or values on practical grounds, so that detailed results mostly derive from the insertion of particular data into general theoretical thinking. In the same way, however the wage system arose and whatever the place of subjection to which it may reduce the worker, the wage problem[1] too is primarily only a similarly special case of value and price theory, a wage is primarily the price of a good and is to be explained in just the same way as the price of all other goods.

Two points to begin with: first, labour was earlier often regarded as a product, which led people to speak of its production costs. But since it is obvious that men are never produced according to economic principles as goods are, and since therefore there is no necessary connection between a wage and the education costs of a man, even if there is sometimes a remote factual connection between them, this view has generally been abandoned today. The national stock of labour is now regarded as a datum – admittedly in part also determined by economic factors, but not by the economic connection described by pure theory – just like the existing stock of raw materials and natural forces, together with which the existing amount of labour in this respect forms a category of goods. It is true that the working population in an economic area is not constant like the quantity of the pictures painted by a dead master (which is the old paradigm for this category of goods), but it is also not variable like other goods through production but changeable according to its own laws, so that from the standpoint of the theoretical system it behaves in the same way as goods that are present in absolutely constant quantities. The second point is this: at least to the extent that we are talking about their industrial application by contrast to 'personal services', labour belongs to the category of goods which do not satisfy needs directly but only indirectly, in that they contribute to the creation of consumption goods. By analogy with a primitive money theory it could be suggested that the price of labour is determined precisely by the valuation that purchasers of 'personal services' set on them: just as the viewpoint was adopted that the value of money is determined in the use of money by the value of gold in its use, it could clearly also be asserted that the valuation of the 'personal services' is directly given, because it causes the direct satisfactions of needs while the price of labour must obviously be the same in both kinds of use or must tend towards being the same, and consequently the value and price of labour in the one is determined with the price ('value in exchange') of the other. But the analogy would not be a great deal of use, because this theory of the value of money is untenable, and consequently no author has attempted to resolve the wage problem along these lines, and the marginal utility theory has in fact taken another direction. The starting-point was the indirect but none the less real use of labour as means of production, and from this was derived the subjective values of the existing resource of labour, on the basis of which the price of labour and thus wages arose in just the same way as the price of consumption goods, so that in this respect labour belongs in the general category of 'means of production'.

There is just one difference that should get a mention at this point. According to the theory of interest which is accepted in the context of the marginal productivity idea,[2] the price of labour corresponds to the full utility of labour or to the currently discounted value of that utility as attained at the completion of the production process. This last conception was introduced by Böhm-Bawerk and is represented not only by authors like Taussig who are in full agreement with his theory of interest but also by very many others (especially Fisher and Fetter) who defend more or less complete derivatives of Böhm-Bawerk's theory. But a discussion of this factor would take us too far out of our way.

This way of looking at theory is fraught with difficulties, which in the conditions in our area of work quickly turned into objections. Only a few of them can be dealt with here.

First of all there is the principle that wages are based on value and value on the productive role of labour, so unparadoxical that we might object to it simply on the grounds that it is self-evident – provided we do not make the mistake of thinking that obviousness automatically entails sterility: that would just be to demonstrate an inability to handle the instrument of the economic system. There is such a vast mass of obvious facts to support this principle that hardly anyone could possibly question whether the worker is paid because he is needed. And the fact that the degree of that need may occasionally be very limited – even though virtually nothing would exist without labour – is no more mysterious than the fact that we do not normally 'value' a litre of water very highly, even though we could not live without water. Yet there are still authors who consider that the application of the marginal utility idea to the means of production is impossible, arming themselves stubbornly against the frightful thought that the means of production might be seen as potential consumption goods, and above all resolutely refusing to admit that any differentiable part of the total product may be 'imputable' to labour. Insofar as this viewpoint turns even against the application of our approach to the case of the closed market producing only for its own consumption it will not be discussed any further here. It is pointless to deny the possibility of the solution of a problem if it has already been solved. It is equally pointless to deny that the manager of such a closed economy would assess the means of production according to its marginal utility and deal with it correspondingly, so that a scale of values could be read off for each of those means and hence also for labour.

But in a market economy the question arises as to how this way of looking at things can be defended in the face of the fact that as a rule neither the entrepreneur nor the worker can evaluate the utility of the company's product. Does it not therefore follow that neither the entrepreneur nor the worker can have that derived valuation of labour which in production for one's own needs would result from the use of the product, and that therefore the quantities of marginal utility which must settle wages in the exchange between entrepreneur and workers are zero for both parties?

For his part the entrepreneur is surely interested only in the level of his profit. All other amounts are of lesser importance to him and come under consideration only in their effect on the amount of profit. But the purchasers of the company's products have a valuation of their utility which the entrepreneur lacks and the price the entrepreneur will get depends on the monetary expression of this valuation of utility.[3] The means of production have value for him as a necessary means to obtain this income, so that his requirement for the means of production is a reflection of the consumers' requirement for consumption goods, and the scale of intensity of the demand for labour arises from this in accordance with the principle of the marginal significance of labour for the production result with the optimal[4] combination of all the means of production. The entrepreneur's whole position as viewed from the standpoint of pure theory (and we can again see the extent of the gulf that separates this standpoint from the sociological one) and the nature of his valuations is thus to be completely subsumed under the category of the position and the valuations of a middleman.

In a free market situation all entrepreneurs alike necessarily value the quantity of marginal labour equally highly in money terms in the sense that in equilibrium wages measure the marginal valuation of all entrepreneurs, i.e. as expressed in money the profit element dependent on a small amount of labour must be the same for all businesses. That this must be so arises from the consideration that otherwise individual amounts of labour would be applied less advantageously than they could be and a more intensive demand would remain unsatisfied, whereas a less intensive demand would be satisfied. That this can indeed be so and that it does not involve the absurdity that an hour of work is only as valuable for a craftsman as for a big businessman, arises directly if we simply reflect that we are talking here not just about valuations but about money expressions of valuations. Just as we can say that the price of bread measures the marginal utility of bread for the beggar as much as for the millionaire, because not only the penny but also the single piece of bread has very different subjective value for each and the relation between the value of the penny and that of the piece of bread can therefore very well be the same for each (though this simple state of affairs has commonly and deliberately been made into an objection against the marginal utility theory) so in our case in spite of all the difference in size and profitability of companies the same may be true. When in elementary presentations of theory there is talk of 'marginal entrepreneurs' and 'marginal companies', this has to be understood as a simplistic form of expression, and one that is very practical in the light of the fact that certain phenomena present more clearly in weaker companies than in others; but it should not make us forget that under free competition every undertaking touches the margins of productivity, while the marginal product is not realised in a single undertaking or the least intensive demand for labour concentrated in the weakest company.

Nor does the worker generally have any valuation of the worth of his own labour, not even a derivative valuation traceable back to an original one. But he has something else, namely a negative valuation of work (disutility) which must at least be compensated for by the satisfaction of needs guaranteed by wages. One might then be content to attribute to this factor the role which is usually played by valuation of the good to be given in exchange. But although it is true both for the individual worker and for the whole workforce of a particular category (even if in a rather different sense in all these cases) that the marginal utility of a wage tends to be approximately equivalent to the 'marginal disutility' of labour, this in fact constitutes just one of the determining grounds for the quantity of work offered. The economic behaviour of the worker cannot be understood solely by means of this instrument, since his weapon in the price war lies in the productivity of his labour and not in the circumstance that it is unpleasant to him. There would be another way again by an analogy with money theory, but this analogy must not be confused with the one already cited. Even though it is hopeless to try and explain the value of the money unit in terms of the value of money material in other applications, once this has settled into its role as money, one can very well see the value of money material in its 'commodity use' as the historical starting-point for the value movement, which then follows its wider destiny under the influence of both applications. Thus one could derive the value of labour genetically from the moment when the transition from production for one's own need – within which labour possessed its own (indirect productive) value for the worker – to the exchange economy, within which this is no longer the case. If we could adopt the view that the peasant, craftsman, etc. metamorphosed into a waged worker under the impulse of a higher prospective income in the form of a wage, there would be an element of the income he earned in the organisation of production he had left behind (taking account of course of the other advantages and disadvantages of the lifestyle in question) – to be put in as the worker's own original valuation of his labour, even if it were not present to the consciousness of the worker. In itself this way would not be as absurd as it seems, for although for the most part the working population was a working population only because it had been driven off the land and away from craft work, etc., and not because it saw a possible better way of life in the calling of the wage-earner, it still applies to a proportion of the workers, albeit perhaps a small one – and it is still true today for a proportion (though a very modest one) of Central European townsfolk or for the Canadian colonists, etc. That the existence of this small proportion of workers is perfectly sufficient for our purposes can be seen by reference to the analogous case of the abstinence theory of interest: there, for us to be able to speak of a 'savings sacrifice' relevant to the level of interest, it is in no way necessary that all saving involve a sacrifice. It is sufficient that the demand for savings capital be big enough to make savings acts involving 'unwillingness' or 'sacrifice' necessary for its satisfaction. *Mutatis mutandis* the same is true in our case.

This way is however far from inviting. Apart from the essentially limited value of a genetic explanation and apart from the fact that these foundations for the individual worker's estimate of his own value are for the most part very remote and inaccessible, it would never enable us to penetrate into the determining ground of wages. It is much more appropriate and realistic simply to accept that the worker does not have any valuation of his own labour, but that in the market economy he is in the usual situation of the man who possesses a good which he does not value in itself but which other people value, and who is determined to demand as much as possible for it on the market. The workers will thus simply want to sell their labour to the highest bidder, then if demand for it is satisfied or diminished in intensity to the person desirous of buying nearest in intensity of demand to that and so on, 'so long as the supply lasts'; and in a market of the (logically) ideal type where there can be only one price for each good, the intensity measured in money of the least intense demand still approaching the sale of the whole stock will set the wage for each quality of labour. Again, this is not to be understood in the sense that a particular distinguishable group of workers of each category serves the least intense demand: 'Marginal Bill', as the Cambridge students have baptised the 'marginal worker', is only a fiction for representational purposes. In fact at each point in time all workers have the position of the marginal worker and where there is question of redundancy, any worker may emerge in this quality: for as a consequence of the 'principle of substitution' individual labour is not valued any more highly than what corresponds to the 'marginal', even with the higher 'intramarginal' demand intensities.

As I have indicated, these equilibrium wages must meet another condition too: the satisfaction of needs it offers must outweigh the highest degree of reluctance to work yet to be experienced. In fact the supply of labour is still elastic even with a given number of workers however uncertain this very condition makes its definition. Our condition must be realised for each worker, though it is tempting to limit its application again to the 'marginal worker' and leave the rest out – especially the workers with higher natural skills. In fact there is also a point in ranging workers on a scale according to the extent of the labour sacrifice they have suffered and allowing to all a surplus of wellbeing above the position of satisfaction of the 'last'.[5] But in addition each must touch the margin, which is given by the equation 'marginal sacrifice = marginal utility of wages' (measured in money) if for each one individually 'equilibrium is to be attained'.

If the individual worker contracts with the individual entrepreneur in a free market, the work opportunity offered by the latter is obviously not the only one. When making an agreement the worker will of course consciously or unconsciously consider other possibilities and especially the one that emerges as the best. With this latter he compares the conditions set by the entrepreneur with whom he is negotiating and he will not work for a lower rate. The worker has a kind of own valuation of his work which arises from the other options available to him for the use of his labour. Insofar as these other options consist only in other opportunities for selling labour, the worker's own valuations based on them are simply consequences of determinate existing wage rates, so that we cannot use them for a foundational explanation of wages. They are merely pseudo-own valuations and not real ones, and they are nothing more than a brief summary of the situation that is useful for the individual case; they reside in the worker's mind or in his behaviour.

But since these are present all the time and serve the worker as a compass, and since the relationships on which they are based in general change only slowly and hence imprint themselves very firmly on his mind, and especially since his whole form of life is moulded by them, they look like established amounts: 'claims' made by the workers that are normal to the place and the time, claims to which they hold very firmly and which the employers expect; for the employers too unconsciously do all the mental labour necessary to establish what marginal amount of labour would be appropriate to the situation. But the employers accept this wage rate (like cost levels in general) as having evolved from long experience and as being more or less appropriate to the marginal amount, changing it therefore only gradually under the pressure of new conditions. Because the workers' claims are thus always consequences of particular wage rates, neither the essence nor the laws of the wage phenomenon can ever be explained by them, but rather the content and the success of the claims must be understood in principle on the basis of wage theory. It is however nonetheless understandable that as a result of their 'inertia', so long as conditions do not change all that much, and especially if law and morals or public opinion protect them (in such points theory has always recognised the direct influence of the power factor) they seem even more plausibly to acquire a real secondary causal role for the individual case. This is a common state of affairs in social life. For example we may refer to a 'nice home', thinking of the attractive behaviour of the members of the family. But once the habit of such behaviour has developed it can become so much a part of life for the family concerned that it affects everyone who comes into the family and so becomes as it were something impersonal and suprapersonal; ultimately it turns into a cause of the behaviour of the individual, when in fact it is only a consequence of the behaviour of all the individuals. Thus the popular view of the causal role of the claims of the workers, which recently has again been made an instrument of scientific analysis, needs to be qualified.[6]

So basically in a market economy no-one has such an own valuation of his labour (an indirect one, appropriate to the means of production character of labour) as the marginal utility theory seems to postulate for its solution of exchange and price problems and therefore also of the distribution problem. Not the consumer, for he values only the bought consumption good and thinks no further; not the employer, for his products have no value in use for him from which a personal valuation of that kind of the means of production could alone derive; not the worker, for he has in general no possible use for his work such as could provide a basis for such a personal valuation – an indirect or derived valuation of utility. In reality the valuations of labour that we can establish directly for workers and employers are a consequence of the fact of a labour profit in money, and they are really different from those that in the simplest case – that of production for the evaluating economic subject's own needs – marginal utility theory can derive from the specific 'share' of individual production factors in the production result. In the case of the worker the valuations of his labour with which he confronts each individual offer of employment are in general given only by the wage levels obtainable in other positions, so that it would be circular to want to apply them generally to the explanation of the fact of wages, even if they do certainly play some part in the explanation of wage levels.[7] This is not the case for the employer: for the return on which his valuation of labour rests is not, as in the case of the worker, the price of labour – which is in fact to be explained by this – but the income from the sale of the product; and this return can very well be set over against the price of labour as an independent determining cause. But this valuation is something other than the valuation derived from the value in use of the product for the producer. In order to show that it too is subject to the law of marginal utility and in order to show that and how it is given a basis by its value in use through the consumer's valuation of the product consumed by him – wherein lies the crucial point of the economic connection between 'production' and 'distribution' – we now need to examine in what precise sense the employer represents the consumer in the role of valuing labour, and how this 'vicarious' valuation of labour relates to valuation of it in terms of its meaning for the company's revenue.

In the mind of the employer then only this latter is to the fore, and even then only if he does not proceed in a purely customary way in accordance with the usual practice of the place and the sector, which is a way of easily supplementing 'subconscious calculation' and keeping one's feet on the ground. He considers the individual parts of the different means of production from the viewpoint of the variations[8] in the profitability of his company which would follow from their loss or gain. This means that the change to be brought about in the gross income from the sale of the product is what is crucial, and not the change in the net income, i.e. the income after deduction of all costs; for the extent of the anticipated growth in the gross income decides what the employer can or will lay out in costs. His 'valuation' of a worker is far from completely accounted for by the pure profit to be realised with his help, any more than my valuation of a cigarette is completely accounted for by that amount of utility expressed in money by which the pleasure from the cigarette exceeds the price paid for it. In both cases it is of course the profit in use which is the object of the exercise, and in both cases the rest of the 'utility' obtained is paralysed through the sacrifice to be offered; but in both cases – and they are completely analogous on this point – the measure of the valuation of worth is given through the whole utility which the good in question brings, and only this amount explains the behaviour of the economic subject and in particular his readiness to make the relevant 'sacrifice'. In the case of the employer it is thus the expected growth in the gross income which is the basis of the valuation of the means of production, it is to obtain this growth that the decision is made to lay out the costs, and it is this growth which emerges as the measure of the demand for the means of production on the market.

This particular 'growth in the gross income' however is nothing but the money expression for the marginal utility of the consumers, which as we have noted must be the same amount for all consumers of a good. For the employer too it is only 'growth in gross income', an amount to which no feeling of value in use is connected, so it must surely therefore owe its existence and its law to the requirement of the consumer: in this sense, according to its inner essence, a value in use expressed in money is firstly a direct value in use of consumption goods, and secondly an indirect value of means of production for consumers, from which the valuation of the individual means of production can then be obtained simply by observation of the effect of variations in the amounts of the individual means of production (with the others remaining the same) on the outcome of production. The two kinds of valuation that we imputed to the employer thus coincide. One is to some extent the pair to the others, the series of earning capacity values and values in use go closely together and variations in profitability always rest on variations in value in use productivity, without the employer having to give a thought to the indirect value in use of a job performance. For his part the consumer has no valuation of labour, but his valuation of consumption goods maintains demand for labour and the economic process functions as if the consumer did have his own valuation of labour. To ascribe such a thing to him is certainly a fiction, but it is based on facts.

Given that employers' demand for labour expresses nothing but a 'vicarious' own valuation of labour and that the worker's valuation of his labour is equal to zero, it follows that wages must be fixed according to the money expression of our fictitious consumer marginal utility at the point that is appropriate to the existing supply of labour.[9] For if wages were lower, a larger number of workers could be advantageously employed at this lower wage than actually exists, so that competition between employers would inevitably drive wages up. If wages were higher, the whole existing number of workers of the relevant category would not be able to find employment at this higher rate without losses being incurred, so there would be unemployment instead, and that would initially drive wages down. Since this is of course valid for all means of production, we come to the principle that is often wrongly regarded (and by Tugan-Baranovskii too) as an intolerable paradox, that in equilibrium conditions the employer neither makes a profit nor incurs a loss. Although it is actually only for the marginal amount of each production factor that price and revenue coincide and an 'intra-marginal' surplus is realised by each, what seems like such a surplus when we contemplate each individual production factor is claimed by the others; the surplus which is realised by labour is the fund for the payment of interest and ground rent, while what seems like a surplus, if one takes land as the variable and 'applies' progressively further amounts of land to labour and capital, is the fund for wages and interest, etc., and it can be seen that in equilibrium conditions the whole 'product' can be comprehensively broken down into parts according to the law of marginal productivity, with no 'residuum' left behind (Wicksteed). Incidentally we see here how 'marginal productivity thinking' extends 'residual thinking'[10] which is so popular in distribution theory, and how it provides a content to a thinking that though formally always correct is in reality quite empty.

I have said that is is wrong to regard the above principle as paradoxical; with regard to the wage problem this leads to the assumption that under conditions of ideal perfect competition[11] and in an equilibrium situation the employer makes no profit out of his workers. We are prone to be obsessed by the fact that the employer may actually keep a considerable part of the income for himself. But if we bear in mind that modern theory distinguishes sharply between the roles of the capitalist, the landowner and the worker on the one hand, and that of the entrepreneur on the other, so that even if he makes no entrepreneur's profit our entrepreneur still always has interest on the capital belonging to himself, ground rent for land belonging to him and an employer's salary for the work he does as well as a risk premium,[12] our principle ceases to be at all questionable. Moreover it is related to an ideal-type understanding of equilibrium and free competition: the nearest approximation to the former that is actually to be found is the 'calm period' which usually follows a depression and leads to a new upswing. Since at such times the entrepreneur generally has no particular function other than the routine work of the settled everyday life of a company, it is perfectly understandable that his income then amounts to nothing more than the sum of the amounts mentioned, and this is confirmed by actual experience. Periods of upturn in particular and times of disturbed equilibrium in general (the most important sources of the profits that so conspicuously exceed these amounts[13]) are what provide him as entrepreneur (as opposed to a mere company manager) with his own particular role, with opportunities for change and innovation in the company, and generally with opportunities for 'speculation'. Other sources of such profits are monopoly, and more generally all those deviations from the (logical) ideal picture of free competition which are to be met with everywhere in practice. Our principle does not deny their existence, it only helps us to distinguish them from the inherent phenomena essential to the mechanism of competition, and hence to understand reality better, something which should of course be regarded as one of the benefits to be obtained from analysis instead of being seen as a ground for objections.

The principle I am defending may look intrinsically absurd in that it ascribes to the entrepreneur a tendency to eliminate his own profit, something frequently asserted by Tugan-Baranovskii himself. That in a free market the entrepreneur's quest for profit destroys profit, that the stimulus of maximum profit is intrinsically suicidal for the profit requiring to be maximised, ultimately wresting it away from the entrepreneur, is a fundamental result that is also a highly unattractive one at first sight. But it only means that in his use of the means of production the entrepreneur is motivated by the need to make the highest profit possible, that this is the criterion on which he assigns them defined values in money, and that under the impetus of the struggle for the fullest exploitation of profit possibilities, competition forces him to invest up to the full level of those money valuations (whereby of course his own work, etc. is invested as well). Because each element of income is dependent on the contribution of some kind of means of production, the whole revenue flows back to this and must (in the absence of any monopoly position) be paid to the owners of that means of production – including the entrepreneur himself. There is nothing here that observation of everyday economic life would not justify. The deeper 'meaning' of the process is that just as the value which we attribute to goods is only a reflection of our poverty and declines in proportion as our milieu is wealthier, so all 'net income' exceeding the sum of the prices of the means of production in the broadest sense is a consequence and symptom of a defect in the production process which prevents the full exploitation of existing possibilities – so that this consequence of a defect at the same time constitutes a motive to overcome it: profit attracts, it is obtained, the means of production necessary to it are correspondingly more highly valued and (in a free market) paid for, so that their new value and price absorbs it – assuming that a fall in the price of the product does not sweep it away first.

All this is extraordinarily simple, and only the 'passive resistance' which even the most practically necessary and technically primitive abstractions encounter can still raise difficulties here. But nonetheless I must dwell on it for a moment, at the risk of burdening the reader with self-evident truths. The question is for ever being raised – and not just by beginners: how can an entrepreneur so foolishly go on producing for so long that his profit is eliminated, how can he pursue possibilities of profit until it melts away to nothing or want to exploit existing possibilities of profit even when that would reduce his overall profit? People sometimes look on this as a *reductio ad absurdum* of the theoretical picture of the profitless undertaking: because it is obviously only the overall profit that is of interest to the entrepreneur and because he will therefore follow the policy that maximises this, they also look on it as a *reductio ad absurdum* of the marginal method. But of course the entrepreneur is not so foolish. He does not desire this result, it is actually produced by the activity of all the entrepreneurs, apart from and in opposition to the will of the individual. It can of course be eliminated by recourse to an overt or silent agreement, for entrepreneurs can set up a cartel, or even without one quietly avoid 'damaging the price' or 'luring workers away from each other'. But this belongs to monopoly theory and is exhaustively dealt with there, so I shall not pursue it here, but I do want to be clear about the inner essence of the market economy. In such an economy the individual entrepreneur never wants to expand his production beyond the point where it will lead to a fall in his overall profit. But if he does not do so others will, so that it makes no difference if he joins in. In a free market every individual is a 'drop in the ocean'; his increased demand for labour does not raise wages, nor does his increased supply of products put pressure on their price. Each individual can therefore quietly expand his production without diminishing his overall profit, indeed he increases that profit, so that he would be dealing uneconomically as an individual if he did not expand his production. But because each man wants to be this individual and all take the same steps, the result follows that none of them individually desires, but which no single individual can stop by holding back. If wages rise and the product price falls, but there is still a surplus, we have the same situation again: overall profit is reduced for everyone, but there are prospects of further profit again for each, and since everyone goes for it, the already reduced overall profit diminishes yet further until finally there is no surplus at all.

New enterprises may be set up which are eminently viable as long as their revenue covers the sum of all the items – and they are profitable for all economic subjects who have no surplus profit to preserve from diminution. Who will set up these new businesses? First all, the owners of the means of production – who, if there is such a surplus profit, receive less than what corresponds to the productive significance of their means of production – will be ready to put these means of production into the hands of people who want to become entrepreneurs, since their involvement raises the price of the means of production in question (of course in the end universally). At present this obviously happens through the medium of bank credit. But there are always capitalists who in such a case become entrepreneurs – as there would to a lesser extent be landowners who would in such a situation go over to doing their own farming. The necessary means of production is thus taken away from the old companies so that their surplus profit disappears,[14] while new capital is constantly being formed and offered (leaving aside other means of production, whose quantity is not explicable on a purely economic basis, so that for the moment we have to treat it as constant, i.e. 'given'). This process can only stop if the type of the profitless entrepreneur is actualised and this could happen only if perfectly free competition were to develop and only if constantly new situations were not emerging in which always new profits were possible before they settled in an equilibrium.

It is very important to have a clear grasp of these simple connections, not least so that we can comprehend that such an expansion of production can never of itself alone lead to a crisis, as is sometimes suggested.[15] For the expansion takes place against a background of falling prices, at which on the one hand the greater product can be sold and at which at on the other hand individual firms are not unprofitable and unable to survive, even the old ones, since they possess a 'buffer' in the surplus profit they have hitherto been making, and this softens the blow, for their net income can never fall by more than this surplus profit as a result of this process; the situation is not the same as what obtains with the other process of the displacement of old-fashioned companies by ones working with modern methods. Furthermore it is clear that lack of capital can never (as is also often asserted) prevent the expansion of production up to the marginal productivity level.[16] Lack of capital may well prevent the individual entrepreneur from expanding his company, although today this can only ever be a consequence of very particular circumstances, so that the normal alert, well-informed businessman usually has no difficulty in this area. But industry as a whole can in principle always reach the point at which in equilibrium entrepreneurs' profit in the narrowest sense disappears, even when the amount of capital remains constant,[17] which is not generally the case.

The case is very clear if we bring into consideration the normally constant inflow of newly-formed capital. First of all this process is the most important result which the tendency towards income adjustment produces not only for capital but also for labour of any quality, that tendency which never attains its goal, which is paralysed by a thousand circumstances, but which reveals an essential part of the life of the economy.[18] Whatever we may think about the essence of capital, the manner of its emergence and the ways this process of approximation – and there are many very different views on the matter – people always have something very real in mind when they say that the new capital which is constantly flowing into circulation and seeking the most profitable use in the light of the different risks, thereby pushes down the profitability of that use and brings it close to the level of the rest. In its wider meaning, in which it also includes amortisation sums, this process is moreover the way in which capital can be 'withdrawn' from one use in order to 'migrate' to another, something that is however possible only at a substantial loss. It is analogous to the movement of workers from one industry to another, which, at least to the extent that we are talking about skilled labour, takes place only in part through the choice of calling of successive generations. Both processes evolve slowly and often only imperceptibly in the face of a great deal of friction and opposition. Hence the very big deviations which there are in reality from 'economic law', and also the necessity for a particular theory for the 'interim period' at the centre of which stands the concept of 'quasi-rent'.[19]

It is this process in particular that makes easier in practice that competition for the role of entrepreneur which in 'quiet periods' wears away at entrepreneurial profit in the narrowest sense, helping to lift wages and ground rent especially to the corresponding level. In this respect its effect is not easy to overlook. First of all it causes a fall in the interest rate, though even that has been contested and indeed by the Ricardians themselves. West's particular argument (1815, p. 21) against it provides a better illustration than most general arguments of the fundamental meaning of the difference between entrepreneurs and capitalists. Only because he lumped both together did he think of interpreting Smith's principle (*Wealth of Nations*, 1950, I, ch. 8), that an increase in capital tends to raise wages but lower the interest rate as a consequence of the competition of the capitalists as meaning that then more is produced so that the product price falls – which is the only way (apart from the effect of the higher wages) that profit can fall. West quite rightly answered that this reason for a fall in the price generally applies to all goods: so it can particularly affect the expression of the exchange relationship in money, but not its 'real' content, and so not 'real interest'. But if one makes this distinction, one recognises that interest too can fall without the entrepreneur's share falling, and that its fall can have other reasons than merely a fall in the 'exchange value' of the product. So it is not difficult to see that an increase in capital must *ceteris paribus* have the effect that those orientated towards practice have always ascribed to it.

Any fall in interest is pure advantage for the entrepreneur, who can only increase his surplus profit. If it is substantial, all the profitability calculations and production combinations change, though in very different ways in different sectors. But there are very complex connections which I do not wish to discuss at present. The process under consideration here evolves gradually and influences the level of interest from year to year but not overtly if growth in capital is significant, for demand for capital is very elastic. But while the advantage for the entrepreneur of the fall in the interest rate grows so marginally from year to year that it can be quietly ignored, the possibility of competition for the role of entrepreneur based on the flow of capital becomes all the more significant in that we are dealing with the penetration of capital into the area of productivity margins, where relatively small amounts can be crucial.

I have now explained and defended my thesis that the entrepreneur makes neither profit nor loss (though a monopolistic or quasimonopolistic position may actually make him a profit, which needs no further explanation from the theoretical viewpoint) and also thereby my principle that wages owe their existence and their law to certain consumer marginal utilities. But there is here an interesting side-light on that most mysterious of all sectors of income, namely on interest, to which reference has been made in passing. Why does it not disappear, just like the entrepreneur's profits in the narrowest sense of the term? This question is a difficult one for me to discuss because I personally believe that in a stationary equilibrium situation of the economy it ought in fact to disappear, and that it owes its existence only to constant 'development'. But anyone who does not share this opinion and who considers it to be a necessary phenomenon inherent in the economic cycle – even if perhaps only in the capitalist form of organisation – must see in it payment for something that is an element of costs or can be construed as such, something necessary for production, a 'productive service' of some kind (of course not necessarily personal). Interest is certainly not the layman's 'profit', nor an intercompany profit arising initially in the 'distribution process', a 'markup' or a fraud by the supplier of some kind of means of production, nor some kind of plunder by economic 'power'. For all such things are either impossible *ab initio* or else they cannot hold up in the light of the processes described above. If interest were something of this kind, it should disappear or show a much stronger tendency to disappear than could be found in the 'historical' fall in the interest rate. This affects even Marx's exploitation theory[20] and still more so Tugan-Baranovskii's. It could well be a monopoly profit, even if only a monopoly profit for capitalists and not for entrepreneurs, but anyone who argues that would have to undertake to prove that a capitalist cartel exists and has always existed.[21]

IV The Social Marginal Product

What then is the economic essence of wages, and what are the most general truths about the grounds of their existence in the market economy? The marginal utility theory will answer: wages are paid because and to the extent that the entrepreneur and ultimately the consumer 'needs' the individual worker. Now if we take this statement only in the sense in which it is intended, it is thoroughly unambiguous and defensible, it says only what is already quite self-evident, that the basis of wage payments lies in the productive meaning of labour, and also that in a free market the level of wage payments corresponds to the current productive meaning of labour, with the same being true for income sectors coordinated with wages. It says that under free competition wages are determined by the money revenue of a company depending on a unit of labour, which not only measures the entrepreneur's valuation and thereby the upper limit of wages, but also actually tends to come to the worker by the play of market forces. To this money income–marginal yield–corresponds a marginal product. This marginal product can be expressed both in products and in values of products and these values are nothing but real consumer marginal utilities for labour separated out from the values of consumption goods by the agency of the entrepreneur and expressed in money, whose level is designated as marginal productivity.

In a free market the marginal product, the productive contribution, marginal productivity or finally the 'marginal efficiency' of labour is crucial for wages, and in an equilibrium situation the workforce shares in the social product according to the ratio between this amount and analogous amounts of other factors of production. These expressions are not to be taken in just any sense among the many they can have, but in a well-defined sense. It is certainly true in other senses that there is not a distinguishable product of a factor of production or that the whole social product is the product of labour, etc. It may perhaps be found objectionable that on this theory the marginal product and thus the productive activity of the worker varies if the other factors of production vary. What happens with the distinguishable activity of labour as the basis of wages if it has to be admitted that wages can change even though the workers carry on performing the same task as before? This is of course undeniable, but it is not an objection. Here the word 'performance' is used in two different senses. In one sense we have the meaning that is closest to linguistic usage and everyday social thinking: performance as the conduct of the performing subject, for only this can be the same 'after as before'. And this meaning, which carries social overtones that make it difficult for us to talk about a distinguishable 'contribution' by the worker, pushes in under the other technical one. In the technical sense performance means nothing but a relative productive utility, with the stress on the dependent productive success. That this and performance in this sense must vary if the quantities of goods involved vary is self-evident, for in general the value of goods changes and what we can do with them changes depending on the stock of other goods which we possess, and the overall and marginal utility of a good is never a function of the quantity of this good alone but always a function of the quantity of all the goods that we possess.

The marginal productivity of labour is one of the most important elements of the destiny of nations and one of the most important indices of the state of society. As long as we remain clear about the fact that it is not 'experienced' by a central social organ, but generally does not exist other than implicitly in consumers' valuations of consumption goods, and explicitly but in alien dress in the level of the entrepreneur's valuation of labour units as measured in money, there is no real problem about calling it 'the social marginal utility of labour'.[1] But we are not entitled to link it to apologetic tendencies, in connection with the thought that the worker is to receive what he is worth to society,[2] nor simply to designate wages as the measure of an indirect social value in use of labour, or at least we must not forget that this amount depends completely on the required property relations in the means of production (especially in land) and would certainly not be the same in every social organisation.

Such an approach all too easily creates misunderstandings in the mind of the reader and sometimes leads an author into errors especially if he is seeking to bypass price theory and to present a picture of a society using its means of production and distributing the result. Such a presentation can highlight both the social meaning of the life process of the competitive economy and the many real analogies which this has with the life process of a collectivist economy. Thus it transpires that in the market economy the national labour force flows first (logically, not genetically) to the production of those goods which satisfy needs whose monetary expression is the highest (the most 'pressing' first) and then moves down the line of gradually decreasing intensities of need expressed in money, until the supply of workers is exhausted; its final waves fertilise the area whose harvest is crucial for the respective significance of all of its waves. A social law is generally discernible in the market economy – and it is a real one, even though it is realised only in the result of the mutual relations between economic elements and in facts, rather than in any consciousness; the crucial feature of this law is the phenomenon of marginal productivity. If a collectivist community were to think of making this same valuation of the urgency of needs the foundation of its economic planning, the result would be just the same (though now of course consciously sought). The difference lies in the fact that no collectivist community would do so and that in a free market economy this process brings about the formation of income automatically and *ipso facto*, while in the collectivist economy distribution would be a special act. Conceptually however it is a mistake to want to find a difference between the two on the basis that in a collectivist economy ground rent for example falls to the workers. For that is also possible in a free market economy since the workers become *pro rata parte* landowners; things are different in the collectivist economy only if the individual's share of consumption goods is removed from any relation to the productive meaning (in the technical sense) of his means of production. This would not be the result of some decree; the new landowners would receive their rents on the ground of the same law of marginal productivity – of the soil – as their predecessors, while as workers they would continue to receive just their wage as before. 'In practice' this may be a trivial matter, but for the scientific explanation of matters it is fundamental.

With some necessary reservations the marginal productivity theory can be developed so well that the whole social stock of labour, capital and land are made to combine and influence each other without respect to the activity of the individual entrepreneur, while the 'marginal products' of these factors are regarded as indices of their productive significance and of owners' share in the social product; and the theory is perfected by the consideration that since the entrepreneur is only a middleman and since consumers and those involved in production coincide, the whole process is basically nothing but an exchange of 'productive activities' or 'potential products'. Ultimately therefore we come back to the fundamental fact of the division of labour, the starting-point for Adam Smith's reflection; and from the viewpoint of need satisfaction production, exchange, and distribution ultimately fuse together in an inner unity, something that has not been achieved in any other theory.

The full meaning of the principle of marginal productivity cannot really be demonstrated from the individual company – at least not if we accept (as is necessary for the existence of a fully free market) that the individual firm is a drop in the ocean, i.e. that its supply of products and the demand it generates for means of production is tiny in relation to overall supply and demand in the relevant markets. Its supply of products exercises no notable influence on their price, nor does its demand for the means of production noticeably affect their price, nor does its demand for labour raise wages much. So the individual company leaves any such effects out of its calculations. Wherever this is not the case, it is a sure sign that we are not talking about a case of a 'free' market. Since the marginal utility of the entrepreneur's profit is fairly constant over the period of time involved in the questions being dealt with here, the action of all the factors which an overview of the whole sector at work reveals is paralysed. For the individual entrepreneur productivity limits result to some extent from the mass effect of the demand and supply of all companies, which affects him too, while at the same time there are very different factors in the foreground, and above all the decrease in the physical productivity of the firm which occurs at a given point if it tries to increase output in the context of a given structure. This fact stands in contradiction neither with the 'law of increasing return' nor with the 'advantages of the big company', but like these is generally observable everywhere, i.e. in all branches of industry, and like them it is connected to particular prerequisites: the introduction of new production methods which are viable only with correspondingly greater potential sales can bring production costs down only so far, for within the new production method the law of decreasing return again comes into operation after a certain point. No matter how many savings are made in the big industrial organisation, they turn into the opposite beyond a certain point – a point which is of course very variable from case to case. For each company (and this is true of agricultural economies too) there may be a period in which each increase in expenditure gives a more than proportional return, but these periods do not enter the picture here, for if an entrepreneur can produce more at falling cost but does not do so, the reason is hardly ever that he is short of capital, but that he is afraid to damage the market. Such a fear makes sense only for monopolists or for anyone who either occupies a quasi-monopolistic position himself or helps to create one for everybody by an understanding with his fellows.

For the individual entrepreneur the position is this: each one combines optimal amounts of labour, land and capital in the interests of the greatest possible profit. It is easy to see that his goal will be reached if he uses so much of each production factor that the profit which could be obtained from the use of a further small quantity of one factor would at least be offset by the price to be paid for it, a price that here where we are speaking purely from the viewpoint of the individual entrepreneur is readily to be accepted as given, so that again in an equilibrium situation the marginal return on each factor of production for the entrepreneur is equal to the price which he has to pay for it, and within the narrow context of the entrepreneur's point of view we have come to the same result as before and to the point at which the entrepreneur's calculation and the social process mesh together.

V Critical Discussion

What I have said is only the ground-plan of a theory of wages, on which is built a tall building part of which has an extraordinarily complicated structure, and it needs to be judged as a ground-plan and as a very general abstraction, a requirement whose fulfilment would exclude the possibility of endless special cases that become objections. Viewed as such as a ground-plan, what has been said is however extremely simple, and if it is nonetheless frequently misunderstood that is both for general reasons and for the particular reason that so many specialists find it difficult to grasp the meaning of the marginal method – as such and quite apart from the form of the marginal utility theory – or to use marginal analysis freely. I shall now say a few words about these difficulties.

In every area the aim of the marginal idea is the comprehension of a process by means of constant quantities: with its help we discover a system in elements that are subjected to constant change, insofar as we establish to which constant quantities they are close at each moment, and insofar as we ossify them as it were and replace them by these constant quantities at each moment. Of course this is a fiction, a 'trick' which could never have appeared in the thought world of most social economists (who would instantly reject it as 'unrealistic') but obviously it was the method that made the whole of mathematical physics possible. It is not simply highly appropriate to the subject of mathematical physics, it is in fact generally of a logical nature. It always involves an 'error', an 'error' which is of no significance only if the quantities involved are particularly small. For such tiny quantities principles are valid on the basis of sufficient approximation that are false or quite meaningless for substantial quantities. So whenever we make use of this quite indispensable aid we must make sure that we are always dealing with these very small quantities. This principle is forever being violated in our area.

I am not going to study the crudest of these violations in the area of our special problem – namely the argument that the whole social product is dependent on labour, and that therefore the marginal productivity idea is necessarily a nonsense. There are all sorts of arguments around today that have no better basis. To give one example, Hobson (1900, p. 145) thinks he is contradicting the marginal productivity theory when he says:

> Now in order to measure the productivity of the last dose of labour, let us remove it. The diminution of the total product may be 8%. This 8% ... we ascribe to the last dose of labour. If now, restoring this dose of labour, we withdraw the last dose of capital, the reduction of product might be 10%. This 10% is regarded as the product of the last dose of capital. Similarly, the withdrawal of the last dose of land might seem to reduce the product by 10%. What would be the effect of a simultaneous withdrawal of the last dose of each factor? ... clearly 28%.

On the following page he puts all land, all capital, and all labour together in one dose and then finds that the removal of any one of these doses eliminates the whole product – and the whole product is certainly not the right measure for the productivity of a factor of production on its own. Such arguments merely go to show that theory has left the stage at which it was comprehensible without any background. What is needed here is not discussion, merely a reference to a textbook of scientific method. We may not love theory as such, but we cannot completely avoid it, and we are obliged to take the trouble to grapple with it and with its assumptions.

Unfortunately many notable authors who would have a great deal to give us go badly wrong in this area to their own detriment and to the detriment of science. An example of this is Schüller, whose articles (1916–17)[1] take the very promising path of researching the structure of demand for and supply of labour in great detail. This is work on the building which needs to be constructed gradually on the theoretical basis I have described. Its value is only partially reduced by the fact that instead of including the special data in that basis, the author places them in contradiction to it.[2] But the critical side of the discussions is completely devalued by the author's lack of flexibility in respect of the essence of marginal analysis. His very first thesis denies the principle that the value of labour to the entrepreneur decreases as he employs more workers, a principle in which, incidentally, to be fair, the words 'from a definite point onwards' must be inserted even if an author occasionally omits them. Schüller (1916–17) however thinks that as a rule the loss of workers has a disproportionate consequence in terms of loss of profits, so that such 'marginal workers' must have had a higher value for the entrepreneur than the others. It can immediately be seen where lies the error – and it is an error pure and simple. Schüller is thinking of the loss of so many workers that an efficient company is thereby disrupted and the pressure of general costs on the product unit greatly increased. In his examples he works with variations of 20 per cent (p. 48), 100 per cent (p. 50), 50 per cent (p. 55), etc., and this of course makes a complete mockery of the essence of marginal analysis. So the principle he is contesting is not affected. If variations in amounts and prices are great, and if they make other company methods the most profitable rather than those that were optimal before, so that a complete revolution follows in the calculation of profitability, of course marginal utilities or marginal productivity that corresponded to the old conditions – conditions with regard to which companies were generally set up in such-and-such a way and not in another – can never be decisive. But this is no deficiency in theory, for theory has in fact the means to describe such processes exhaustively. If a particular production method assumes an absolute minimum of workers, so that the unavailable workers have the role of the well-known fourth horse for the carriage-and-four or the equally well-known second glove, it is clear that their significance for the entrepreneur in a given case is in fact greater than the significance of the others who without them are useful only for a less lucrative application – but this does not constitute a contradiction of the marginal utility theory. Schüller recognises this analogy with consumption goods, of which a minimum is absolutely necessary for a given use, but following a casual remark of Wieser's he considers the case with those an exception, while treating it as the rule with means of production. Even if that were correct, no objection would follow from it, but it is not correct, and in fact both kinds of value phenomena regularly go together in the case of means of consumption as well as in that of means of production.

Be it only to introduce the melancholy question what we are to expect from all our dilettantes, when this happens to Schüller's green timber, there is a lot to be gained from consideration of a few more points in Schüller's critique, even where they have no direct connection with the idea of marginal analysis. Let us go back to our author's last comment. He says that the law of the decreasing value of further increases in goods cannot be valid for means of production too, because the entrepreneur needs a definite quantity of them for his company, not more and not less. But in the first place (to keep to the subject of labour), do we really have to begin by producing examples to show that each company, however inelastic, will employ a different number of workers at different wages? Is labour not applied to the care – e.g. storage – of raw materials, the care of machines, the cleaning and improvement of buildings, the 'presentation' or general fine tuning of the product, inspection, general service and errand-running functions, etc., the costs of which become non-economic expenditure as soon as wages rise a little? Admittedly this makes only a small difference – but it is precisely such small differences that are crucial; for there is also the mass effect of such variations, and this is of course related to the most favourable case thinkable for Schüller's argument (as a rule companies are of course not so 'rigid'). But in the second place, is it not obvious that quite apart from this the viewpoint of the optimal combination of means of production is decisive for the choice of a type of company from all those known and possible in a given situation, and that this their mutual suitability will ultimately be fixed by marginal processes, so that the company, however 'rigid' it is once it is up and running (with changes in conditions such rigidity leads to all the multiply interconnected effects contained in the word 'quasi-rent') is adjusted to a definite marginal productivity of labour? This is in no way affected by the circumstance that on technical and other grounds it is not always possible either to stop with the marginal worker or to reach him. (Consider the sale of a good in the normal minimum market quotas which force the buyer to buy more or less corresponding to his marginal utility). The supposed inelasticity of demand for labour founded in such a way is the basis for Schüller's most important practical results.

There is no implication that the individual entrepreneur has consciously to perform marginal profitability calculations all the time. He always has other companies in view and also an old stock of economic experience available to him, which generally means that he does the right thing – just as in spending our income each of us only exceptionally makes particular conscious observations or even 'hesitates', for the relevant mental work is already embodied in our habits. There is a circumstance here on which Schüller lays great emphasis when in fact it is not very relevant, namely that the entrepreneur values his workers only overall and neither can be nor wishes to be informed about the value of an individual worker to him. Generally speaking this would have no meaning for him, and marginal utility theory no more asserts that he has such information than it asserts that he sounds the depths of the phenomenon of costs. For him cost is a comfortable condensed expression he is quite happy with. And he does not generally require any explicit valuation of the individual worker, it is enough for him and for us that his conduct does actually imply such a valuation.

There is a lot more to be said about the interpretation Schüller gives of certain circumstances, e.g. the fact that individual entrepreneurs very often buy raw materials of the same kind and quality at different prices, or about the concept of differences in production costs of the company as 'profit', etc. This would take us too far out of the way, but we cannot leave unanswered his second critical foundation thesis – his rejection (p. 38) of the principle

> that the least value that the workers of any one entrepreneur have defines the value of all workers of the same kind for all entrepreneurs, and that this marginal value alone defines the intensity of demand and its influence on wages. In fact work has different values for individual entrepreneurs and the resulting gradations are expressed in forms of demand and in their effects on wages.

The marginal value of workers of the same kind is of course not the same for all entrepreneurs, because the money expression in which it is manifested means something very different for each one. But that does not prevent this monetary expression itself from being the same for all and this is all that matters. Anyone who wanted to deny it would fall into the same error as those who object to marginal utility theory's assumption that the marginal utility of bread is measured by the its price for both millionaires and beggars. And only this monetary expression defines the intensity of demand for more labour in the neighbourhood of the margin. What is different for the different entrepreneurs – the extent of their demand and their individual features – will become visible with substantial changes in price or in the level of supply, and these will be the cause of effects on wages which call for particular investigation.[3] This is another question however and it would not be denied by anybody.

Schüller's critique of Clark (pp. 732 ff.) is tenable only at one point – his rejection of Clark's tendency to present the equilibrium wage as 'fair' on the basis of the productivity idea. But the misjudgement of the meaning of the law of diminishing marginal productivity that I have been talking about is worryingly prevalent in the writing of the great American theorist. It should be noted that in fact it is not completely correct to say that the 'first' worker has the greatest value. For most companies can of course hardly do anything at all with one worker and he would therefore have as little value as an infinitesimal quantity of most consumption goods. But such expository carelessness is pardonable. The inspired negligence from which Clark's brilliant exposition cannot generally be absolved left Schüller with the impression that it was being asserted that the 'stratum of demand' whose intensity is the smallest would be the 'broadest', so that if there was a wage increase very many workers would have to be let go. This is not necessarily so, and it is certainly not what Clark means. It does not follow from the passages adduced by Schüller, and in any case it is irrelevant for the principle of the theory: it may be so or not so, it may be so sometimes and at other times different – in any case we are talking here about a concrete fact to be investigated in terms of statistics, a fact which certainly can and must be embedded in theory, but which does not follow from theory. Schüller's other objections against Clark have been dealt with already. They are reminiscent of the style of argument of Thornton, whom Schüller quotes approvingly – and since Thornton's own inability to hit the mark did not prevent him from being listened to, I wanted to counter a very similar kind of enterprise, so highly do I prize the merits of its author.

As befits his major role, Clark has been exposed to many attacks which it would be instructive to discuss.[4] I now want to pick out those that were made by von Zwiedineck in his review of literature 'Neuere Literatur zur Lohnfrage' (1916–17, pp. 640 ff.). First of all he too denies that there is a fall in the marginal productivity of labour on the grounds that if a worker can produce a given product with a given amount of capital and then a second worker comes along, the product may conceivably be doubled and more than doubled. This is certainly not to be excluded, and it can indeed happen in two cases: first of all if the one worker was not sufficient for a rational utilisation of the amount of capital, and secondly if this multiplication of the quantity of labour makes possible 100% new forms of operation. Otherwise not. And neither of the two cases – in which moreover the crucial factor of value productivity would first need to be investigated – has anything to say against Clark (nor do I need to explain why). Again the error of the critic lies in his unsufficient grasp of the meaning of marginal analysis.

The same is true of von Zwiedineck's second objection, a much more disturbing one. He finds a contradiction between the two following principles: if the number of workers increases, overall productivity decreases if capital remains the same and falls where there is a decreasing amount of capital allotted to the unit of labour. And if the number of workers remains the same while capital investment increases a decline in overall productivity will be observable and productivity falls with an increasing quantity of capital being allotted to the unit of labour. There is no contradiction because in the two principles the variable is different. The principle that if the unit of labour combines with a consistently decreasing amount of capital, productivity falls, does not in the slightest contradict the principle that if the unit of capital combines with constantly decreasing labour, the same result ensues: in both cases there is one production factor that is constantly less exploited but in the two cases it is a different one and the effect on 'overall productivity' must be the same in both. A contradiction would be present only if in each principle a decrease in productivity were attributed to the same factor.

Tugan-Baranovskii's critique of Clark is also totally misguided. First of all he (1913, p. 61) presents us with the well-known objection we have already seen in our discussion of Schüller's works; that the entrepreneur makes a valuation of the workers as a whole, so that the product of the marginal worker is not crucial for the wages of all, and that for most part it is not a smaller but a more than proportional part of the profit that depends on the availability of the last partial amount, and I do not want to go into this again. But he thinks that even if we admit that a real meaning is to be attributed to the marginal product, wages cannot rise above it but can fall below it and the competition between the entrepreneurs does not prevent that. But it does prevent that, as we have seen above, and as price theory demonstrates with all the certainty desirable. Finally there is absolutely no substance to the argument (1913, pp. 63–4) that capitalists would have no motive to employ workers if they made no profit in doing so. Only with the employment of the marginal amount of labour is no capital income involved, and this does not mean that in general no capital interest is gained with the help of the workers – not even if (as with Clark) this interest is linked to the productive role of instrumental capital, for then too the employment of workers is necessary in order to obtain it, just as the use of instrumental capital is necessary in order to obtain the marginal product of labour. Tugan-Baranovskii can only explain the principle of the profitless use of the marginal worker in such a way that Clark either overlooks the fact that capital consists not simply in tools but also in the workers' means of nourishment, or else is of the opinion that capital of the latter kind is available to the capitalists in unlimited quantities so that wages costs are generally not felt by them, and therein lies a scarcely comprehensible misunderstanding of Clark's analysis, and the mere fact that such a misunderstanding is possible is a condemnation.[5] Nor is there anything to be said for Tugan-Baranovskii's polemic against the principle that supply and demand determine the wage level (pp. 34 ff.). In particular it is wrong to assert that the price of labour does not affect demand for labour and that equilibrium can prevail at any wage level. But it is pointless to go into this, for Tugan-Baranovskii himself admits that more workers are taken on if wages fall, that wages rise with rising demand (p. 40), and that the productivity of labour has an effect on wages (p. 43), and this is quite sufficient to demonstrate the contested connection. Yet the formula of supply and demand is compatible with any wage theory including Tugan-Baranovskii's,[6] so that there was no ground for him to oppose it. It is not true that attempts to influence the level of wages would be meaningless if that level was 'determined' by supply and demand.

VI Peculiarities of the Labour Market

Again: up to now we have been talking solely about foundations and only about the foundations of what is relevant 'in principle' or 'in essence' to our problem, i.e. what relates to the principle of explanation of the (economic) essence of the wage phenomenon. With regard to 'praxis' all that has been said is only a 'tendency' or, as applied to 'practice', only an extremely crude 'first approximation' which requires not only a consideration of the concrete circumstances of each individual case but in many areas a general theoretical refinement. Regardless of the impossibility of ever exhausting a real phenomenon theoretically, the 'practical' value of this fundamental theoretical knowledge is actually much greater than is usually admitted, for it throws indispensable light on a whole series of practical questions; nonetheless in essence it is so abstract that in many cases it performs only one practical service, which is however much more important than is accepted by those who consider theory to be destroyed by a reference to deviant facts; this service involves facilitating the diagnosis of such deviant facts. For as we have seen it makes a very big difference to know whether a phenomenon belongs to the essence of the free market economy or whether it is to be explained in terms of a structure different from the one inherent in the free market economy.

Although this applies to the whole area of economic theory (and to all the exact sciences in general) I shall cite a few particular forms here that such 'deviations' assume in the wages problem. I exclude obvious phenomena like 'indolence', a deficient overview of the market, etc. Many things, such as the factor of the stability of wage levels, explicable in terms of habit, etc., or the way that social processes sometimes make it impossible for the worker to exploit his economic position, have already been discussed. What remains can be classed under the heading of difficulties in the mechanism of the free market.[1]

First of all it would be a prerequisite for a perfectly free market that each worker could contract with each entrepreneur. But quite apart from the fact that the geographical locations of companies, etc. are an obstacle to this, each worker is as a rule clearly forced to let one entrepreneur have his whole labour power for a given minimum period, even though it might be far more advantageous for the worker to work part of his time for one entrepreneur and part of his time for another. It is however evident that where many workers and many entrepreneurs are involved, this factor cannot play any significant role.[2] Moreover the circumstance that the worker is usually placed in the position of having to choose either to accept a given working day or else not to be employed at all has the consequence that equality between the marginal utility of wages and the marginal sacrifice of labour is not easily achieved for each individual. But it is more or less clear that factory systems have to give in to the pressure that the workers exercise in this direction, and that length of the working day is generally not far from what for most workers roughly corresponds to the point where there is such equality. In addition it needs to be remembered that the labour market differs from many other markets in that the marginal utility of money is not constant in it for the 'buyers', the workers. This raises many difficulties for the application of theoretical aids, which are appropriate only where the marginal utility of money in exchange is constant. But the most important consequence is that a rise in the level of wages can have the result that less labour is on offer,[3] as can be observed with sudden sharp wage rises – at world fairs for example.

Then of course demand for the complete mobility of labour is not met so that the workforce breaks up into numerous non-competing groups – as they have been called since Cairnes; though we must not of course forget that the consequences of this are partly made good again through the mobility of capital. These consequences are that the labour market breaks up into partial markets for each of which the law of productivity is valid, though the same marginal productivity does not apply to all together, a circumstance that weakens the reality that underlies the concept of the social marginal product and that is expressed in the fact of different wage levels for work of the same difficulty and the same unpleasantness.[4]

First of all let us take the appropriate case of imperfect mobility – imperfect geographical mobility of labour of the same kind in the economic area – and let us discuss an interesting question in relation to it; whether the establishment of perfect mobility would be good or bad for the workers. Obviously a range of institutions work towards this result and the great majority of them indeed with the aim of thereby furthering workers' interests. These certainly are furthered, and especially that 'sector' of them which looks to a social product as extensive as possible. But the workers' share in the latter may thereby be diminished, possibly to such an extent as to outweigh the advantage for the workers of a greater social product. This possibility is apparent from the fact that with the establishment of full mobility very small islands of high wages that exist in odd places for various reasons disappear, without this necessarily producing any obvious advantage for the other workers. The gain to the latter in such a case is imperceptible, while the loss to those previously advantaged is significant – so that there is a debit balance for the workers overall, which may of course be compensated for or overcome (but not necessarily so) by the simultaneous elimination of similar small islands of lower-than-normal wages. Moreover it is obvious that the benefits the labour force acquire are all primarily obtained in isolated jobs and that therefore the existence of full mobility is not always favourable to the workers (even apart from the case in which organised workers are undercut by non-organised workers, where this is self-evident). Another point is however much more interesting: perfect mobility means that the potential of the whole quantity of labour present in the economic arena is fully exploited. The social stock of labour is the more truly productive in that it is promptly and unfailingly devoted to the most profitable uses. This means just the same as if it had become greater without becoming more mobile, and this can have the effect that its marginal significance is now smaller than the (favourable) average of marginal amounts on the partial markets was, and that the relative share of the labour force in the social product therefore falls.[5] The absolute share and real wages do not need to fall because of this and will in fact almost never do so, indeed as a rule they will actually rise. But they can fall – it depends on the elasticity of demand for labour. I do not want to say thereby that a greater mobility of labour is damaging for workers in general,[6] but it can be damaging in individual cases, and it is difficult to decide what is true for any given case. There is a wide field here for crucial practical special studies involving the constant 'insertion of concrete data into theory' for which in principle theory offers every assistance.[7] It sets the agenda for fact-gathering and obtains the answers to our questions from the facts gathered – assuming that these questions are not so simple that they can be answered simply by a consideration of the facts and without any technical assistance – or, better, it gives alternative pre-determined answers appropriate to different concrete circumstances and from which we select one or another on the basis of a study of the concrete circumstances of the individual case. To give a simple example: if in our case the mobility of labour increases to the extent that overall output expands as much as it would if the number of workers had increased by

1 per cent, the overall sum of wages will always fall and the workers as a whole suffer a determinate 'loss' provided that over the relevant period the elasticity of demand for labour is less than 1 – i.e. provided that wages also fall by more than 1 per cent in response to this 'increased' supply. If over the relevant period elasticity is greater than 1, the overall wage sum is greater, so that the workers derive an 'advantage', which of course does not prevent their relative share in the social product from falling.

Increased mobility of labour is definitely a good thing for the capitalist interest. It may of course damage the individual entrepreneur and the individual capitalist, i.e. the profitability of companies based in an area of abnormally low wages, and existing fixed capital may occasionally be thereby devalued – particularly in areas of abnormally high wages. There may in particular be damaging effects for very big monopolists who previously governed the labour market of a whole district; hence the frequent efforts of entrepreneurs to reduce their workers' freedom of movement by exploiting techniques for the organisation of labour in their own companies to make the workers as useless as possible for other companies and sectors. So monetary benefit can definitely be assumed for the labour force as a whole at best only in the final analysis and in the long term – namely for the time in which the advantages accruing to capital have been translated into demand for labour – but this applies directly only for one of two possible cases; whereas monetary benefit is promised for the capitalist interest taken as a whole, in any conditions and quite directly.[8]

All this applies not just to the geographical mobility of the workers but also to mobility from industry to industry, which is always limited if there are particular qualifications to be acquired that are quite valueless or considerably less useful in other sectors. Where such acquired aptitudes are involved, we have a case of quasi-rent for intervals of time for which the career choices of new generations are not effective; once 'investment' has taken place it can be cancelled only with difficulty and at a loss and within the limits of these losses such workers must passively accept the wage which the temporary situation on the limited market thus created allows them, without being able to migrate to other parts of the overall labour market and thus correspondingly reduce supply on the partial market. The law of marginal productivity is not nullified but living contact with the marginal productivities of other such partial markets is paralysed. If Schüller and Tugan-Baranovskii had said that, they would have been able to explain all the facts they had in mind on the basis of theory.

The difference in the natural aptitudes of workers is not be to taken as a hindrance to mobility. What we have here are simply different kinds of 'labour as commodity',[9] just as peas and beans for example are different consumption goods, and there are connections between their values and their prices but these are very complicated. It fits with one of the many concepts of rent to speak here where applicable of higher efficiency 'rent' (rent of ability), and in fact that is just as much justified as it is to regard the rent of more fruitful soil as a surplus over and above the 'marginal yield' of the soil in general, only in neither case is there much to be gained by doing so. It would be more useful to study the connections between the values and prices of different categories of labour; such a study would look primarily at the partial replaceability of these by one another in one relation and their complementarity in others, also at the repercussions of wage rises in one of them on the others. This is scarcely even a beginning but all the theoretical aids for it are ready to hand in our price theory.

Social and national borders on the other hand are very much hindrances to mobility, only it is often difficult to establish in practice which of the three cases discussed applies – i.e. whether we are dealing with a vocational qualification (education, habit, nationality, individual adaptability to given tasks) or with differences in innate aptitude, or with social and national barriers – or which of these three is the most prominent, since all are generally found together. This difficulty is especially noticeable with the 'vertical mobility' of labour. It is still not clear to what extent a higher position in economic life (and even more so a higher position in other spheres) requires other types of capacity or simply a 'higher' capacity of the same kind or in general no different aptitudes from the subordinate ones, how these 'capacities' ranged on some kind of scale relate to one another, and which of them is innate, which is acquired, or which is simply triggered by opportunity – or indeed absent. Nor is it clear how the capacity to obtain a job relates to the capacity to do it well or how the level of remuneration of the activity relates to its position on another scale.[10] Here there are sociological and biological problems involved in our area, among others the question what role is played by special talents and whether in general – or at least in the area of non-manual work – there is something like a general ability/aptitude in the sense of Spearman's 'central factor' which asserts itself in all or most areas in more or less the same manner. In all these areas there are many obstructive prejudices and biases and theory can only seldom contribute anything to the answers; it usually has to wait for such answers in order to use them in its own domain. Here we touch on a topic covered by the Galton School.

There is however a brilliant piece of work in this field, Moore's *Laws of Wages* (1912), which I reviewed in this journal. The great idea of studying the relations between wage differentials and differences in qualifications opens up powerful perspectives. There is a new way here that is steep and rough, but it does require to be traversed. All this however I cannot pursue any further in the context of the present work.

VII The Wage Theorem of Unilateral and Bilateral Monopoly

In my discussion so far I have kept the case of the free market in the foreground for reasons which I have stated: even if no such state ever existed in practice, it would still be necessary for our understanding of processes to establish what is inherent in the essence of the market mechanism and what is not. To know this is essential not only for the diagnosis of the individual case, but also for the resolution of very practical questions; taxes or wage rises lead to very different results depending on whether we are dealing with industries which reach the productivity margins or industries that realise marginal profits.[1] Without some consideration of this difference there can be no real insight into things and one of the commonest mistakes in this debate consists in asserting of one of these cases what applies only to the other.

Thus if within certain limits or generally an entrepreneur or his combination of entrepreneurs has a monopoly of demand on the labour market, his valuation of labour is always to be understood as the same as that of an entrepreneur in competition with others – whether or not he also has a monopoly of the supply of his product (e.g. as a result of a prohibitive duty) does not affect the basic law of the process, although it does however constitute a particular case. But this valuation (which would in principle derive as much from consumers' valuation of utility in this case as in a free market) – the 'marginal product' of labour – is then no longer determinate for wages. Why should the entrepreneur offer a wage at the level of the marginal product, since the factors that in the competitive economy force him to do so are no longer present? Wage levels would in fact be undetermined here. Otherwise the monopoly price is clearly determined, but only as a consequence of the circumstance that those who contract with the monopolist vary their demand or their supply according to the prices determined by him. In our case this would not be possible for the workers. If they had to rely on demand from the monopolist as the only opening for the utilisation of their labour and really had to go hungry if he did not employ them, they would have to accept any wage level. Economics alone could not demonstrate what that level must be (over and above the necessary minimum for the physical existence of the number of workers required by the monopolist). The monopolist would inevitably need a greater number of workers to obtain his maximum profit than were directly available, and he could attract the extra workers through higher wage offers. But if there is quite simply a determinate number of (competing) workers available, no more and no less, we cannot hope to make up for the missing regulatory piece by dragging in the factor of the disutility of labour. For although the workers certainly would like to measure the amount of work to be done at any given wage rate in terms of the law of the equality of the marginal utilities of wages and the marginal reluctance of labour, if the monopolist stipulates an output and a wage, e.g. per day or week as an indivisible whole, he can force on them a level of performance for which that law is nowhere near realised, with respect to the value of those wage elements on which the preservation of life can be said to depend, a value that is higher than any known amount.[2] Therefore here the economically comprehensible factor becomes less important than other factors like fear of potential bitterness, respect for public opinion, morals, ethical considerations, etc. This is moreover an extreme case, and monopoly positions as actually occurring in the labour market generally have very narrow limits – or else the possibility of workers being attracted from elsewhere or something similar comes into the picture.

More important for practical purposes is the case where entrepreneurs have a monopoly position on the product market. Here the workers' interests are affected only to the extent that the monopolistic entrepreneur produces less and therefore generates a smaller demand for labour than would come from the relevant industry if free competition was the rule.[3] Here too the entrepreneur's or trust director's valuation of labour is a derivative of a consumer marginal utility. But in the first place this consumer marginal utility is now greater – because in general less is now produced than would be produced if there was free competition under otherwise similar circumstances – and secondly, in its effect on the entrepreneur's valuation of labour it is influenced by the possibility of replacing individual workers by others from industries where free competition is the rule. Only this 'substitution marginal product' is here determinate for wages, and the extent of demand is determined here by the number of workers that gives a maximum profit at this wage. With a given production method one and only one maximum corresponds to each such wage level. If all industries were organised monopolistically there would be a tendency for wage rates for the same kind of work to even out as a result of the competition between all these monopolists on the labour market, but the level itself would not be clearly determined.

In practice these cases are linked to all those cases of limited competition in which the latitude allowed by the pure economic law is always more or less substantial and which in fact occupy a broad area in the economy. It must again strike the reader how near our argument comes here to Tugan-Baranovskii's and in fact we are now dealing with those same facts that he must primarily have been thinking of when he allotted so much space to the 'power' factor. Schüller's observations are also closely connected to the whole area of limited competition. This is particularly evident to the observer who studies shorter periods. Schüller is primarily interested in the behaviour of companies in the temporary situation; not the flat surface of the level to which the economic sea tends but the stormy waves of the present moment. It is a standpoint that has something to be said for it. What must be stressed here in relation to both Tugan-Baranovskii and Schüller is that none of this contradicts the foundations of theory, and we must not allow our understanding of the essence of competition mechanism to be clouded by it, though we would not really get very far if we did not investigate anything else but that essence. The main features of a thing and its essence are one question, while the manner in which these are revealed through a small part of the thing is another. Both need to be studied, but to line the results yielded by the two up against each other is pointless.[4]

If the workers are organised monopolistically, wages are again clearly determined – with given methods of production – by the point at which the overall sum of wages is at a maximum. Whether in order to reach this point the overall supply of labour must generally be limited and if so, how substantially, is a *quaestio facti* and depends on the elasticity of demand. In any case here the workers do not need to put up with the wage which corresponds to the marginal product of labour, since they have power over the intramarginal value of labour[5] and can present every entrepreneur with the choice either of employing the marginal workers at the wage they seek or of taking on no workers. But since in the equilibrium situation these intramarginal surpluses will be taken up by ground rents and interest on capital, the wage demand, if it is to be maintained in the long term, is of course subject to limitation in the light of the effects of a withdrawal of rent and interest on the supply of land and capital (if private ownership of land is the rule, the supply of land is variable in view of its other possible uses – hunting, park land, etc. – according to levels of return). I shall come back to this topic shortly. Apart from this however wages can also rise above the measure given by the marginal product if the supply of labour is not restricted – assuming that individual entrepreneurs can be subjected to such a condition. If not, there remains only the restriction of supply which reduces the availability of labour artificially and therefore raises its marginal product artificially. In the form of the shortening of working hours such a restriction is a real weapon in the hands of workers' organisations.

Where monopolistically organised workers face an industry that is monopolistic with respect to demand for labour, there is an exchange between two monopolists – an 'isolated exchange' like the one between Robinson Crusoe and Man Friday – and there is no clearly determined wage level. But different circumstances, like the fact that the leader of each party has to watch out for the possibility of certain followers breaking ranks, anxieties about the ultimately devastating effects of endless conflict and about the consequences of demands pushed beyond a certain level for economic development etc. set limits to shifts in wage levels[6] (assuming we are not talking about a hypothetical war of annihilation but only about achieving a durable result within the capitalistic way of production). There is a particular advantage for the workers in this case: where they face competing entrepreneurs, they can only impose on the individual entrepreneur the restriction that he cannot dismiss any worker even at the higher wages if he wants to produce (though they cannot generally prevent individual companies from being closed down) but here they can impose the restriction on the whole industry.

As with all monopolies there needs to be careful differentiation. Each monopolist can raise his monopoly profit if he is not obliged to fix a uniform price but can establish a price system which exploits the greater buying power of many buyers, without excluding those with less buying power (as a uniform price at this level would do), a price system which is not too demanding for the weaker buying power of other buyers and attracts them without (as a lower uniform price would do) preventing the monopolist from possible exploitation of buyers with greater buying power. The same is of course true for a purchasing monopoly. The monopolistic seller of labour could proceed in an identical way and introduce wages differentiated in this manner afterwards and share them equally among workers of one category. The monopolistic purchaser of labour does in fact proceed in this way sometimes and wage differentials for the same work (as between men and women, workers of one nationality and foreign workers, young persons and mature persons) are explicable out of tacit quasi-monopolistic agreement.

VIII The Problem of the 'Artificial Rise' of Wages

If we now put some flesh on the theory we have sketched out and apply it properly to the available factual material, the results obtained on the old questions of 'artificial wage rises', the shortening of the working day[1] and the law of the movement of wage income are really much fuller than is generally believed. I want to say a few words about the first of these topics, leaving aside the relation between wages and quality of performance and assuming the latter to be unaffected by the relevant wage rise. As befits its practical significance, the problem has been discussed very frequently, and it has of course always been a storm centre of opinions hostile to theory – a whole series of prejudices against theory and what it allegedly teaches have their roots here. There is no other place where the nature of economic discussion is so clearly apparent, and more especially the fact that those obsessed with practicalities do not generally even take the trouble to understand a scientific theory, but are content to bandy around cliches and catch-phrases.[2] If this were not so, the general question of the 'possibility' of artificial wage increases could not have been raised, for no-one could have disputed it. At most it could have been said that 'artificial' wage increases have certain effects which may damage their potential long-term effectiveness. And yet no less an authority than Tugan-Baranovskii himself has ventured the opinion that if the theory were right it would demonstrate the pointlessness of all such attempts, concluded that it must be false because in fact they actually do succeed, and looked for a new theory.

We have to be clear as to whether we want to talk about the effect of an 'artificial' wage rise (e.g. one resulting from a legislative enactment) in relation to the case of a monopoly, to the case of limited competition, or to the case of a completely free market, and we need to know which of these applies *in concreto*. With the case of a free market, we need to be clear whether the rise takes wages above and beyond an equilibrium situation or whether not such position is reached at the moment of the rise; then whether we are studying temporary or long-term effects, and whether we are thinking of wage rises in only one sector or across the board. We must moreover always distinguish between the effects of wage rises on the social product and the effects on the share of the workers – both relative and absolute. A very general question like: is an artificial wage rise possible? or: how does an artificial wage rise work? doesn't really have any meaning. We need to discuss a few of the more important cases and outline the chief general ways of looking at them.

If workers face an entrepreneur who has a monopoly over the market for his product – the case of a monopoly of demand for labour solves itself – there do not need to be any repercussions and the wage rise can be maintained in the long term, as long as the workers are able to resist pressure from other workers. The monopolist could find it advantageous[3] to raise the price of his products, with the consequence that demand for them falls, and consequently the monopolist's demand for labour falls too. But within certain limits he may be able not to raise the product price without overall production becoming unprofitable for him (Montemartini).[4] If not, sooner or later it will come to lay-offs, for with altered production costs the point of maximum profit (Cournot point) is generally different. The possibility of this condition is advantageous for the workers, but does not mean that their position is more favourable in relation to a monopolist than in relation to an entrepreneur with whom other entrepreneurs are competing; for the social product is smaller in the former case than in the latter and in general it is only the fact of a profit gained at the cost of all consumers, especially the workers – which offers an advantage at this point. If all sectors of industry are monopolised and if a general rise in wages occurs, the situation of the workers becomes even more favourable, to the extent that there is now no undercutting to be feared on the part of other workers. In either case moreover the monopolist may have an interest in varying his output, even if he does not raise the product price, and even more so in changing his production method, for the most advantageous combination of the means of production at the previous wage level is so no longer.

The same situation applies everywhere where there is restricted competition or some kind of unspoken agreement between entrepreneurs, and hence especially in underdeveloped countries. Here there are still profits everywhere, even at the margins of productivity, which serve as a 'buffer' and reduce the pressure of a wage rise on the overall organism of the economy. This applies almost everywhere, particularly for short periods, and these circumstances explain why we can agree with Schüller's conclusion that 'within the practical limits under consideration wage rises can generally cause only a relatively small fall in demand for labour' (1916–17, p. 743), without of course approving his reasons for the principle. There is also a partial agreement here with Tugan-Baranovskii's practical conclusions.

If we turn to consider the case of competition we must first of all ask whether intervention by authority in wage settlements will succeed in an equilibrium situation or not. Very often in fact the appearance of success results from the fact that for some reason or other wages were not at equilibrium level. An intervention that brings this about does not of course have any unfavourable repercussions. A specially important case is that of the depreciation of currency which has been going on since the mid-1890s and which is being powerfully reinforced by the events of the day. Here wages usually follow changed conditions only at a greater or smaller interval and there ensues a temporary fall in real wages that is quite unjustified, i.e. quite unfounded in the real conditions of wage levels. If that is now corrected by government intervention, the situation that results is exactly the one appropriate to the mechanism of competition. Perhaps in such cases – and they are very numerous – it is not quite correct to speak of an apparent success, since many unnecessary frictions, battles and miseries are actually eliminated thereby. The time you do get a merely apparent success is when there are government-imposed or otherwise 'artificial' wage rises in a period of economic upswing such as would in any case produce wage increases; such artificial raises only 'work' because the equilibrium position of wages shifts upward anyway. Therefore the satisfaction of nineteenth-century social planners about their activities was in part a delusion. But in any case the real problem of 'artificial wage rises' occurs much more rarely in practice than the problem of the rise in a wage level that has remained short of its point of equilibrium.

My different approach is sustainable thus far: the only point open to dispute might be the solution to this 'real' problem, which contains the theoretical kernel of the matter even though it is much less significant in practice. If in a particular industry governed by free competition wages are raised above equilibrium by government intervention and the press of workers from other sectors is kept away, the marginal amount of products will now be produced at a loss and decreases, so that the product price rises. There is another way to the same result: the entrepreneur 'knocks on' the wage rise onto the price, so that demand decreases and the price falls again from this level, but not quite back to its earlier position; a partial passing on to the consumers takes place and – through reduced production – a further partial passing on to the owners of the means of production, and therefore to the workers. If we were really dealing here with a 'profitless entrepreneur', both passings on would have to make good the rise in wages. The process does not continually need to take place step by step in practice, but the entrepreneurs can skip one or some links in the chain and anticipate its result.

I want to point out with respect to this result that it is perceptible only if a simultaneous development does not change the data of the relevant equilibrium situation, with e.g. demand for the product of the relevant industry rising. Because this is normally in fact the case, a passing-on process will generally be overshadowed, even when as is generally the case there is no 'buffer' of quasi-rent and surplus profit in the industry in question, but that does not mean the process is unreal and can be ignored. It is often argued that coffee prices fell after the introduction of coffee duties, so that the duty did not in fact influence the prices at all, but in fact without the duty the coffee price would obviously have fallen much more; it is equally obvious in our case too that a similar reply is not only theoretically correct but also necessary in the interests of our understanding of a practical case.

The process described only happens if the demand for the product in question is not too inelastic. If it is, the fall in demand occurs elsewhere in the economy and may then easily be invisible to the eye of the observer.

It might be argued that a reduction in production would be an appropriate reaction to the wage rise from the entrepreneur's point of view only if the costs of the product unit were thereby reduced and industry followed a law of decreasing return. But this is not so. Even if the curve of successive supply prices bends downwards in the industry under consideration and follows a law of increasing return with the costs of the product unit rising as production contracts, e.g. as a result of the larger proportion of general costs falling on the unit, there is a point at which the demand curve falls permanently below the supply curve and this is the point of stable equilibrium. If the supply curve then shifts upwards parallel with itself because of a wage rise, a look at the well-known shape shows not only that a general reduction in production is still always an appropriate reaction of the entrepreneur to the wage rise, but that the havoc caused by a disturbance of equilibrium, whether that is constituted by a wage rise, by the imposition of a tax, or by something else, will for the most part be much worse if that industry follows a law of increasing return than if it follows a law of decreasing return. There are complex cases – the case of multiple equilibrium situations among others – but all these questions have been carefully discussed by Marshall, Edgeworth and their circle, so that ignorance of the relevant conclusions is absolutely unforgivable today.

Objections of the kind made by Schüller miss the point of the argument here too. Certainly in our case an entrepreneur cannot reduce his 'demand for output per square metre' by giving up a square metre of the piece of ground on which his factory stands. For short periods here the economic process encounters very substantial friction and resistance which may occasionally bring it to a halt, and theory has ways of understanding this.[5] The entrepreneur has to bear in mind that he can expect the ceaseless movement of economic life to bring his company back to profitability without him doing anything about it. Theory – especially modern theory – has never asserted that the problem is resolved simply by the articulation of fundamental principles. Moreover a superficial view of the effects of a wage rise suggests that some companies will be unprofitable and will slowly sicken and that others will thereby gain breathing-space, so that the effect of the economic connections is visible only to an overview of the whole social process and not to a study of the behaviour of each individual company.

The variations to which my account refers are to be regarded as relatively very small, so that the foundations of the company organisation and the application of income in the economy are not changed through them, and this again applies primarily to relatively short periods. The practical usefulness of the results is not thereby altered, for wage rises of the kind being considered – i.e. wage rises above the equilibrium level of wages in an industry in which perfectly free competition is the rule – are in fact always only small. But if we then consider greater variations – which however may still not be so great that a catastrophe or a complete collapse of organic relations to existing things occurs – and on the other hand we consider longer periods of time, changes in the manner of production and the supply of capital have to be taken into account. Another combination of factors of production will now be optimal and the coefficients of production are modified. It will be advantageous to apply more capital and land in relation to labour. The multiplication of the amount of capital per worker takes place mostly in the form of an extension of the mechanised company,[6] and obviously wage rises are one of the most important reasons why ever-increasing scope for mechanisation of the production process is sought.[7] *En passant*, this may affect two interesting cases: firstly, where as a result of the complete change of all the elements, a much greater amount of production than before will be optimal in the entrepreneur's calculations: where previously a smaller amount of production was optimal, and no greater amount had been advantageous even with mechanisation of the production process – rather, such mechanisation would have been unprofitable at the earlier wage level, whereas now at a new wage level mechanisation and with it a bigger output offers the best hope of profit. This case does not necessarily happen but it may do so, and then not only does it have the result that workers profit as consumers, but also that a kind of secondary demand for labour is triggered, which does not wholly restore the previous overall demand for labour but only a part of it. This potential extension of production does not contradict our principle that a rise in wages tends to follow a reduction in production. For that principle is generally valid only on the assumption of truly constant production methods, while the case discussed above rests on the opposite assumption. Both cases are equally real, both fit in well with the foundations of the theory, but both are related to different series of facts which are in reality always superimposed one upon the other. Likewise it is no contradiction to say as we did that as a consequence of the tendency for wage rises to be accompanied by restrictions on production, demand for capital falls, whereas we now see that it may also rise. Broadly speaking the one result occurs with small changes and relatively short periods, the other with bigger changes in the wage rate and relatively longer periods. The question might be raised as to what is the use of a theory which answers a 'clear question' about the effects of wage rises with such a mass of contradictory possibilities: and it would indeed be wonderful if the same people who for are for ever complaining that theory distorts many-sided reality with its simple formulae, when shown that from these simple formulae an elastic living system of results covering all possible cases can be derived, wanted to get indignant all over again and to turn the different possibilities into contradictions undermining theory – *guarda e passa*! But if this question is actually asking what effects a wage rise would have in practice in a concrete case or approximately in the present and in the domain of capitalistic culture, it is evident that our theory can (like all theories) formulate its results only hypothetically, and this question never comes up independently but only with the necessary facts included in it. But even then a theorist who really has a grip on theory will be careful not to be too 'absolute'. In other areas too insight does not always go hand in hand with prompt judgements about the individual case; the promptest diagnosis is given to a patient by the town barber; while the man of science often shows 'uncertainty' in diagnosis, something which normally and properly redounds to his credit.

The other case I wanted to discuss in this connection is where with a reorganisation of production such as is involved in the mechanisation of the production process, completely new possibilities very easily emerge that no-one had thought of before, so that a further reorganisation of production follows, which can have the consequence (among others) that at the new wage level demand for labour reaches its previous level again or indeed rises above that level. From the viewpoint of the causal connection under discussion here this would need to be described purely as an accident, but it is an accident that happens very easily.

The multiplication of the amount of capital per worker does not necessarily need to take place in the form of an increase in existing capital, even though that is the most important case. Fewer raw materials can be held in stock for example, or the finishing of products reduced. The most important case of the multiplication of the production factor of land is of course the transition from an intensive to a more extensive form of company. These cases demonstrate very clearly the nature of one aspect of the theoretical problem which we always have to be aware of. The effects of wage rises are conditioned by the fact that we are talking about two different kinds of relations between the values and prices of labour on the one hand and capital and land on the other: all three are complementary goods and furthermore all three are up to a point competing goods.[8] A paradigm of the first kind of relation is that between the values and the prices of sugar and coffee, and a paradigm of the second is that between the values and the prices of coffee and coffee surrogates. Both cases were discussed in depth a long time ago,[9] but their combination presents particular difficulties, so I shall not go into them any further here.

Absolute capital yield does not necessarily fall as a result of a wage rise, but this basically only applies to small variations and short periods of time, where the reaction to the wage rise consists purely in a lengthening of the production period. But to the extent that it does fall there arises the question how that affects the supply of capital. If it contracts, in general and in particular the result must primarily be a transfer of the burden pressing on capital over to the workers, and in fact for a very long time artificial wage increases were said to result automatically in people 'not saving any more'. This view was however always (and now by Tugan-Baranovskii) countered with the assertion that within certain limits a fall in capital yield can bring about a rise in 'savings activity', an argument that is justified. If we take the position that capital comes about through saving and that this – of course only at the margins – involves a 'sacrifice' that must be compensated by interest income, it does not follow that if interest falls people will inevitably save less. For even though marginal capital yield must be the same as the marginal sacrifice of saving, this equivalence can be achieved at very different interest rates. With interest at a high level the curve of marginal utility of increasingly large amounts of savings obviously goes downwards faster than with interest at a low level. If we now treat the curves of the marginal utility of the increase of income and the curves of the disutility of savings as identical in the two cases, it may be that with a higher interest income equilibrium will be reached with a smaller marginal sacrifice, and thus a smaller overall amount of savings than with a lower interest income, because the marginal utilities of the faster increasing income growth can be compensated earlier by a 'reluctance to save' in the first case than in the second case. And if there is no decrease in saving, there cannot be a transfer of the burden to the workers in this sense, indeed it can even happen that more is saved than before and interest is thus put under more pressure.

Too much may however be asked of this argument. For most of the authors who operate with it the argument has the particular disadvantage that it shows the possibility of an interest rate reduction without any reduction in saving necessarily taking place thereby, while at the same time it also shows the necessity of interest in order that there can be general saving (leaving aside the very small part of the required amount of capital which we can assume would be 'put aside' entirely without interest as a reserve against misfortune, etc.). This cannot be used to show that any reduction in the interest rate will leave the supply of capital unchanged or raise it only if interest generally remains above zero, for that is true only for limited intervals and to a different extent for the different motives for saving and classes of savers. Even within these limits we can apply it safely to individual savers, but not to the overall social sum of savings. Where that is concerned it must be borne in mind that even though many people save less at higher interest rates than at lower, at higher rates of interest many people join the ranks of the savers – especially 'little' people – who would generally not be saving at the lower rates. This makes the issue very uncertain, and one cannot say that the facts speak very clearly in favour of the argument under discussion. The fact that up to now falling interest rates and increasing taxation of capital income have gone hand in hand with increased saving proves nothing.

For in the first place a habit of saving once acquired persists for a long time even if its rational foundations have been lost; in the second place, we are dealing with a historical process in the course of which all the data have changed fundamentally, and particularly in that so many people have been in a position to save for the first time after previously living on the subsistence level, while others have made entrepreneurial profit as never before, so that nothing can be proved from it; thirdly, it is not clear whether the reluctance to save that appears here and there in certain circles which were previously more inclined to save does not have amongst other causes that of the weaker impulse of a lower interest rate. Finally however – and this needs to be especially emphasised – nothing is proved by the argument under discussion against the abstinence theory, for this theory can be fully reconciled with the fact on which the argument rests so that it does not matter whether or not that fact is certain. Tugan-Baranovskii all too easily concluded that if an interest rate reduction may have either an increase or a decrease in the supply of capital for a result, the abstinence theory of interest is refuted. I do not intend to defend this theory at present, – I too find it unsatisfactory – but this 'refutation' is beside the point.

So far we have been thinking of an 'artificial' wage rise in one single industry. But since we have eliminated as all too obvious the effects of pressure from workers from other industries – clearly a real difference between this case and that of a general wage rise – what has been said applies to a great extent also to the latter. Only one point remains to be cleared up. The popular opinion is that in this case too entrepreneurs simply 'pass on' the amount of the wage rise to the product price, and one of the preferred theories about price increases in the last fifteen years has been that they are to be explained precisely by rises in wages. But the question is clearly not so simple, for when there is a given amount and a given circulation velocity of units of purchasing power, surely all prices cannot rise at the same time. Some economists criticise laymen for believing they can, but there is of course an answer to those economists. If overall costs increase for all entrepreneurs and all have the intention of demanding higher prices, they will now get even bigger loans from their banks, e.g. be able to discount greater amounts of bills of exchange. By means of banknotes or newly-established credit balances the amount of the means of circulation is then permanently increased – to the extent that repayment of loans is usually followed by renewal of them – and as the laymen always thought, all prices may indeed climb at the same time. This is one of the many forms of the modern abuse of credit and one of the reasons why it is so difficult for banknote banks to avoid gold speculation. But such a rise in all prices is illusory and no entrepreneur will profit from it, not even if his own income rises, since the prices of all the goods that he would like to buy with his higher income also rise, at least with this reservation – and it is an important one in practice: apart from the intercompany profits which currency depreciation produces for the circle of entrepreneurs (but not for the capitalists as such). As Ricardo pointed out, it is impossible for all the exchange relations of commodities to rise at the same time, something which is not really affected by another fact emphasised by Ricardo, that wage rises move exchange relations in favour of commodities in which a relatively large element of direct labour is involved, at the cost of those that are produced with a relatively large amount of fixed capital. This last principle is however a very important element in our problem. At the time when it occurs, the shifting of exchange relations produces profits and losses which have nothing to do with the main currents of the effects of the wage rise and may completely conceal them for the individual enterprise; it gives us an example of how differently a wage rise affects individual enterprises – another example is the big difference that it can make whether a company is governed by a law of decreasing or a law of increasing return. A third example is how elastic the demand for its products and its demand for labour are. What we have here is a hopeless tangle of effects and repercussions. Although it is true that apart from the case of 'abuse of credit' we have discussed not all prices could rise at the same time, it is nonetheless still true that they may do so if a reduction in production occurs, to which again we would need to add: below the level it would otherwise have reached. If this happens, the workers as consumers will again be robbed of a part of the advantage which they have gained as producers, so that it has very much more than purely 'nominal' effects. Such a reduction in output also means that the wage increase does not need to fall purely on capital (and land), although with a general rise in wages the tactical position of capital is thereby made worse in that it cannot migrate – although it can still 'mechanise'. If at this point Ricardo apparently came to a different conclusion, that has to do with certain particularities of the only cases which he considered, namely the 'unreduceability of wages' and partly to his primitive value theory, which made it difficult for him to have real insight into these things. It would be easy to show that his conclusion is 'correct' within his data system and does not in the slightest contradict the conception being presented here; and the same is true for Schüller, whose conclusion is the same as Ricardo's; the facts he addresses easily fit in with theory, even though his general approach cannot be defended in the same way as Ricardo's.

The effects of a general wage rise are in fact the same whether it results as we have assumed from the intervention of authority or from organised action on the part of the workforce (with or without a strike). In the latter case the workers have a more or less complete monopoly position and this is covered by what has been said on that score. What we spoke of earlier as being accomplished by external power (and here at least the 'power' factor is in its place and clearly distinguishable from the effects of economic factors) is accomplished here by the fact that the intramarginal values of labour are exploited. In this case the workers would have no interest in raising wages above the equilibrium level, since that in any case marks the maximum of the overall amount of wages to be obtained – whether temporary or permanent. A particular feature of this case is that it is easier to avert both personal losses for workers made redundant and the wage-push threatened by them by keeping them on or sacking them as appropriate.

In practice the danger is temporary, and if as a consequence of government regulations or labour organisation dictats wages cannot fall, permanent unemployment is much lower than it would be if the theoretically basic case of a rise in wages above its equilibrium level in an industry otherwise operating under fully free competition were actually the rule. But the danger does exist, and when in England – where industrial life comes particularly close to the free market model – very substantial 'artificial' wage rises occurred in the immediate pre-war years, there were numerous cases of unemployment which were explained in a whole variety of ways. Tugan-Baranovskii also noted this phenomenon, but without any suggestion of an explanation which could allow us to suppose that 'England's bold quest to introduce this policy on a grand scale' (1913, p. 82) does not say so much for the unlimited power of social policy as he thinks. To the determined social planner who does not want to listen to counter arguments and does not want to see facts that contradict him, any such hint would be futile. But of someone of the stature of Tugan-Baranovskii we may expect that he be able to look fairly and squarely even at unwelcome facts[10] – and that he not speak carelessly of a high level of wages 'in spite of substantial levels of unemployment', as if there were no connection between the two.

Now we need to sum up the most important practical heads of our argument regarding the effects of 'artificial' wage rises. We can see that in very many cases such rises may have lasting success, while in other cases the success is only apparent, but ultimately no damaging consequences ensue for the workers. In my opinion these cases constitute the majority of all the practical experiments attempted, and that is what the classic writers would have expected. For this very reason it is not correct to say with Tugan-Baranovskii (p. 83) that if 'wages were determined by the law of prices' it would a 'very great mistake to try and alter wage levels by socio-political legislation', even less so to make this a reason for calling for a 'change in the theory' because the old theory 'contradicts the actual facts of social life'. Even for the theoretically basic case theory has never preached the 'impossibility' of these wage rises with such insistence.[11] If a theorist occasionally does so we should not be too quick to throw the blame for it on theory. The legitimacy of this distinction lies in the fact that the foundations of theory must be judged in themselves and according to their potential results and not purely according to what an individual author derives from them, still less according to what the herd of hack writers finds in them. The fact is that it can be clearly demonstrated from the classics that socio-political experiments may be successful in this case too, and this is still more applicable to today's theory, if we only make the proper use of it. It says only that these wage rises set off certain repercussions which on certain presuppositions rob the worker of a part of the overall profit and on other presuppositions of the whole profit – a very different standpoint from the one that Tugan-Baranovskii is opposing.

Then we saw that it is possible to use both organised action[12] and legal measures to raise the share of the workforce in the social product.[13] First of all, with small wage increases which leave the basis of the settled policy of the company unchanged, it is possible that the 'reduction' in production consequent on the wage rise to below the level that it would have reached without the wage rise, and the corresponding 'reduction' in demand for means of production to below the level that it would have reached without the wage increase, primarily or (in a conceivable if extremely rare marginal case) wholly, alters capital and land utilisation, and it is certain that (other than in the thinkable but extremely rare marginal case) they do have this effect, so that in the vast majority of cases the number of workers made redundant is not big enough for their supply of labour to push wages back down to the earlier level, or (if that is not possible) so that their loss of wages would balance the profit in money made by the others.[14] The inner meaning of this process is that as a result of the intervention either the relative marginal productivities of the means of production will change – and indeed generally to the advantage of the workers – or that workers' wages will be emancipated from the marginal product and the intramarginal value of labour will be exploited. Moreover it is possible (even if less easy) for substantial wage increases leading to a change in production methods to influence the marginal product of labour favourably, and particularly thereby its relative share in the social product, and maybe even the overall wage total – its real amount – and in the most favourable case thereby encourage still further wage rises. Does this amount to preaching the fruitlessness and pointlessness of social planning?

Of course there are limits to all this. A blind striving for wage increases can certainly be pointless – at least economically pointless – for as a resource in the social and political battle to destroy Capitalism constantly-renewed wage demands may well have a point, something that Tugan-Baranovskii overlooks if he thinks that the potential economic pointlessness of wage demands implies their general pointlessness.[15] But apart from this a much greater prudence and foresight is necessary in these things than the popular-humanitarian social planner is accustomed to exercise. Certain repercussions that rob the worker of a share of his success almost always occur if we are dealing with a case which corresponds closely to the theoretical basic pattern. Above all the workers as consumers lose a part of what they have acquired as workers. As a rule wage rises have the consequence that the social product becomes smaller than it would otherwise have been. And we cannot be too confident that the loss will fall on all economic subjects while the profit accrues only to the workers. For to an extent we are dealing here with a loss of consumers' rents, affecting everybody but doing no-one any good. Of course we need to consider the effect on the supply of capital and the possibility that at least in the short term the industry's process of adapting to the higher wages is a bad thing for the workers. If the effect of the wage increase on demand is not so serious as many theoreticians believe, the danger is nonetheless very real from this quarter.

If a short answer is now wanted to our question, we can say that small wage rises for the most part and substantial ones in numerous cases (only we are speaking here more of the theoretical basic case, not of the case of monopolised industries nor of those cases where the wage to be increased is below the equilibrium level) affect the relative share of the workforce in the social product favourably, leading to a rather (and sometimes substantially) higher overall wage total; that for the most part such rises have a negative effect on the size of the social product and that the satisfaction situation of society overall sinks below the level – expressed in money – that it would otherwise have reached, but that the real amount of the workers' share may increase; that the direct and indirect repercussions of the wage rise rob workers generally of a part and often of the greater part of the success they achieve, but almost never of the whole of it; and that if measures are taken for the care of workers made redundant so that their supply cannot put pressure on the wage obtained, a lasting result can also be achieved in this way. A general assessment of how significant this success can be, and especially of how substantial must be those 'relatively small' wage rises by which the workers' chances are optimised, is impossible. In every case it will depend on a very complicated system of conditions. Especially if we reckon the elasticity of demand for labour over the crucial periods to be substantial – or again, if the equilibrium level of wages was reached even before the intervention and no supporting wave of economic activity begins – we may quite rightly find very narrow the boundaries within which lasting success is to be hoped for.

But can anyone wonder at this? Is it not basically self-evident and is it not precisely the cornerstone of the socialist critique of the market economy that within that system – capitalist if you want – with its private possession of the means of production and its reliance on the individual drive to acquire, etc., options for this kind of social planning must be limited, however extendable those limits are? Is it not precisely the task of science to set the limits and can the layperson not expect precisely that of science? The slogan about the social relations of power has no part in this task, and we have now seen its total emptiness. For if we want to know something about the effects of wage rises which even a blind man can observe in a thousand ways in practical life, it remains quite simply dumb, and at best has only 'popular economics' to offer us. But as we have seen it is not right that theory should renounce this task or that certain facts should be inexplicable from the theoretical viewpoint. Of course it is true that theory does not offer all we could wish. But that instead of marching forward from operation to operation it is for ever falling over itself and that even what it does is not understood or even known about is purely a matter of the way it is tackled and the passive resistance which it seems to elicit quite automatically. The time has come to put an end to controversies that lost any meaning long ago and for us all to collaborate on a common task in an area that is quite neutral and on which we all must move in the same direction, whatever our political orientation.[16] It is time to break with the childish attitude which only wants to see what is comfortable and for which the dogma of the all-powerfulness of social planning is sacred. It is above all time to relearn the theoretical craft and pursue theory in an orderly manner, since it is something we cannot avoid. This is the area where we are most deficient. Everything else would then be in place for a true social theory of distribution.

Part II
Equilibrium and Power

I Power and the Economy: The View of an Anti-Schumpeterian

1 INTRODUCTION

What is meant here by 'power' is all social power, in the broadest sense, thus implying both economic power (power which can be exercised over others through the supply of goods) and extra-economic (non-economic) power. What I am concerned with here is only the latter of these two. The word will therefore be used here only in the sense of extra-economic power. Extra-economic power (and the word social power also means this when it is contrasted with economic power) is sometimes identified with authority (influence). To make this identification is on the one hand a misunderstanding of the essence of authority, and on the other nothing other than a crude abuse of the term when it comes to analysing extra-economic forces, but I will not go here into the details of my opinion on this matter.

The relationship between power in this sense and the economy has been dealt with by scholars numerous times up to the present, and as far as the majority of academics is concerned, there is a widespread acceptance of what must be regarded as an established theory. This states that the economy – the market economy – is a self-regulating entity, and that power is a prerequisite (a datum) for the existence of that economy. However, once this prerequisite is satisfied, an economy develops according to its own logic (i.e. its own laws). There is therefore no scope in economic theory for taking account of the operation of power, because it does no more than formulate in the form of laws the movement of the economy according to its own particular logic. This is the so-called Monroe Doctrine of economics. It can be said that even where this actual term is not used, almost all academics would subscribe to this dominant view.

This is not the case with those views which are grouped together in economics under the name of *Machttheorien*, or theories of power; these contend that power plays an active role in the economy. As far as its relationship with power is concerned, an economy is thus not autonomous; it is not something which possesses its own logic, totally detached from power. Adherents of these theories take the view that economic theory, and particularly price theory, can only be clarified if they take into account the influence of power. Tugan-Baranovskii [1913] is a recent representative example of this view. The economic theories of Oppenheimer are frequently categorised as theories of power, but even though he regards power as one of the major reasons behind the formation of a monopoly, he recognises throughout the autonomy of the mechanism which he establishes, all prices as monopolistic prices. It is therefore not appropriate to count this as a theory of power. It is correct to see E. Dühring as a supporter of theories of power, but his price theory associated with theories of power is constructed on an inadequate explanation of marginal utility, and is distinctly crude. Any attempt to dissect it using the techniques of modern academic analysis would be very difficult, and would serve almost no useful purpose. That, at the very least, is my view. This does not mean, however, that we must reject the view that takes Tugan-Baranovskii theories as representative of theories of power. To my mind, nevertheless, the Tugan-Baranovskii standpoint is too lukewarm. He is totally committed to marginal utility theory in determining product prices. It is only in relation to distribution theory, and the theory of producer goods prices, that he tries to look at the influence of power. However, if we accept that the latter are directly governed by power, the same is also almost certainly true for the former. My own perspective on theories of power is that price formation as a whole is directly determined by power. I believe that my interpretation is the only one that incorporates the ideas of marginal utility theory and marginal productivity theory, while at the same time trying to take account to the same extent of the influence of power. We may, of course, point out that there is an aspect of F. von Wieser's price theory which must be regarded as a theory of power, although in this case, too, very little significance is assigned to power. I myself always regard Tugan-Baranovskii's views as the precursor of my own perspective.

Even with Tugan-Baranovskii's theory of power, however, there are a lot of fundamental criticisms to be made. These criticisms, moreover, also naturally apply to my own ideas, which go far further than Tugan-Baranovskii did in making claims for the influence that power exerts upon the economy. If I am going to try and follow through my own assertions, I have no choice but to make my way forward by overcoming the criticisms which have already been made. In terms of theory, the sharpest criticism is perhaps that of Schumpeter. If I can take up, and sufficiently refute, this representative view, then I shall regard myself as having largely achieved the defensive side of my task, namely that of proving my theory of power.

2 SCHUMPETER'S VIEW OF THE ECONOMIC EFFECTS OF POWER

Schumpeter's position is constructed largely on the basis of marginal analysis. On the one side, like Menger, Böhm-Bawerk and Wieser, he stands firmly in the tradition of marginal utility theory, but he is at the same time strongly influenced by the Lausanne School. The influence of this school brings to the study of economics the approaches of physics, in particular those of mechanics. Now marginal analysis may be said to have a wide range of applications in physics. Transferring this approach to the study of economics means that marginal analysis is before long bound to become its core principle. Thus any price theory founded on marginal analysis, and hence on the marginal principle – although it of course acknowledges general equilibrium and relationships of mutual dependence – is at heart a theory of marginal utility where consumer goods are concerned, and a marginal productivity theory where producer goods are concerned. It is, of course, the case that when things are looked at as a whole, the prices of all commodities can ultimately be explained by reference to marginal utility, but this is not something which I intend to discuss here.

From this perspective, the criticisms which can be made of the theory of power, that is, of the assertion that power intervenes directly in the economy, and therefore plays a part in determining prices, are naturally denials and critiques of this very fact. Of course, this is not to deny that power has some influence on the economy. It is merely that this influence remains no more than a precondition for the development of the economy in accordance with the theory of its own autonomous mechanisms. It is no more than a given condition, a datum. However, what is the significance of its influence as a given condition, or, to put it another way, what is the real significance of its being a given condition?[1]

I am not going to attempt here to show Schumpeter's view on this subject by going through his references and his arguments clause by clause. I am just going to outline his perspective. From the point of view of people in general, and from Schumpeter's point of view as well, the effect of power on the economy may, I would suggest, be broadly summarised as follows:

1 Extra-economic power develops the social structures within which the economy operates, and hence also economic structures. The quantities of goods which constituents of the economy hold, and hence the amounts of goods they demand, are determined within this framework; once these are taken as given with the economy, then prices and the volume of goods, which are the core of the economy, are determined in so-called purely economic terms. What is meant by 'purely economic' is no more than by means of exchange, or 'by means of a process whereby it may reasonably be assumed that in return for a specific good a second good may be acquired'. This means that even if the word 'economic' is construed in a somewhat broader sense, but still as a concept which conflicts with power, then there is no question of any direct coercion upon the other party, merely exchange.

2 If power develops social structures and influences the economy through them, it is only what might be called an indirect agent. However, even today there are circumstances under which power performs a direct function. These are (a) the determining of prices, and the implementing of transactions by laws or compulsion, as in the case of, for example, official prices, a minimum wage system, or a levy according to a fixed indemnity cost; and (b) the use of prestige to increase or decrease prices, or to promote or hinder transactions. This would include, for example, accepting that servants are paid low wages because they are regarded as having a low status, being constrained by the prestige of another to part with something which one does not really want to sell, or, conversely, buying something which one does not really want. If the economy is going to be 'pure', and the so-called laws of economics, that is, the laws governing exchange, are sufficient agent, then this kind of intervention of power does not occur. It will only occur where the economy is not pure, where the operation of the laws of economics is impeded.

3 Workers' wage demands play an important part in determining wages. This is certainly so where custom and morality underpin these demands. In this case we can of course recognise the direct impact of power on the economy. We must consider, however, how such demands are formulated. They are, in fact, determined by economic laws, formulated according to the so-called wage inertia determined autonomously by the economy. They are therefore no more than secondary elements derived from the economy.

Broadly, then, this approach takes the view that variables (quantities and prices) in the economy are directly determined only by the economy itself, or, to put it another way round, only by the logic of the economy itself, merely by exchange. Only where there cannot be pure exchange, or where power acts as a secondary, reactive agent, will the direct influence of power affect variables in the economy. Basically economic entities, that is, variables in the economy, are determined by the economy itself. If we limit ourselves to mechanisms which directly affect the economy, then it is the economy which determines itself. Herein lies the autonomy of the economy.

Of course, economic organisation itself cannot be considered detached from the exercise of power. However, in principle power only exerts a determining influence on variables in the economy indirectly through this economic organisation. In this sense, power is no more than just one precondition of the laws of economics.

3 CAN PURE ECONOMIC THEORY CLAIM TO HAVE AUTONOMY?

It does not immediately follow from this statement, however, that we can assert the autonomy of economic theory. What Schumpeter meant by this autonomy was that economic theory does not incorporate within itself factors relating to social power. I would like to note that this is certainly the case as far as the present problem is concerned. The fundamental basis for this argument must now be considered.

According to Schumpeter's opinion, the real state of an economy is diverse and determined by a range of factors. It was for that reason possible to construct a single theory by focusing on some of these factors and pursuing considerations from there. Current economic theory is an example of this. In this case, the other factors are controlled and regarded as given conditions. By doing this, we can observe movement in the economy following from the operation of a specific factor, and this is exactly what contemporary economic theory does. From this perspective, when movement in each subject is regarded as movement according to the principle of exchange, or the principle of maximisation, the inevitable result is a theory of marginal productivity. Thus far this insistence on the non-functioning of power is very close to the statements of Böhm-Bawerk. Consideration of other factors is now regarded as the task of economic sociology. Viewed from this perspective, economic sociology is a residual concept, and no positive provision is therefore attributed to it. Since it is a kind of residue which remains after we have extracted from reality everything that is purely economic, it may vary widely. It must be possible to extract one factor from these, and to examine the economy in terms of this one factor. An economic theory depending on power can, of course, also be formulated as a result of such investigations. On this occasion things which are purely economic are fixed as a given datum.

It is therefore possible to formulate a single 'methodologically autonomous theory' with respect to the operation of each of the various causes which we have to be able to distinguish in this way. The other causes now have to be dealt with merely as given conditions. We will now consider just the operation of these two sets of causal factors, namely the economic ones dealt with by economic theory and those which come under the heading of power or other 'social laws' (to use Karl Diehl's words). This does not mean that we regard the economy and power as acting together equally as determinants of economic variables. It does not permit of moving from the parallel exercise of social power and the laws of economics to the attainment of economic phenomena. Sets of problems which can be quite different each have their own methodological autonomy, and when one thing is being looked at, the other is regarded as given.

Having examined the original theories relating to interest, Schumpeter explained this as follows. The relationship between power and economic laws should not be seen as the parallel functioning (*Nebeneinanderwirken*) of the two along a single line, but rather as a mode of functioning in which the different factors which go to make up the chain of social cause and effect function in tandem with each other (*Hintereinanderwirken*). These elements influence each other, but remain methodologically autonomous from each other. In order to elucidate this (for the sake of economic theory, and not to achieve a sociological perspective), we may appeal to some sort of analogy. Winning or losing at cards is decided by two things; the cards which are first dealt out and the skill with which each individual player uses his or her cards. If we call the latter the fortune bestowed by skill, the former the fortune of the cards, then it is these two which together determine the result. It is then possible to take the fortune of the cards as a given, and observe what result will come from the fortune of skill alone. This would be a theory of the fortune of skill in cards. If we look for the outcome only of the cards, with the fortune of skill as a given, we have a theory of the fate of the cards. Contemporary economic theory is like explaining the results of skill, with the fortune of the cards as a given. Alternatively, we could also have a theory whose aim is to observe the results of the fortune of the cards with the given being this time the skill. This can be interpreted as being Schumpeter's position, but we cannot thereby establish any organic unity between each of these theories. So how then can we establish a foundation for the significance of traditional economic theory? My own belief is that we have no alternative but to achieve a unity between two, three or four theories through some kind of Paretian successive approximation. That is to say, we have no choice but to incorporate into the vacuum we call the pure economy the elements referred to as power, undertaking a secondary approximation. This is the way which I have used in my previous works.

Summing up the above argument, we are led to the following. It is not just economic laws (dealt with by economic theory) which determine economic variables. A great many other things are also important, one of which is power in society. If we take one of these two and observe its functioning, the other has merely to be regarded as given. However, consideration of the former, i.e. economic laws, has furnished us with a methodologically autonomous theory. Exactly the same can be said if we look at the functioning of the other side. For this reason, as long as we are concerned with economic laws, i.e. development according to the logic of the economy itself, or, to put it another way, as long as we are concerned with the determining of economic variables by those things which determine them directly, power will be put in the background as a precondition and its functioning will not be brought out into the open.

This way of dealing with social power, which we find in the ideas of Schumpeter, rests on two basic grounds. One is that as long as we are considering the influence of one set of causal factors in the economy the other set of causal factors can only be dealt with as a given. The second is that power does not belong to those causal factors which are incorporated into the laws of economics, but is classified as belonging to the other set of causal factors. Now while there are a range of other things here which need investigation, I think that it is the first of these two basic grounds which needs to be pursued. I cannot, however, admit the second ground of the argument, and will try and directly address this fact.

Is it not the case that any assertion that social power is not one of those causal factors which can be brought within the remit of economic laws, but must be regarded merely as a given as far as the laws of economics are concerned, means that we are closing one eye to the functioning of power? My feeling is that there are two ways in which the functioning of social power has an influence on economic variables. One is the functioning generated by power through social organisation or, more strictly speaking, through economic organisations. From the viewpoint of economic variables this is not direct intervention, but rather indirect operation. The second mode of functioning is the direct command over economic variables within the mechanism of exchange.

If we assume the latter does not exist, we are, of course, bound to end up regarding power as a given condition for economic laws or economic life. Let us take again our previous example of cards. There is no scope in the dealing of the cards for the operation of individual skill, and no further dealing takes place until victory or defeat has been determined by means of skill. If the deal and skill are in this way entirely separate from each other, then we may decide the numbers of points players get by taking one of these two factors as the explanatory variable and regarding the other as given. If, however, we were to assume that the deal itself was influenced by skill, could we really then regard any observations from the perspective of the deal, i.e. an observation of how the points were determined by the deal, as being totally separate from skill? The answer to this must, of course, be in the negative.

Therefore, even if we accept the premise that where we are observing the operation of one of multiple causal factors, the remainder have to be regarded as given conditions, the conclusion that power is no more than a given condition in economic theory is only correct if we regard power as something with no direct influence on the determining of economic variables – or, to put it another way, it is only correct if we deny that power, as a precondition for the formation of economic organisations, has also a direct influence in their decision-making. This is exactly what Schumpeter's perspective was; it has also been the perspective in general of economic theorists who treat power only as a given.

Why is it that if a person embraces this view of economics, his economics is recognised as *the* orthodox economics? We are aware that an economics which is focused on power is likely to be constructed as power economics, while an economics focused on geography will end up as geographical economics. What is the reason, however, why contemporary economic theory has to be *the* economic theory? For me this assumption of Schumpeter's is a hopeless pluralism.

The problem is therefore no longer a methodological one, but a substantive one. Is it conceivable that social power does *not* exert a direct influence on economic variables, and in particular on prices, which are their very core? Is it likely that this influence will merely be a purely secondary factor, or only operate beyond the confines of pure economics? Schumpeter answered this question in the affirmative. On what grounds, however, was this assertion based?

4 POWER AND THE PRICES OF FACTORS OF PRODUCTION

Schumpeter has taken the view that, just as the price of products is determined by their marginal utility, so, likewise, the price of producer goods is determined by their marginal productivity. He acknowledges that power has a great influence on the formation of economic organisations, but once power has been regarded as a precondition for the conduct of economic life, it is necessarily reduced to being an impassive, idle spectator. Everything is determined in a purely economic fashion (*rein ökonomisch*), that is to say by means of free and spontaneous exchange between individuals. This perspective is also found in the older economic theories, in the ideas of Marx and Oppenheimer, who are regarded as having placed great emphasis on the operation of social power. Even in the case of Marx, it was always value, and hence the volume of work society deemed necessary for production, which determined the price of a commodity and the level of interest. There was no question of price and other economic quantities being influenced by the power relations between individuals. For Oppenheimer, too, while the overall capacity of power was demonstrated in the very drive to establish influence and wealth, and in the formation of monopolistic relations, when he came to discussing the working of the economy subject to this basic premise, the determining of all prices as monopolistic prices was merely by means of attempts to pursue utility and profit, i.e. by purely economic means. Schumpeter acknowledged this fundamental position, rejecting only the labour theory of value for product prices, and taking up marginal utility theory. As far as the prices of producer goods were concerned, Schumpeter's adoption of marginal productivity theory was a necessary consequence of a marginal analysis perspective, and an essential supplement to marginal utility theory.

Producer goods cannot initially possess utility for anyone. Nevertheless, the perspective of marginal utility theory suggests that if we take away utility we can have no price. How can we therefore solve this problem? According to Schumpeter – and this is a point of view shared with marginal utility theorists – in the final analysis it is the utility recognised by the consumer which counts. However, consumers do not even know what particular producer goods are needed for the production of a good, so how can they attribute a utility to that producer good? In answering this Schumpeter argues as follows. The consumer cannot directly acknowledge the utility of a producer good. The consumer can, however, discern the utility of a product, that is to say of a finished good. The demand function is determined in accordance with that utility, and the price is in its turn determined on that basis. It is on that basis that the entrepreneur sets a value on the producer good. The entrepreneur determines the demand price for the producer good on the basis of the amount of value which it will bring to the enterprise. Thus the final factor in deciding the prices of producer goods is the marginal utility of consumers (*Konsumentengrenznutzen*). This being the case, the entrepreneur, in estimating the value to himself of the producer good, is doing so as a proxy for the consumer. This is nothing other than a proxy, but proper valuation (*vikarische Eigenwertschätzung*) on behalf of the consumer. Ultimately the price of a product based on the marginal utility of the consumer is reflected in the producer goods through the medium of a proxy valuer in the form of the entrepreneur, and it is by this means that the price of a producer good is determined. While this may be an indirect mechanism, the demand, and hence the price, are determined in accordance with the utility estimated by the consumer.

The problem, however, is the way in which this utility is reflected. Marginal productivity theory has been selected as the most appropriate means. The entrepreneur values the producer good in accordance with the principle or perspective of so-called *Variationen*; in making an estimate of value, he estimates its earning power (*Rentabilität*). That is to say, he looks at the amount by which his income would be decreased or increased by taking away or adding that specific means of production without any improvement in the organisation of production itself. The income earning function of producer goods is obtained such that it represents a change in the volume of income with respect to a change in the amount of a producer good used. Predictably this gives to the entrepreneur the demand function of a producer good. According to this demand function, it is the productivity accounted for by the final unit of the producer good (and *de facto* its income earning power) which determines the price of that producer good. Let us now look at this from the side of the supply of producer goods.

It is always bound to be the value for the supplier which will determine the supply price, and hence the supply function. This is because the supply function is always the reverse side of the demand function. Now under a situation of capitalistic production, it is generally the case that the owner of the means of production makes no specific estimate of either utility or income earning power. The supply price is essentially zero. Therefore the suppliers always accept on the market the demand prices which are decided by the entrepreneurs. That is to say, the supply prices represent the prices at which the means of production can be bought and sold in all other dealings. For that reason, if we look at the supply function for a means of production across the society as a whole, we find that it is ultimately determined by the demand function. Thus in the final analysis we have to say that the price of a means of production is determined by the demand functions and the quantities of the goods to be produced.

It is not my primary object here to explore how far marginal productivity itself can explain the price of a means of production. I merely intend to examine the form of theory essential to the theory of marginal productivity. And in this we find that as far as producer goods, that is to say means of production, are concerned, they are powerless to determine their own prices. It is the quantity of supply alone that is the determining factor in all economic quantities. The active, controlling role is played by the utility of the consumer, and the consumer demand. The entrepreneur, acting as a single proxy valuer, allocates the price of a product based on the marginal utility of the consumer to producer goods in accordance with their marginal productivities. The suppliers of producer goods passively accept the prices which have been so determined. This, then, is the general perspective.

Let us now take (from the previously mentioned work) one or two statements by Schumpeter which demonstrate this viewpoint:

> But the purchasers of the company's products have a valuation of their utility which the entrepreneur lacks and the price the entrepreneur will get depends on the monetary expression of this valuation of utility. The means of production have value for him as a necessary means to obtain this income, so that his requirement for the means of production is a reflection of the consumers' requirement for consumption goods, and the scale of intensity of the demand for labour arises from this in accordance with the principle of the marginal significance of labour for the production result with the optimal combination of all the means of production.
>
> Given that employers' demand for labour expresses nothing but a 'vicarious' own valuation of labour and that the worker's valuation of

> his labour is equal to zero, it follows that wages must be fixed according to the money expression of our fictitious consumer marginal utility at the point that is appropriate to the existing supply of labour. For if wages were lower, a large number of workers could be advantageously employed at the lower wage than actually exists, so that competition between employers would inevitably drive wages up. If wages were higher, the whole existing number of workers of the relevant category would not be able to find employment at this higher rate without losses being incurred, so there would be unemployment instead, and that would initially drive wages down.

Wages are paid because the entrepreneur, and, in the final analysis, the consumer, needs each individual worker, and they are paid only in so far as there is that demand. In as far as this fact is comprehended, in the sense of its being thought about at all, this manifestation is totally clear, and ought to be able to be supported. It is not merely an expression of the fact that – and this is self-evident – the foundation for the payment of wages rests in the productive significance of labour. It also shows how the level of wages in a situation of free competition is suited to the productive significance of labour, and how this fact also holds good for income types found side by side with wages. This demonstrates that in a situation of free competition, wages are determined by the monetary profit accruing to the enterprise from one unit of labour. This monetary return is a measure of the entrepreneur's valuation, so it does not merely set a limit to the upper bound of a wage, it also tends toward the amount awarded to workers in reality by the operation of various forces in the market.

This monetary marginal revenue corresponds to the marginal product. This marginal product is expressed both physically and in the value term. Moreover this value is nothing but the consumer's marginal utility of labour, being extracted from the value of the consumer goods and expressed in monetary terms. The intensity of this marginal utility is referred to as marginal productivity.

Schumpeter's original position *vis-à-vis* the theory of power was not, unlike Böhm-Bawerk, a purely negative one. Just as the attitude he adopted towards Marxist doctrine and towards socialism was a highly complex one, so, too, was the perspective he adopted towards the functioning of power. There was no question of an intrinsic, unconditional denial of the operation of power, rather what we have is a denial of it in terms of economic theory, a denial of its position within the parameters of economic life according to the principles of exchange.

Schumpeter was never among the narrow-minded academics who went so far as to deny categorically the very functioning of power; his field of vision extended to society as a whole. In one conversation with me [in 1931] he said: 'The functioning of power is conspicuous within the field of dynamic economics. However quantification of the factor of power is virtually impossible.' My own response to this was 'Quantification may not necessarily be impossible. It is no different from dealing with the concept of technology. Moreover a static state is a limiting case of a dynamic state, and apart from its functioning in a dynamic situation, we must also recognise that power functions in some form in a static situation.' I hold to this opinion even today. I consider that a static theory which does not incorporate power cannot actually apply its analysis to the present-day changing world. This being the case, what really needs to be done is for us to reconstruct [theory so as to] incorporate power into it. We may mention J. M. Keynes as someone who actually did this unconsciously, or, as it were, smuggled power into his theory. I shall discuss this again elsewhere. Also, in order to say enough of Schumpeter's theoretical attitude towards the functioning of power, I must recount the perspective, whereby there is achieved an equality relationship between the discomfort of work, i.e. the marginal sacrifice of labour, and the marginal utility of the wage in a situation in which leisure and work are balanced against each other. However, since our major concern here is with a separate point, I will not try to embark on it here.

5 COUNTER-CRITICISM OF SCHUMPETER'S THEORY

Let me now go back to Schumpeter's critique of the theory of power. There is no categorical denial of the functioning of power. Nevertheless, he did not deal with the functioning of power within the scope of economic theory. He looked instead for the results of economic behaviour, or effectively exchange behaviour within the confines of what might be called pure exchange. Though power may be able to operate, it is put in parentheses as a given and its functioning is, as it were, put to sleep. Thus, Schumpeter's disregard for power in a static theory may be dealt with in more or less the same way as Marx's disregard for utility in his economics of supply and demand, namely by removing the concept of use value to 'a special study, that of the commercial knowledge of commodities'. (I hope to have an opportunity of returning to this point again at some future date.) The postulate that power does not function within the proper territory of economic theory thus becomes a basic premise. The final conclusion is therefore not that far from Böhm-Bawerk's, whose theory of the price of producer goods rested on a theory of imputation, and hence adopted the theory of marginal productivity. It may be expected from Schumpeter that if there is an insistence on wages over and above marginal productivity, one part of the labour force will become unemployed and the wages demanded will collapse from that side, so that power is ineffective.

I next want to examine whether this standpoint is actually permissible. My own opinion is quite simple. Schumpeter asserts, first of all, that the price of a producer good is determined wholly by the marginal productivity of that producer good. How, however, are we to determine that marginal productivity? If no price can be assigned to a producer good, as long as the whole thing remains undecided, as it were, we are unlikely to be able to consider the marginal productivity of a producer good. Without the price of a producer good there is no marginal productivity, and it is logically contradictory to talk of determining the price of a producer good by means of its marginal productivity. It is just this assertion that I shall try to explain next.

So what is marginal productivity? It is regarded as the amount by which income increases or decreases when a specified producer good is taken away or added under the most favourable combination of producer goods. It is the phrase '*optimale Kombination*' as used here which is the focus of the argument. The criticism can be made of marginal productivity theory that where a specified amount of a producer good is taken away there is a very great loss (maybe tens of per cent) of profits, i.e. in product prices, and consequently these lost earnings cannot determine the price of the producer good. Schumpeter's reply to this is that this result is because the amount of producer goods taken away is excessively great, and this would happen only 'where rational management is thrown into disorder'. If we take this away we end up with a totally new method of management (a new combination) and a 'total revolution in the calculation of profits' (*eine völlige Revolution in der Rentabilitätsberechnung*). In that case it must necessarily follow that we cannot determine wages according to marginal productivity. Following that perspective, the ascertaining of marginal productivity must always be undertaken in accordance with a fixed principle. As long as the method of production itself is specified, or, to put it another way, as long as a specified combination of producer goods continues to be used, then the removal of the marginal unit of a producer good will result in an according diminution of revenue. It is this diminution of revenue which has to be regarded as the marginal productivity of that producer good. It is not my intention here to consider the fitness of this kind of perspective. It is sufficient that we should be aware of how far, for the sake of marginal productivity theory, the concept of the most favourable combination, as a fixed combination of producer goods, may possess a considerable degree of significance.

The most favourable combination of any means of production is subject to two basic premises. One is the level up to which technology has developed. The other is the prices of the many producer goods. At a given level of technology a product can always be produced by a variety of combinations of producer goods. If, in the same way as it is only possible to produce one unit of water by mixing two units of hydrogen and one unit of oxygen, we could only get a certain product by mixing specified producer goods in a specified ratio, the problem would be an extremely simple one. There would be no need of having to make a choice among numerous methods of production or combinations of producer goods. However, this is not in actual fact the case. There are many potential combinations. To choose the most favourable one among these, the prices of producer goods must inevitably be given. That is to say, the firm must be able to estimate them. If we think along these lines, we must say that where we are ultimately unable to estimate the prices of all the producer goods, we will not be able to determine what is the most favourable combination, and hence their marginal productivity. For that reason, if we cannot predict the price of producer goods, or, to be more exact, if we cannot estimate them, we cannot think of marginal productivity either.

Now one thing that can be noted in Schumpeter's view is his explanation of the constituents of power embodied in workers' demands for wages. He does not, of course, deny the operation of power here. He merely regards it as playing the role of a secondary factor in explaining prices. Demands made by workers are not sufficient in themselves to explain the essence of wages; they are, rather, the result of wages. They are no more than something which ought to be explained by wages. Even if we could explain wages by these demands, if we accept that the demands themselves are no more than the result of wages, the explanation ends up by being circular. This was the criticism made by Schumpeter of Schmoller's theory of wages, and it can be regarded more generally as a criticism of theories of power that place considerable emphasis on workers' demands.

However, we are bound to take this view of Schumpeter's position as well. The assumption is that wages are determined by the marginal productivity of labour, and the marginal productivity is premised on the most favourable combination of producer goods. This very combination, however, may be expected to assume a certain level of wage. So by what, then, is the wage determined? There can be only two positions on this. One is to look for the origins of wages by emphasising a degree of mutual interdependence. For myself I would not deny that wages may be determined by a mechanism of mutual interdependence; however I consider that we need to go further and search for its origins. The factor behind it, then, can no longer be marginal productivity. My view is that this is nothing but a recognition of the status of the worker, and of extra-economic power. The attitude of the worker, and hence the supply function of labour, cannot merely be a reflection of the demand function; it cannot be seen as something purely passive. If we were talking about something purely passive, then marginal productivity could not be uniquely determined, and the determination of wages moment by moment would be a matter of pure chance.

If we take this sort of view, then wages are calculated in accordance with the workers' demands which accompany the supply of labour, i.e. their demands which reflect their social position, and it is these wages which are paid. It is this wage which makes possible all production plans, and hence a favourable combination of the means of production. Marginal productivity is thereby determined, and exerts a reactive, corrective influence on that wage. This makes possible the establishment of general equilibrium. For that reason the functioning of power is not merely a given condition, on the basis of which purely economic processes go forward. It is part of these purely economic processes, and effectively and directly determines economic variables. In as far as it exerts this influence, power is not a basic premise of the economy, but an element which is alive and operative within it.

Now Böhm-Bawerk's and Schumpeter's contention that power does not function (a contention repeated also, I think, by the Neo-classical school) was, on the one hand, the inevitable consequence of the tradition which maintained that producer goods, too, were commodities. On the other hand, however, it was a reflection of the atmosphere of the time. There can be a variety of visions as to what constitutes an ideal type of capitalism. The actual status of a worker is bound to be more than a simple commodity. What we have is not status which leads to valid demands in accordance with marginal productivity, but rather something which starts off low, then reaches more or less to that position, and gradually attains to a position of power above that level. Such is the tendency in society and politics. Austria in Böhm-Bawerk's time, and perhaps Central Europe more broadly, can be said to have reached a position where relations with others could be conducted on the basis of equal contracts. This was the social basis for his recognition of the principle that power did not exert influence. We must be aware, however, that such a status marks a stage of historical development. There is also a time both before and after the marginal productivity wage period. Before it the wage awarded is less than productivity, and life extremely hard. Such a situation is best shown by Japan during the Meiji period. In all countries after the First World War wages exceeded marginal productivity (i.e. the marginal productivity at a time when all labour could be employed), and a period of high unemployment consequently followed. From a general perspective power is always operative, and even when it has been regarded as not having any effect it has functioned in a manner which even to outward appearance can be seen to have some effect. In this case the principle of the non-functioning of power has in actual fact thus ceased to work. There appeared a situation in which the unemployed did not reduce their wage demands, but endured unemployment. We thus came to be in a situation in which economic theory needed to incorporate the elements of power. Power has a considerable significance in relation to the determining of dynamic phenomena, and the changing character of the economy compelled economists to contemplate a change in the nature of economic theory.

II Why Can Wages be Rigid? An Alternative Foundation for Keynes' Premise

1 KEYNES' SUPPLY FUNCTION OF LABOUR, AND HIS UNCONSCIOUS SUPPORT FOR POWER THEORY

It goes without saying that Keynes' wage theory possesses specific characteristics because of the distinctive nature of the supply curve for labour. Because it adheres to a fixed monetary wage, the supply curve forms a straight line parallel to the horizontal axis showing the quantity of labour, and is regarded as rising from the point of the specified volume (the point showing full employment). Certain doubts may attach to the latter half of this proposition, but I shall avoid discussing these here. In any case, it is a feature of Keynes' wage theory that the money wage demanded (the supply price of labour) is fixed and is not reduced even by unemployment, i.e. there is no elasticity of wages. For that reason it is possible to conceive of equilibria with varying degrees of underemployment. Stagnation was often said to denote a situation near to equilibrium, but to actually understand this as equilibrium is clearly a major change in wage theory.

Considered from this standpoint, it is Keynes' idea of an equilibrium under circumstances of underemployment or imperfect employment, and his concept of the singularity of the supply function for labour, which led to his categorical denial of the principle of the non-functioning of power found in Böhm-Bawerk and Schumpeter. Indeed, we can take the view that a stage had been reached in which the very reality of the involuntary unemployment with which Keynes was concerned rendered orthodox criticisms of the theory of power totally ineffectual. There are various views regarding the reasons for the appearance of an equilibrium in conjunction with underemployment. There are many who take the view that such a situation is caused by a deficiency of effective demand, and hence of investment. If we seek the reasons for this deficiency, there is also the view that it stems from an insufficient lowering of the rate of interest. My own view, however, is that it is rooted in the realities of the labour supply function since the time when the *General Theory* was published [1936], a time during which, despite unemployment, the supply price of labour has not fallen in accordance with the circumstances of demand. Ultimately, if the supply price of labour rises and falls in accordance with the existence of unemployment, there will be no involuntary unemployment. It is the absence of such elasticity which creates this kind of unemployment. By this means, too, the deep-rooted criticisms of a theory of power lose their very basis. What follows is an explanation of my own standpoint on this matter.

While Keynesian economics (here the *General Theory*) puts an emphasis on macroscopic perspectives, it cannot be considered to have modified the traditional view of the theory of exchange. It cannot, moreover, be considered to have incorporated into economic theory elements such as coercion or power. All dealings are regarded as being carried out according to the principles of exchange. What happens, however, with the sale and purchase of labour, or employment contracts? Those who are seeking labour decide to pay at a level which accords with marginal productivity, notwithstanding however many workers they may hire. Wages are therefore regarded as being determined by marginal productivity. However the marginal productivity which determines the wage on this occasion has fundamentally to be regarded as the marginal productivity in a situation where the whole of labour is employed. This is because if this is not the case the wage demanded by labour will rise and supply will increase. What, then, is the meaning for labour supply if wage demands should exceed the disutility and pain of labour? One preliminary hypothesis can be suggested regarding this.

This hypothesis places emphasis on a certain kind of money illusion, and the prestige of money. Even if there are changes in the purchasing power of money, there is adherence to a fixed money wage, or satisfaction with a fixed money wage persists. This is because it is driven by an after-image of the purchasing power of money or an assessment of money itself as an inertial force. The supply of labour is thus not a function of relative prices, but of absolute prices. This perspective is in accordance with some interpretations of Keynes. I myself cannot accept this. Even if the gap between the marginal disutility and the utility of the marginal remuneration of labour is based on an illusion regarding money, then if that is the case, we would expect that illusion to be equally influential where the sale and purchase of other goods are concerned, and not just in the case of labour. If that disparity based on illusion is equally operative in the case of other goods, then we probably cannot expect there to be an absence of homogeneity only in the labour supply function. We are, at the very least, likely to be unable to explain this peculiarity of labour supply.

I myself regard this as the functioning of resistance due to the existence of power. Let the marginal pain of labour be a, and the marginal utility of the wage demanded be b. What does the disparity between a and b signify? It is what labour aspires to gain through the exercise of power. Since labour considers that amount of money wages as that which befits its position, and as a symbol which can denote that position, it is seen as necessary to secure that level of wage. Keynes expresses the difference by assigning two meanings to the disutility of labour. However, while this diversity of meanings may have enabled a grasp of one facet of the balance between the marginal disutility of labour and the marginal utility of wages, it took no account of the character of wage demands as being influenced by power, and hence Keynes believed that it was possible to explain involuntary unemployment purely from the standpoint of utility being equal to productivity. In the final analysis the factual recognition of involuntary unemployment is correct. Through this analysis Keynes, arriving at the portals of a theory of power, renounced a cause and effect explanation of the problem. Only a theory of power may be considered to be able to furnish this explanation. The argument below is an attempt to shed light on Keynes' labour supply function by an appreciation of a theory of power.

2 A RECONSIDERATION OF WAGE THEORY

A necessary rule of economic theory is that under specified given conditions the existence of a specified fact will give rise to other specified facts. Whether or not this is the case can be judged according to two yardsticks. One is whether the substance of the rule is coordinated and whether or not it embraces any contradictions, the other is whether or not the rule is of any use in trying to explain reality. To put the second of these two points another way, I mean the extent to which it can profitably be used to explain actual trends. Marginal productivity theory must, of course, be acknowledged as the hitherto dominant academic theory. However, I want to leave aside here the question of how far its internal theoretical construction holds within it any contradictions, and consider the question of how far it is of use in explaining wages in the real world.

I have been observing closely the fluctuations in wages in Japan in recent years. I shall avoid all references here since I do not have adequate data, and would like to put down just one point which I can summon from my memory. Around six months after the end of the war [1945] several organisations (companies, public offices, etc.) witnessed a succession of wage rises. Rather than resulting from spontaneous decisions on the part of the organisations' leaders, these rises were based on collective demands. They were characterised by a dramatic rate and level of increase. I recall feeling a considerable sense of shock when I saw in a newspaper that workers in one municipal office had secured a roughly 500 per cent rise. Such, however, was the phenomenon that a more or less similar scale of the multiple was widely insisted upon, not merely where other public organisations were concerned, but in companies as well. The shock which reading about this incident gave to me was more of a theoretical nature. My question was how marginal productivity theory, despite its widespread support in the academic world, could be used to explain such phenomenal jumps in wages. However, such sharp increases were not limited to that time. I now remember, for example, that wage increases in 1947–8 were far more rapid than the increase in commodity prices, and over a specified period real wages increased by anything from 50 per cent to 100 per cent. Such an occurrence can hardly be fully explained by any theory of the marginal productivity of wages, and may be considered to necessitate a reappraisal of the theory itself. Take, for example, an increase of 500 per cent. There is no question of the marginal productivity of labour leaping up by 500 per cent, from ¥200 to ¥1,000, within the space of a single night. It is extremely high even when the high rate of inflation that was going on is taken into consideration. In fact, it is more likely that marginal productivity was declining quite considerably around the time of these wage increases. This being the case, we end up merely with a 500 per cent increase in wages, and no discernible rise in marginal productivity. It is not merely that I believe that such changes in wages cannot ultimately be explained by marginal productivity theory. I would go further and say that it is not just that it cannot explain these changes, but I believe that it cannot clarify the structure of the static determination of wages either, as this is a limiting case of dynamic change.

My own standpoint is that of a theory of power which holds that wages are primarily determined by the relations of power. The influence which power has on the determination of wages is laid bare and exposed at a time of social upheaval, like the postwar catastrophe. Under such circumstances the power-based negotiations between the suppliers of labour and those who have a demand for it, and hence the relations of power between them, will determine the level of wages. As the exercise of violence and other extra-economic means is gradually brought under control, the negotiations between the two sides will again come to be marked by a character of exchange. Marginal productivity theory seeks to examine the supply and demand for labour purely as a form of exchange, but in reality dealings include a range of extra-economic elements, so marginal productivity theory only holds good for a certain ideal type of situation. Generally speaking, at the deepest level of reality wages are determined by the relations of power, and the case where marginal productivity theory is applicable is just one specific case of such wage determination.

Only if we take this view, can we, I believe, explain the wage rises that occurred in the period of these dramatic increases around the end of the war. Even if we take into account all the changing conditions normally used in a dynamic explanation, such as changes in technology, changes in tastes or changes in population, even then we do not have sufficient explanation. In order to make clear the theoretical scope of the theory of power, I want to start my discussion with an analysis of Keynes' notion of unemployment.

3 INVOLUNTARY UNEMPLOYMENT IN ITS TRUE LIGHT

Keynes' concept of unemployment can be divided into two parts. One is voluntary unemployment, and the other involuntary unemployment, sometimes referred to also as non-spontaneous unemployment. My view is that involuntary unemployment according to Keynes should be understood as follows. Namely labour supply is a function of money wages, and, moreover, up to a certain point possesses unlimited elasticity. That is to say at the current wage even if the demand for labour should increase the supply can also increase by the same amount. The labour supply function is shown as a straight line running parallel to the horizontal axis (see Figure 1).

In Figure 1 money wages are measured along *OY* and the amount of labour along *OX*. *S* is the line of labour supply, which we can regard as being determined by the real pain (disutility) of labour, while line *D* shows the demand for labour. Now the supply price of workers

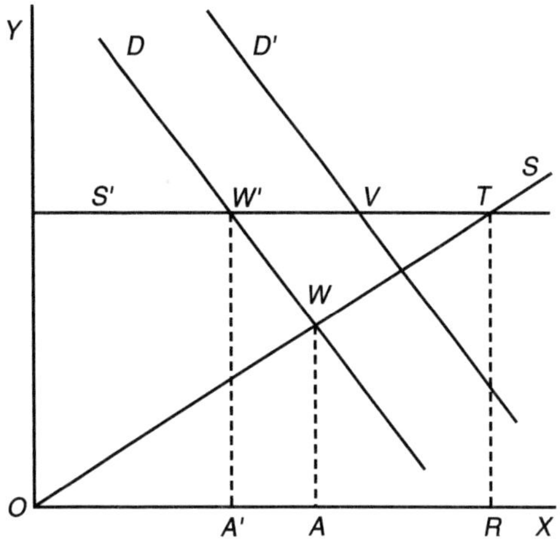

Figure 1

which actually operates, that is, the wage demanded, is not shown by *OS*, but by *S′T*. Under a situation of demand *D*, only *S′W′*, that is *OA′* can be employed. Although labour to the extent of *A′R* would like to work at a wage equivalent to to *A′W′*, and in spite of the fact that the utility of the wage exceeds the disutility of work, they become unemployed. This group becomes involuntarily unemployed. If prices rise the demand for labour will increase to *D′*. Employment will increase to *S′V*, and *W′V* will be absorbed. Such is Leontief's interpretation, and this understanding must be broadly correct.[1]

There are various views as to what is the central concept of Keynes' *General Theory*. While the dominant view is that it is the consumption function which should be emphasised, economists like Leontief cite the characteristic labour supply function driven by money wages and the nature of the demand for money, and highlight these as the basic points where Keynes' theory diverges from the classical school. Whatever view one takes, what is beyond doubt is that the *General Theory* took this nature of labour supply as the starting point of its enquiry. Moreover it forms the basis for the explanation of involuntary unemployment, and at the same time acts as an important prop for Keynes' opposition to the classical school (including Pigou). However, at least in Keynes' case this is an empirical assumption, and not something which can be explained theoretically. Such a significant factual assumption surely requires an intrinsic scholarly foundation, in effect an explanation. Needless to say under the system of the classical school demand and supply are not determined by absolute prices. It is all a function of relative prices. The so-called postulate of homogeneity runs through it. Keynes, however, maintains an exceptional position in arguing that labour supply falls outside this. The clue to the explanation for this would seem to be provided by money. This is what we can call the inertia of the value, or of the prestige of money. This is something which, in the present era of inflation, is widely experienced. It is apparent that the purchasing power of ¥100 today is less than that of ¥0.5 before the war, but it is still considered to be far greater in value than those goods that could be purchased by the old ¥0.5. The lingering odour and image of the old purchasing power of ¥100 persists. We should also consider that as a means of payment old debts can rationally be discharged by this means. One may consider, therefore, that this inertia of prices can explain the nature of labour supply. It is difficult to deny that there are cases which can more or less be explained in this way. It is clear the real purchasing power of wages is reduced when money wages are left constant, notwithstanding a rise in commodity prices. Moreover, money will possess a quite separate value as money in itself, and this value will not change in line with prices. That being the case, labour supply does not quickly respond to rising commodity prices. However, there are various other things which have to be considered in this context. The amount of income which can be directed to any use apart from the purchase of goods, for example, debt liquidation, will be very small, and the inertia in value arising from this will consequently be very weak. More broadly, there is also the influence of the image of the value of money that prevailed before the rise in prices, but this is unlikely to persist for long. As one might expect, it vanishes with time. It is obvious that we cannot use something which is temporary to explain something which does not change over a long period. Thus the kinked labour supply curve should not be explained by money illusion.

There is, however, an alternative approach to this problem. If we think of where a labour supply curve of this nature ultimately comes from, my own belief is that it must be founded on the quest for power. I have long held this view, and have yet to be persuaded of the need to change my opinion. A certain amount of money wage means on the one hand that a certain volume of various commodities can be purchased thereby, and on the other can also be regarded as representing the treatment of that person or that kind of person in the society. Thus a salary or a wage has two aspects: one as the material compensation for the person's work, and the other as the treatment that is appropriate to his social status. Where the rationality of the economy is still at an early stage, the significance of wages is entirely as treatment. As rationality progresses it moves towards becoming material compensation. At that point, if we regard money as no more than a veil, and carry through this perspective of counter-compensation, marginal productivity is likely to hold good. The element of treatment is certainly resonant of a communal society, and has pre-capitalist overtones. However, as long as the suppliers of labour are not reduced to machines for calculating the material disutility of their work, this element is not going to disappear completely.[2] This is the reason why the modern method of remuneration is to measure labour in terms of time. Since, while rationalisation is limited, the compensation for labour is characterised less by the idea of sale and purchase than by service and counter-service, a worker will work as much as he can throughout the day, while the employer provides him with reward consonant with his status. As the economy becomes more rational, labour is increasingly sold and purchased as a commodity. However the spirit and essence of reward persists strongly in the case of non-manual labour. This is perhaps because a kind of respect and mutual relationship develops between employer and employee because of the employee's ability and education. In any case, where this element of reward for status, reward according to prestige, remains predominant, the supply price of labour is not determined by any calculation of material utility. Rather it is determined by prestige, and hence aspirations to power. The extent of this demand for prestige and reward commensurate with prestige is a kind of phenomenon of social consciousness. It is a demand common to the workers concerned, one which is at the same time accompanied by a tacit recognition on the part of society. This being so, we are not talking about differences according to individuals, but something which is in general of the same magnitude. It is here that we find the origin of the infinite elasticity of the supply curve.

Let us return to Figure 1. Let the labour supply line *OS* show the labour supply function determined in accordance with the marginal disutility of labour, and hence determined in a purely rational manner. S' shows the supply function determined by the demand for prestige. The fact that this is a perfectly straight line must be regarded as stemming from one or both of two things: either the demand for prestige is the socially conscious manifestation of a kind of public opinion, or it is based in addition on labour union demands. This results in a peculiar characteristic relating to involuntary unemployment, namely the fact that the marginal utility of wages is greater than the marginal disutility of work. Where there is involuntary unemployment, *S*' is higher than a corresponding point on *OS*. This gap denotes the difference in utility. It is a characteristic of involuntary unemployment that the labour supply price does not fall despite such excess utility. This gap can be said to be the utility gap stemming from the desire for power, i.e. prestige. If we regard the satisfaction of this demand for prestige, that is to say the satisfaction of formal desires, as utility as well, then we can say that in one sense involuntary unemployment will no longer exist. Such was not Keynes' intention.

4 THE ECONOMIC BEHAVIOUR OF PEOPLE WITHIN THE FRAMEWORK OF THE SOCIAL ORDER

Let us now examine the view of the orthodox school, which uses the concept of monopoly to explain the particular character of labour supply discussed above. (Schumpeter has more or less a similar view.) The method of explanation was to argue that it was turned into a monopolistic supply through the organisation of labour unions. Indeed, many scholars regard current wage rises as a form of labour offensive which can be explained by this means. There are, however, many shortcomings in this perception.

(A) (a) Labour unions do not embrace more than a certain part of all workers, but even so the fixed nature of money wages is recognised right across the labour force.

(b) It is recognised that even where labour unionisation has scarcely advanced, there is inherent in labour supply a character of resistance accruing from the desire for power, for example the phenomena of high real wages in times of slump.

(c) In advanced capitalist countries there is the conspicuous existence of high real wages at a time of stagnation among unskilled workers, who must be regarded as unorganised labour. This phenomenon, therefore, must be due to class- or workgroup-based identities which go far beyond unions. Individual workers' resistance to power is, rather, driven in parallel by a self (or socially) admitted norm consciousness that is due to workers' insistence on their status.

(B) In the case of a supply monopoly, those with demand have the freedom to choose whether or not to purchase, and the freedom to decide how much to purchase. They respond freely to the supply price. However, in what might be called a labour supply monopoly, the purchasers of labour do not always have the freedom to determine the amount purchased, but are in a position to decide whether or not to purchase a specified amount of labour as a package. This includes an element of compulsion which goes beyond the concept of a simple supply monopoly. Then there is social and political pressure, and the whole goes far beyond the framework of the free economy.

(C) In a capitalist economy, and hence in a free economy, supply and demand prices are only notified between the suppliers and the demanders. This is the case even for a monopolist. However, where there is what might be termed a monopolistic supply of labour, many other means of negotiation apart from notification are adopted. What we have is almost the same as the case of political conflict. Although elements of this kind hardly intervene at all in the sale and purchase of products, it is recognised that political power is bound to be a part of modern wage negotiations. This is not something appropriately dealt with by the concept of monopoly. From this it can also be inferred that it is a mistake to regard wage negotiations as mutual monopoly. In short, the attempt by traditional economics to deal with the labour supply function, and particularly with increased wage demands, purely by the concept of monopoly, cannot be carried through. When labour's status becomes higher, wage demands are bound to rise, regardless of whether or not labour is unionised. This cannot be explained by the notion of monopoly.

(D) Earlier economic theory attempted to explain the functioning of power by utilising the same notion of monopoly from several angles. By putting social and political relations of power in the formula of class relations, Oppenheimer considered that the intervention of power within the economy could be dealt with monopoly-theoretically, as he regarded class relationships as a kind of monopoly. Had he been able to succeed in this attempt, he could well have provided a new explanation for the labour supply function which lay firmly within the structure of past theory. However, the mere use of the term monopoly for it has brought about no improvement in the actual state of affairs. There is a considerable difference between labour suppliers' resistance to power and a supply monopoly. Oppenheimer's contribution was to call attention not to the collective agreement of wages, but to class exploitation, and there seems to be no need to discuss this point further.

Oppenheimer's concept of monopoly may be regarded as simply a successor to, or an extension of, the concept of monopoly found in

Marx in the form of class relations or private ownership of means of production. There is an insistence on monopoly by Oppenheimer in the form of exclusive ownership of the means of production, for example capital or land (*Bodenmonopol*, *Kapitalmonopol*). However, this does not mean anything more than the ownership of capital and the ownership of land; there is no implication of sole possession of all capital, or all land, or of any monopolistic supply of them.

As economic theory has become conscious of itself as something which follows scientific laws, and hence as it has advanced along the path of explanation based on 'understanding', constructing for itself an identity as an exact science, its direction may be said to have become more psychological. The Vienna and Lausanne Schools are representative of this tradition. However, this psychological trend has tended to abstract the individual from society, regarding him as an isolated, Robinson Crusoe-like person. So, while economics may have advanced in its 'understanding' through exploring what might be called the everyday mentality, it is from the perspective of the isolated individual; and social demand and supply, and in their turn both price and quantity, are regarded as being determined by individualistic utility calculation. This being the case, the world of the capitalist economy is formed by a tangle of individual utilities. Although some opposing elements were recognised by the traditions of Marshall and the Cambridge economists, in as far as the supply side represented the sufferings of workers, the economy was regarded as a tapestry of utilities. However the capitalist economy possesses a fundamentally complex social structure, and the economic activities of individuals within it are all circumscribed by that society. They are thus of quite a different nature from the behaviour of Robinson Crusoe. The understanding of economic theory should not start from an understanding of the behaviour of the isolated individual, but rather from an understanding of the behaviour of the social individual. That necessity is of greatest importance in the analysis of supply and cost.

What I mean by a social individual is not merely a person within the framework of the social order. It is an individual who, along with the individualistic pursuit of material and spiritual objectives, seeks power and predominance within society. This desire for power has to be acknowledged first and foremost on the supply side. It is the view of the 'power doctrine' theory of economics that it is this which has to be incorporated into the analysis of labour supply, which is the most basic element in supply as a whole. We would then have something which might be called a sociological economic theory. From this perspective the economy is no longer a tapestry of utilities or of choices in the normal sense. Herein lies the true significance of Marshall's parable of the two blades of the scissors. It is a tapestry of utility and power resistance. If the warp is composed of utility, then the weft is resistance, or power. We are mistaken if we see the only example of this resistance in the case of a strike by a labour union. It is in permanent, if concealed, operation in the daily functioning of the economy.

Many scholars, while recognising the functioning of such elements of power within the economy, take the view that they should not be incorporated into economic theory on the grounds that they are extra-economic, and argue that they should be brought in by treating them as something qualitatively different from the economy. However, up to now the economy has not been wanting in concepts such as utility, technology or population. Neither production nor the development of the economy can be analysed without some consideration of the concept of technology. However, these factors are themselves extra-economic. It is merely that they have to be absorbed into a theoretical explanation as the starting point for explanation in order to clarify how economic factors are determined. An economic explanation is said to have been made if some economic phenomenon has causally been analysed in terms of some pre-economic factors. This is exactly the same as an explanation in biology being nothing but a causal explanation of biological realities such as growth and heredity in physical and chemical terms. Utility is not itself regarded as something economic, but we need the pre-economic as the determinant which explains how economic things are determined. Power, too, has a very similar position.

If we take our consideration a bit further, the contemporary economy embraces to a marked degree elements of control and planning. With that, the functioning of power strongly intervenes in the development of the economy. Nobody is likely to doubt that the power or offensives of the working class change the face of the economy or influence the pace of expansion of production and business cycles. Now it is not possible for an economic theory of utility calculation such as that of the orthodox school to provide a unitary explanation for the results of either state intervention in the form of controls and regulations, or labour offensives. Such things are not merely put beyond the bounds of theory, but are forced into a position where they do not even attain to organised scholarly treatment. This results in the gulf between economic theory and the real economy being excessively wide, the measurement which can be reached by economic laws being of no use, and the part which falls outside this range tending to rely on nothing more than common sense explanation.

At the same time, the fact that Keynes' labour supply function faithfully reflected within itself the operation of power relations marks a great leap in economic theory which must not be forgotten. It has not, however, provided us with a full explanation. Thus Keynesian innovation needs to be extended; the extension needs to absorb the factor identified as power within economic theory, and to achieve a rationalisation of the non-rational elements in the actual economy, that is, those elements regarded as non-rational from the perspective of the orthodox school. Keynes' theory, apart from being an innovative attempt in the direction of a new macroeconomics, is also the first step towards a sociological economic theory.

III Why Interest Remains Positive even in Static Equilibrium: Another Anti-Schumpeterian View

1 INTRODUCTION[1]

There are three things which should be regarded as the major issues in theoretical economics. One is the question of prices, second the question of interest, and the third the dynamics of the economy, in particular the question of trade cycles. However, as Schumpeter pointed out, while there exists a broad unanimity of opinion regarding the question of price, supply is the most unclear part of economic theory when we come to look at the details. There is a range of conflicting opinions regarding duopoly pricing, and there continue to be opposing views regarding marginal productivity theory as well. However, as far as the general position is concerned, things can be said to be fairly settled on general equilibrium theory as the form, and marginal utility theory as the content. The question of the dynamics of the economy is, as it were, virgin soil, and although many theories from the classical school onwards have dealt with it, it cannot be said that we have ended up with any clear statement regarding the issue. In recent years trade cycles have become a topic of investigation, and it has even become a topic of discussion whether or not such investigation should as a result form a part of economic theory. The development of dynamic theory is something for which we must look to the future. By contrast the question of interest has been explored since long ago. However the situation is one of a confusion of different views with no unity between them. It is not that scholars have not concentrated their efforts on this area. Indeed, scholars such as Böhm-Bawerk devoted their very considerable abilities to investigating the problem. Scholars such as Fisher (1907), Landry and Knight (1934) left behind major works on the subject. The same can hardly be said for the theory of value and price. Nevertheless, such a confusion of different views has resulted from the complexity of the phenomenon, that it makes the problem very difficult.

I have had an interest in this difficult problem for some fifteen years, and have, moreover, pursued some observations relating to Oppenheimer's monopoly theory, Clark's marginal productivity theory, Schumpeter's dynamic theory and Böhm-Bawerk's agio theory. I have been particularly influenced by Schumpeter's dynamic theory, and have consistently upheld this theory since 1921. However, while I remain as ever a supporter of dynamic theory, my attitude towards other theories has undergone several changes. I started off by totally rejecting other theories of interest and advocating dynamic theory. In recent years, however, I have come to the view that interest is at the same time the result of power. I believe that what we have is, so to speak, a double-sided relationship between a dynamic theory of interest and a power theory of interest. When Professor Schumpeter lectured on the theory of interest at Kobe University [1931], I suggested that his dynamic theory might permit of the opposite interpretation, making it a theory of exploitation, and Schumpeter was probably somewhat startled at this. Since I became absorbed in the study of Böhm-Bawerk's theory of interest in the spring of 1932, I have tried to reinforce my original opinions by modifying his theory of the rate of interest from the perspective of a theory of power. His theory does, of course, need to be modified in other respects as well, but I do not want to go into that here.[2]

Lindberg found it impossible to accept Böhm-Bawerk's theory of the rate of interest as it stood, and it ultimately led him to the theory of the minimum wage. Let us explore this a bit further. According to Böhm-Bawerk, as long as the productivity of producer goods, i.e. the scale of surplus earnings, is fixed, and the volumes of capital and labour are also fixed, both interest and wages will settle into a fixed position. Lindberg, however, took the view that interest is unlikely to settle down at Böhm-Bawerk's equilibrium point; rather wages will settle at the minimum wage, and interest will be determined in accordance with this level. My own view is that Lindberg's equilibrium point is not the true equilibrium point, yet I cannot accept that interest will settle at Böhm-Bawerk's equilibrium point either. I have therefore thought that ultimately, as long as the economy is pure and unadulterated by the operation of power, there can never be such a thing as an equilibrium interest. I have thus provisionally suggested that power relations are an indispensable element in determining equilibrium interest.

There are, however, certain deficiencies in the theoretical construction of this assertion, and I have been compelled to come to the view that it cannot possibly be sustained. Lindberg's view, as stated earlier, has both a positive side and a negative side, and while I have rejected the positive side, I have not yet rejected the negative part, i.e. that relating to the denial of Böhm-Bawerk's equilibrium interest. Indeed, in that area, I have gone rather too far, and have had to summon up the courage to retreat from those excesses. Under the hypothesis established by Böhm-Bawerk, I accept that equilibrium interest will be the true interest, and hence that the determination of that equilibrium interest does not assume the intervention of power relations within the economy to be necessary.

I have thus been compelled to abandon my attempts to modify Böhm-Bawerk's interest rate theory by applying to it a theory of power. I cannot, however, go as far as rejecting the belief that interest, too, is the result of power, and do not acknowledge the necessity of doing so. My aim is to take as it stands his interest rate theory in as far as it assumes the conditions established by him, and to retain at the same time Schumpeter's dynamic theory, and by tying these to a theory of power, to construct an organic and unified theory of interest. It is certainly not my intention to combine these theories and to craft them into a kind of mosaic. I hope that I have been able to grasp the common points which serve as their basis, and from there I am making a bold attempt to reach a synthesis.

2 THE PRODUCTIVITY OF CAPITAL, AND CLASS RELATIONS

This statement is by itself, however, not sufficient to clarify the characteristics of my theory of interest or its position in relation to the various other theories of interest. Are we right to regard productivity as being effectively destroyed by Böhm-Bawerk's critique of it? The original productivity theory merely recognised the technical and physical productivity of capital; it was unable to take the discussion further, to its value productivity, that is its capacity to create value in excess of compensation. And then, any recognition of the principle that the value of products is attributed to the producer goods, and hence that the two attain to an equal value (which can be called the law of cost), leaves no room for the existence of a surplus generated by productivity. We may accept that this perspective has become a widely held view since the time of Böhm-Bawerk. From such a standpoint all efforts to explain interest by means of productivity would seem to be in vain.

Schumpeter's dynamic theory is nothing but a carrying through of this law of cost, or the following through of the theory of attribution to its final conclusion. If the whole value of the product is attributed to producer goods, where is the space wherein there can exist a differential between the values of the two, i.e. a surplus? If there is no such margin, the surplus can be created only through the dynamics of the economy. I do not think that it is possible to deny this assertion. The question then becomes, though, what kind of elements in the dynamics of the economy we are actually talking about. In this respect there are points on which my own personal opinion has to dissent from Schumpeter's theory of interest. As I see it, the perfect functioning of the law of cost can only be recognised where we have no power relations or no class relations. Where class relations do exist, this functioning is to a certain extent impeded. In as far as it is impeded, the product price will be higher than the price of the producer good. To that extent we can say, as it were, that there exists productivity in capital. To put it another way, the question of whether or not capital has productivity is the samc as the question of whether or not class relations predominate. There is productivity in capital in accordance with the predominance of class relations. Not only that, it must be said that it is that very productivity which enables capital to be what it is.

My own view is that this perspective of trying to explain interest by means of productivity is in effect a standpoint that tries to explain interest by means of class relations. However, that by itself is still unlikely to offer a sufficient explanation. If, as a result of class relations, the value of producer goods should be reduced to a point below their productivity, is it not then the case that the value of the product, i.e. the value productivity, will follow in its footsteps up to the point of the value of that producer good? Given that competition will reduce the product price to the price of the producer goods, it is possible for this view to be taken. However, our response to this question must be in the negative. Whatever the value of the producer good, the value of the product will not follow in its wake, since it has its own peculiar method of determination. To explore this aspect is the task of a future occasion, but what we can do is substitute for this point the assertion that physical productivity is, in effect, value productivity. In short, the relationship between the value of a producer good and the value of the product is that while the former may follow in the steps of the latter, the reverse is not the case. Thus when there is anything which impedes this relationship, we are bound to end up with a situation where the gap between the two can exist in perpetuity.

As I mentioned above, I have virtually abandoned any attempt to explain interest by means of productivity. Even so, in regarding productivity as the result of class relations' impeding the functioning of attribution, I would like to think that it is that very productivity itself which is the true key to the explanation of interest. In this sense my own opinion must be regarded as a revived version of the interest productivity theory generally regarded as demolished by the criticisms of Böhm-Bawerk and Schumpeter.

Although Böhm-Bawerk went a considerable way in advancing destructive criticisms of productivity theory, his own theory of the rate of interest can be regarded as a type of productivity theory. By this I mean that the concept of the 'scale of surplus return', on which the theory was founded, was, in effect, nothing other than productivity itself. Without this basic premise the whole explanation ceases to hold. What is more, this assumption of productivity is made without any proof whatsoever. The only support for the assumption comes from experience. This fact inadvertently demonstrates that the construction of interest theory inevitably has to be based on the circumstances of productivity, and that it is impossible to achieve a satisfactory explanation of interest in the absence of productivity theory. In that case, how can the existence of the productivity of capital be established on the premise of class relations?

The fact that capital possesses value productivity is in effect the inadequate implementation of the attribution process, and the inadequate implementation, as long as we tackle the matter separately from the functioning of the agio – or rather, as I would be inclined to state, as long as we deny that there is a general tendency towards a lower valuation of future goods – signifies a scarcity of capital. I fully endorse this way of thinking. As it is limited by the scale of capital, the product value cannot all be attributed to the producer good. What I wonder, though, is why this inadequacy of capital should be inevitable. This is a result of class relations. Class relations inevitably provoke a shortage of capital, and that shortage produces a surplus, and hence productivity of capital. In that sense we can say that class relations bring about the productivity of capital. Why is it, then, that class relations are bound to cause a shortage of capital? This is a question which will have to be clarified later on.

Now the explanation outlined above claimed that the value productivity of capital was the other face of class relations, but it at the same time amounts to a denial of previously held opinions, namely the perspective regarded since Böhm-Bawerk as an unshakeable proposition, that technological and physical productivity do not signify value productivity. This point, too, requires fuller analysis, but I am inclined to defer this to a later section as well.

3 THEORIES OF POWER SINCE EQUILIBRIUM THEORY

When I refer to power relations, I interpret the term very broadly. Class relations should be understood as one aspect of power relations. The current view of class relations is of conflict between the propertied and propertyless, and it takes in its turn the form of the relationship between enterprises which can make use of capital, and their workers.

If we are to try and explain the productivity of capital by means of the shortage of capital, we need to place considerable emphasis on that characteristic of the capitalist economy which can be called the advance payment economy. As long as we are looking at it from a pure economic perspective, any inability to realise a sufficient attribution of product value is due to a scarcity of capital. However, if the emphasis is placed on class relations, we have to take the following view. As long as wages are paid in accordance with the status of the worker, even when wages are not paid in advance, but after the final completion of the product, there is still likely to be a surplus there. Only when there is advance payment, and when advance payment becomes a necessary condition of the carrying out of production, i.e. when production is undertaken as an enterprise, does this surplus become a surplus based on capital. Class relations on the one hand create a surplus (and this is true of pre-capitalist economies as well), and on the other take the form of organisation we know as the capitalist economy. As a result they not only necessitate advance payment (due to those class relations workers are not provided with sufficient clothing and food), but limit the size of capital in relation to population, thus impeding adequate realisation of attribution. What I am saying is that class relations necessitate the existence of a surplus, and this in turn means that there has to be an accompanying shortage of capital.

On this point I find myself compelled to recall Gustav Schmoller's explanation for the level of wages:

> Power relations between social classes are manifested in the level of wages. Class discrepancies, which are transmitted through the popular consciousness, established and made apparent in people's lives, and which change only gradually and incrementally, are reflected in the overall income distribution, and in particular in the overall wage level and the differing wages of various groups of workers.[3]

If we suppose that wages are determined in this way by class relations, and that this determination results in an insufficient realisation of the pure economic process of attribution, then here for the first time there will be scope for capital to possess productivity. There is no scope for establishing the productivity of capital apart from in an advance payment economy, and in the low wages which accompany it, i.e. apart from where perfect attribution is impeded. As long as we only consider pure economic relations between equals separately from the relations of capital it will be impossible to think of the continuing productivity of capital.

The attempt to explain interest by means of power relations is, of course, certainly not at all new. To take only contemporary theories, scholars such as, for example, Stolzmann and Tugan-Baranovskii, were clearly supporters of this view. Stolzmann's theory, which did not adopt the perspective of marginal utility theory, incorporated a large number of very obvious errors, so I do not intend to go into it. Tugan-Baranovskii, however, while using marginal utility theory, also propounded an explanation which focused on the central role of power in the determination of wages. However wages are the price of a single producer good and hence, apart from the fact that they form a part of the cost of production, any movement in them must necessarily have an influence on both the price and quantity of the product. Such a theory, which ignores this mutual relationship and, moreover, fails to make clear the extent to which the law of cost functions, can only be called excessively naive. If Stolzmann's perspective can be called pre-marginal utility theory, then Tugan-Baranovskii's can only be called pre-equilibrium theory. Like Schmoller's exposition mentioned earlier, what we have here is no more than a fragmentary description, one which cannot be considered to have any theoretical organisation. My own theoretical position is that what I am attempting to do is to provide power theory with a post-equilibrium theory form.

Tugan-Baranovskii provides no proof for why the product price determined according to marginal utility should exceed the producer good price. It is assumed from the start that it is greater. He does not regard this as something which is in need of proof.[4] Likewise, as we well know, Marx's position, with its great emphasis on class relations, was to use the labour theory of value to ensure and explain how the product prices which could be obtained exceeded wages set at a level equal to the cost of reproduction of the labour force. However, unless we do take the labour theory of value as our basic premise, the size of the product prices that produces positive profits is bound to be a problem. As I said before, this question can be answered by, on the one hand, making it clear that producer good prices cannot be set properly due to class relations that impede the adequate functioning of attribution. It can also be answered by on the other clarifying how the law of cost cannot operate where attribution is not made thoroughly, meaning that even where the producer good price is low, the product price will not follow in line. This then leads to the conclusion that we cannot confirm Schumpeter's dynamic theory of interest in its unmodified form. In short, in order for a 'post-equilibrium theoretic' theory of power to be able to explain interest, it has to be able to elucidate two aspects relating to surplus product value. One is the negative one that, however much competition there may be, producer good prices do not follow in the wake of product prices, hence the existing surplus does not disappear. On the positive side there is the point that product prices do not follow in the wake of those of producer goods, since the former create a surplus according to their own particular circumstances of determination.

Schumpeter's dynamic theory depicted a process whereby attribution and competition operated side by side, with competition lowering the product prices themselves and attribution bringing about a rise in the price of producer goods. The assertion was that as a result of this pincer movement from above and below profit was completely eradicated.[5] It is my contention in this work that competition cannot be allowed to possess such a function.

4 THE DYNAMIC THEORY OF INTEREST AND POWER THEORY

The discussion up to this point necessitates that I make clear the sense in which I am a supporter of a dynamic theory of interest. I recognise that as long as the static state is one in which perfectly free competition can operate, i.e. as long as there is perfect attribution of product prices to producer goods, it can be said that there is no interest there. In the real economy, however, the attribution will never be perfect. I will now attempt to account for some of the reasons for this failure of attribution.

Schumpeter considers that the fact that attribution is inadequate is due to new combinations, or insufficiency of the diffusion of new combinations, that is, of their imitation. However, even if the imitation is carried through sufficiently, the price attribution can still not be sufficiently implemented. Price attribution, that is the realisation in terms of price of as much value as can be attributed, necessitates the provision of a specified amount of capital, and that is not necessarily available. This can easily be inferred from looking at the theoretical construction of Böhm-Bawerk's interest rate theory. As long as there are fixed limits to the amount of capital, however great the diffusion of new combinations, there is still likely to remain a surplus. This being the case, if the law of cost causes product prices to follow the prices of producer goods, this assertion is likely to be disproved, but otherwise it does hold. We must thus say that capital scarcity prevents sufficient progress of attribution, establishing a surplus. Nevertheless, if we go a bit further, we have to ask whether there is not anything which perpetuates and makes inevitable this inadequate attribution. That is to say, if the pure economy predominates, and hence the surplus is one based on a scarcity of capital, it will disappear along with the replenishment of capital. In this sense, it is in the nature of the matter that it should be temporary and fortuitous. As mentioned above, however, where power economics predominate, and hence where there are fixed social limits to the price of producer goods, that attribution cannot be adequately achieved whatever the volume of capital. Let me try to demonstrate this by putting it another way. As long as we have class relations as a basic premise, then I think it is possible to recognise such elements within it, i.e. those elements which make a surplus inevitable. My perspective is that there are things which prevent prices being attributed in full to producer goods. The most fundamental of these is power relations, and hence something which is not pure economics. If this obstacle were to be removed, enabling sufficient accumulation of capital, then the product price could be attributed totally to the producer good, leaving no surplus at all.

It must be conceded that any theory of interest with a substance of this kind is quite a long way from that of Schumpeter, which can be referred to as a dynamic theory of interest in the sense that interest is regarded as something which cannot exist in a static state, but only in a dynamic context. Nevertheless, we may still say that although the contention that the inadequacy of attribution is due to power relations is very different from Schumpeter's own perspective, the standpoint of looking for the origins of the surplus in the impediments to attribution can be regarded as a different form of his dynamic theory.

My earlier statement that 'the explanation of interest by means of power is in one respect a dynamic theory of interest' and that that dynamic theory can be interpreted as a theory of power, is also in effect an expression of this state of affairs. As an extension or revision of Böhm-Bawerk's theory of interest, Schumpeter's dynamic theory was originally totally independent of the functioning of power. Not only did it elucidate the reasons for the existence of interest quite separately from the operation of power, but it made the basic assumption that the intervention of power could exert no influence on interest. In that sense Schumpeter's theory and any power theory relating to interest seem to be what might be called diametrically opposed to each other. When we come to analyse these dynamics, however, we find that the mechanism for the setting of interest called for by power theory is, as one might expect, included as one part of them. Moreover, my view is that without this part we cannot say the interest will inevitably arise from a dynamic state. This is because, supposing differences in profits between enterprises, and supposing what are called excess profits can be explained purely by what Schumpeter referred to as those new combinations, it is surely not possible to provide an explanation for general profits and hence interest.

Thus the above assertion that interest can exist as a result of power relations, is at the same time a kind of interest productivity theory and a kind of dynamic theory, because Schumpeter's dynamic theory implies that interest is possible only when the economy is out of a stationary equilibrium. The inadequacy of price attribution is caused by power relations, but because this is the case capital possesses value productivity and inevitably accompanies the profits resulting from the dynamics of the economy. The functioning of power gives rise to a surplus in the form of value productivity. I am not just recognising that as regards interest, productivity theory and dynamic theory have a common foundation with power theory. I think that we can also discern some similarities in relation to Böhm-Bawerk's interest rate theory. What, then, are these similarities?

5 NEW WAGE FUND THEORY AND POWER THEORY

My view is, that out of the two sections of Böhm-Bawerk's theory of interest, it is the second part, i.e. the theory of the rate of interest (from one perspective his new wage fund theory), which will last. It is not just that the first part, i.e. the theory of the causes of interest, is the subject of many differing opinions; it is that some of the theoretically essential connections between the two sections are lacking. He ends up by constructing his interest rate theory without incorporating any element of agio. That alone seems to be a brave statement, but I would certainly not make such an assertion myself without any basis. However, the proof of this must wait until later, and I shall try and advance the argument on the basis of this proposition.

Böhm-Bawerk's interest rate theory clearly assumes fixed productivity (a scale of surplus income accruing from one month's labour by means of roundabout production). It is, so to speak, an interest rate theory which does not prove how the productivity of capital is bound to exist, but which rests on the assumption of that productivity. Of course, he directed the most fundamental criticisms at the productivity theory of interest, resulting in the apparent retreat of that theory, but he himself, however, was very flexible towards any recognition of the productivity of capital, and made this assumption purely on the basis of empirical experience. He then assumed fixed capital and a fixed population. Then, on the basis of this supposition, he defined the point at which the natural interest, i.e. interest in a situation of equilibrium, would settle, and hence the point at which, in a situation of equilibrium, wages would also be able to settle. That defines the mechanism whereby, by means of advance payment, attribution is insufficiently carried out, and hence the accompanying mechanism which makes inevitable the establishment of interest. What, then, is the reason whereby interest can be established under such circumstances? The fundamental condition is advance payment, and an insufficiency of capital is the direct cause which makes interest inevitable. The insufficiency of capital renders inadequate the attribution of price, having applied, as it were, a block to it. It is at this point that the surplus, i.e. the interest, is produced. Such a representation does not, needless to say, in itself accord with that of Böhm-Bawerk. From his standpoint, such value attribution undergoes a transformation in a situation when products can only be obtained in the future.[6] There can be attribution of the price minus the interest, i.e. of the value, but this does not mean that the attribution of the price will be sufficient. However, this is, in the end, no more than a difference in expression. From my perspective, putting things in the above manner does not in the least distort the meaning of Böhm-Bawerk's theory.

As I mentioned earlier, my basic intention is to explain interest by means of power. However, I use general equilibrium theory as the basis of my proof, and am not seeking to establish this for the world prior to equilibrium theory. In this sense we have to understand the structure of the theory devised by Böhm-Bawerk to determine the rate of interest in the market, and incorporate this understanding into our analysis. Since his argument includes a number of unrealistic propositions, I shall try and deal separately with the considerations which must arise from this point. Apart from this, there is no need for any prior assumption of the productivity of capital, as in Böhm-Bawerk's assertion, and so what has to be clarified is why there has to be such a thing at all. This is something which I have already explained. However, there is something indisputable in the assertion that, under given circumstances of productivity, the extent to which the product price is attributed to the producer good will be limited by the volume of capital. Looked at from the other side, though, leaving asidc the question of whether or not Böhm-Bawerk was aware of this himself, a shortage of capital becomes an obstacle to sufficient attribution. Regarding this point, I explained previously how I thought we needed to define the reason why such an obstacle is inevitable, and therefore why such a thing is not necessarily dependent on the volume of capital.

However, we know that Böhm-Bawerk's interest theory embraces a fundamental denial of the functioning of power. He maintains that even though power may exert an influence on interest and wages as a chance occurrence or a temporary distortion, power cannot exert a lasting influence upon these things. In this respect there is a conspicuous gap between my own views, which emphasise the operation of power, and a theory of interest of his type. Nevertheless, when we view this as the result of Böhm-Bawerk's characteristic theoretical construction, and scrutinise further these theoretical assumptions, then even by in a way accepting Böhm-Bawerk's view, I think it is possible to establish my own.

Schmoller, with his advocacy of the utmost loyalty to the facts of history, declared that wages were nothing but a reflection of power relations. It is taken for granted in equilibrium theory that interest functions in line with wages, and hence is influenced by wages. Although it is demonstrably the case that both interest and wages are driven by power, Böhm-Bawerk's theory of interest resolutely asserted that power exerted no influence in relation to interest. However, is reality alone a sufficient reason why we have to reject his theory of interest? For myself, I do not think so. His theory of interest concluded that power had no influence on the basis of the theory's own specific assumptions. If we substitute for these premises the conditions which actually prevail, then we have to lay aside the conclusion that power is of no influence. We have no choice but to acknowledge the reasons why both interest and wages are controlled by power. In his interest rate theory both population (the volume of the supply of labour) and capital (the resources for life) are assumed to be fixed. For this reason, even if there is an attempt to boost wages through the use of power, or a similar attempt to increase interest rates, things are ultimately bound to return to the point of equilibrium. This is because the increase in wages brings about unemployment, while the rise in interest produces a shortage of labour. However, the conclusion that power is powerless is derived from the premise of fixed capital and fixed population. Böhm-Bawerk himself recognised that such a rise could become an actual fact when there was an increase in capital or where there was some shift in the working population. He merely stated that under such circumstances economic conditions (pure economic mechanisms) would make this possible, and indeed would make it inevitable even in the absence of the functioning of power.

Nevertheless on this occasion the question of the extent of the operation of power must be understood first and foremost as the question of whether or not the impulse (*Anstoss*) or motive force behind the movement in wages lies in power. If we should once recognise that there exists in power any active function, i.e. any impulse which can serve to drive up wages or interest, then when economic conditions (e.g. an increase in capital) make this possible, it is likely to be as an enabling condition, and not the motive power behind it. Moreover, even where we do get such economic conditions, we must also take into account the fact that as long as the wage increases are not demanded on the basis of power relations, they cannot be realised. It is evident that the present situation shows the existence of this very tendency. We should in particular take note of the fact that demands based on power for such things as wage rises will facilitate such circumstances. Now such facilitation is always bound to occur. The size of the population will tend to be directly influenced by any increase in wages. Supposing that unemployment results, an increase in the size of the population will be checked by the unemployment, or it may even result in a decrease. A fall in the rate of interest resulting from a jump in wages is likely in general to stimulate an increase in capital accumulation, and even though this may be accompanied by the appearance of conditions elsewhere which will check the trend, this remains a separate question. Schmoller's comment on the vulgar view that a wage rise is likely to provoke a fall in the interest rate, and that a fall in the interest rate gives rise to a decline in capital accumulation, is as follows. Namely, the view that regards a drop in interest as bringing about a decline in capital accumulation, when subjected to close scrutiny, does not stand up to the test of reality. In a period when interest rates have been at an all time low, that country with the lowest rate has enjoyed the highest level of capital accumulation. There is no question of people saving less and consuming more purely because the interest rate is low. Even should the interest rate stand at 1.5–2.0 per cent, accumulation is unlikely to cease, indeed those who plan to subsist on future interest are likely to strive to accumulate all the more because of any decline in the interest rate.[7]

If we make the assumption of Böhm-Bawerk's interest rate theory, namely that both capital and population are fixed constant, then that theory is incompatible with the theory of power. But this premise does not hold true. In fact, the amount of capital is not a constant, because where the rate of interest is set too low, some of the capitalists will eat up their capital by increasing their consumption. Also population, i.e. the number of workers who want to be economically active, will increase, because overtime work is made and more women join to the labour force when wages are set too low. Thus both capital and labour are essentially functions of interest, wages and productivity. Let us then use the approach of regarding capital and labour as dependent upon wages and interest as influenced by power, and refer to the interest and wages determined in Böhm-Bawerk's way by the flexible supply of capital and population, as the equilibrium interest and the equilibrium wages, respectively. If these are not equal to those interest and wages which are amicable to social power relations, then the latter will not be realised in the economy; power is powerless as Böhm-Bawerk insisted. That is to say, as long as we stick to the assumption of Böhm-Bawerk's interest rate theory, namely that both capital and population are fixed, then that theory is incompatible with the theory of power. However, if we acknowledge that both capital and labour supplied are flexibly adjusted to those levels of interest and wages that are compatible with the power relations, then the equilibrium interest and the equilibrium wages are adjusted such that they finally become equal to those set by the power theory. In that sense I believe that it is possible to rewrite Böhm-Bawerk's so-called new wage fund theory to form the basis of a theory of power. Any economic theory which is bound to deny the indisputable historical fact that both wages and interest are determined by relations of power, can surely not discharge its appointed task as economic theory. So, for it to be able to discharge this appointed task, the new wage fund theory must modify its basic premise, and must become a historical wage fund theory embracing what might be called a basic premise assigned to it by history, i.e. a historical assumption. We shall return to this problem later in section 10 below.

My own theory of interest is thus at one and the same time a historical wage fund theory, a power theory, a productivity theory and a dynamic theory. These various theories, which would appear to be mutually conflicting, in fact contain at root a common nucleus of truth. My intention is to extract this nucleus from past theories and to put it all together in one systematic theory.

The reconstruction which I intend to undertake of Böhm-Bawerk's theory of interest goes beyond what I have suggested above. In this the time element referred to as the period of roundabout production becomes the focal element. Now both the intensity and volume of capital are analysed according to all time elements. This, too, can be regarded as one of Böhm-Bawerk's scholarly achievements. From my point of view, however, this is the result of his excessively abstract representation of the means of production. Seen from this perspective, any analysis of the composition of capital to the point of the production period would appear to be unacceptable. This point, however, will be dealt with in detail elsewhere.

6 THE MEANING AND IMPORTANCE OF THE SOCIOLOGICAL EXPLANATION

Since I have up to now been concerned with explaining my own position, I now want to attempt an explanation of interest itself. I will here first try to clarify what are the conditions which give rise to interest. I will then proceed to try and explain the fundamental basis which makes these conditions inevitable, and hence the true causes of interest. I regard this source as something originating in society, something which can be identified in social organisation. I am not looking for this in purely individual psychological or technological factors, such as the sacrifices entailed in waiting for something, the low estimation of future goods, or the productivity of roundabout production. In this sense my position is that I am attempting to explain interest by means of social factors, i.e. it can be said to be a social explanation.

My assertions in relation to this point are divided into three stages. I first of all need to clarify the nature of the interest which, out of all the various kinds of interest, needs to be taken as the focal point of explanation of any theory of interest. Here it is production interest that is important, since consumption interest has a subordinate status. It is production interest which the theory of interest has as its focal point of discussion. My first task is to give an explanation of this point. What I need to do second is to clarify the nature of the conditions which give rise directly to this production interest. This will be the second stage of my discussion. I then have to go on to explain what these conditions are ultimately rooted in, i.e. where they actually come from. Such a clarification will enable us to confirm the fundamental causes of the existence of interest. This will be the third part of my discussion.

Let me add something here, however. I am not categorically denying that interest is something which has to be verified by the productivity of capital. While I am opposed to any recognition of the productivity of roundabout production as the core principle in the explanation of interest, it goes without saying that interest can ultimately only be explained if we recognise the value productivity of capital in some sense or other. However, can we really work on the assumption that value productivity is something that is just given, that it is something which does not require explanation? This is, of course, possible if we accept that it is something produced merely in accordance with technological conditions, something which is independent of any social conditions, and does not need to be explained by reference to social actions. This is no different from adopting as a basic assumption the law of diminishing returns. However, while the value productivity of capital does, of course, on the one hand need to be based on technological factors, it can on the other not be established outside of social conditions, or, to be more specific, class relations. Moreover, I will go further to say that these technological factors are conditions which operate everywhere, but do not by themselves, of course, give us value productivity of capital. It is only when we add to them social factors in the form of class relations that it comes into existence. Seen in this light, we have to incorporate the value productivity of capital into any explanation of interest; we cannot assume that it is given. And if we start explaining it, we ultimately find that it is social factors that give rise to the value productivity of capital, and thus inevitably produce interest. When it comes to looking at what determines the level of interest, I would accept that it is essential to take into account the various circumstances which act together to decide the rate, in particular such conditions as the state of technology, the scale of capital and the size of population, but when it comes to finding a solution to the question of what it really is that is the fundamental cause of the existence of interest, we must provide a 'social' explanation in the sense I have indicated here.

7 THE SUBSIDIARY NATURE OF CONSUMER DEMAND

Interest can from one perspective be divided into consumption interest and production interest. If we look at the history of the development of interest, we find that interest first appeared for the purposes of consumption. Up to a certain point in time, therefore, interest meant merely interest for the purposes of consumption. The appearance of interest for production does not necessarily presuppose the existence of a capitalist economy. However, as capitalism developed, production interest did become the main form of interest. Nowadays interest for production does not merely account for the greatest proportion in terms of amount; its importance is without doubt likely to increase in the future. The general rise in income is likely to bring about a decline in the proportion of demand for capital service going toward consumption use. Capital accumulation is likely to result in an increase in borrowing of capital for production.

The perception that consumption interest is of a subsidiary nature is not merely based on the fact that its volume is proportionately small in the context of interest as a whole, and is likely to become progressively smaller in the future. Whereas, even without demand for capital service for the purpose of consumption use, as long as there is demand for the purpose of production use, interest must necessarily appear, in contrast it may be regarded as impossible for interest to appear given the total absence of demand for production use. For one thing, the demand for consumption use, that is consumer demand, cannot appear as long as consumers are sufficiently rational, so that it cannot be anything more than a chance event. Secondly, in anything like an actual situation of the absence of rationality on the part of individuals, the appearance of interest can hardly be considered as inevitable. Thirdly, if we assume that the tendency in the development of the economy is for consumer demand gradually to decline in relation to income, then it will therefore also gradually decrease in relation to accumulation. Fourthly consumption interest does not have its own permanent source, from which it needs to be paid. Thus if we only have interest for the purposes of consumption, it cannot be a perpetual and hence a normal phenomenon. I will try to explain these points one by one.

First, let us suppose that the consumer in the economy acts in a sufficiently rational manner. As long as he attempts to live within the confines of his income and to plan his life rationally, any demand for capital for the purpose of consumption will arise only as the result of accidental or unplanned events. Suppose individuals are all rational and prepare for such events (for example, by means of insurance). Even so, there may be demand for savings from those whose consumption has to exceed their incomes due to some accidental event. Then there may equally be those who will undertake windfall savings under similar circumstances. In such a case we cannot say that interest will inevitably arise. Moreover, the fact that consumption patterns are not sufficiently rational, for example because of people being weak-willed, is ruled out by the assumption and should be treated separately. If we should predict such rationality in the behaviour of individuals, and if, as a result of consumer demand, interest should still appear, this must be due merely to unforeseen circumstances, such as an unplanned turn of events resulting in a need for consumption in excess of that planned for such eventualities.

Now for the second point. Even if we remove the assumption that individuals are sufficiently rational, and assume that apart from accumulation undertaken to guard against diminishing reserves of goods in the future (diminishing of income in proportion to desires), and unexpected turns of events, such accumulation is undertaken for the requirements of social power, we find that even where consumption demand for capital results from an increase in future stocks of goods, or from an actual disaster or irrational tendencies (such as weakness of will), the scale of this cannot necessarily be thought of as exceeding the supply of capital. This applies, moreover, even in a situation where accumulation has been undertaken over the course of several generations. In short, it is impossible to take the view that interest will then inevitably come into existence.

Thirdly, it is assumed that the tendency in economic development is for modes of life to become more rational as standards of living gradually increase, resulting in a progressive diminution of the need to borrow for the purposes of consumption. Looked at in particular in the light of a progressive increase in accumulation, the need to borrow declines in proportion to income and accumulation increases in proportion to income, so consumer demand *vis-à-vis* accumulation is likely to decline.

Fourthly, if we only have consumption interest, or, to put it another way, if we only have consumer demand for capital use, there is no independent source for paying that interest. This is likely to have to be paid from out of the income needed for living expenses. However, when the accumulated capital is equivalent to as much as many tens of times national income, as is the case today, the principal and the interest on it cannot possibly be paid out of income or, moreover, out of wages, which are the income of the main classes who demand capital for the purposes of consumption. In this sense it cannot be a perpetual, normal phenomenon for consumption interest alone to be interest.

Of course the existence of consumption interest is an undeniable fact, and the determination of the level of interest is to a conspicuous degree guided by the consumption demand for capital. Hence if the theory of interest is to become something comprehensive and complete in itself, we do, of course, have to deal with consumption interest, but we cannot make it our focal object of consideration. It is production interest that lies at the heart of interest. As I shall try and explain next, production interest does not only have its own independent source, from which it is paid; even if there should be no consumption interest, it remains a perpetual, normal phenomenon. If production interest can be explained, then this can be said to constitute the major part of the theory of interest. I thus believe that nowadays we are likely to find little objection to making production interest the core object of analysis in constructing a theory of interest.

According to Schumpeter, the existence of interest in any static state is an abnormal phenomenon. He says that in that situation interest – and I at least regard this as something of a positive amount – may or may not exist according to the circumstances (hence in the latter case some amount has to be paid to the borrower). Interest in a static situation is thus regarded as not being an essential element in this state. Now Schumpeter's static state is where there is no new production demand for capital, or, to put it more appropriately, a state where there is no net demand for capital. A static state is hence one where borrowing is necessary purely for the purposes of consumption. Such a perspective regards interest fundamentally as being production interest itself.[8]

In Fisher's theory of interest there is an explanation of both the first approximation and the second approximation. In the case of the former, income is regarded as fixed, and on that basis the circumstances which give rise to interest are explained purely in terms of time preference, that is, the tendency of subjective evaluation to discount future goods. From this point of view the level of each time preference is determined by the situation regarding income and consumption, and the rate of interest is primarily determined by that level. This takes no account of the situation relating to productivity, the argument being that there is on the one hand consumption demand for capital and on the other capital accumulation (and hence supply), and interest is determined where these two factors are equal to each other. This perspective means that interest is in no way dependent on the productivity of capital, coming into existence purely because of the time preference itself, or, so to speak, because of consumption demand. Not until we come to the second approximation do we find any analysis which takes into consideration any agency founded on productivity.[9] The very construction of this way of reasoning, since it appends no preliminary scrutiny of what actually is the core element in interest, may be regarded as being of such a character as to make impossible any grasp of the nucleus of interest theory. However, a detailed examination of Fisher's theory of interest is given elsewhere.

8 THE CIRCUMSTANCES UNDER WHICH PROFIT IS ABSORBED AS INTEREST – THE SEPARATION OF CAPITALIST AND ENTERPRISE

I have already made clear the reason why production interest should be the focal object of analysis in interest theory. Henceforth when I refer to interest it is mainly to be taken as meaning production interest. What, then, are the conditions which give rise to interest? I will divide this problem into two elements. If interest is mainly production interest, there is no source out of which it can be paid apart from profits on capital. What, then, are the conditions which produce the profits which are the source of interest? Secondly, what is it that transforms the profit from capital into interest and, as it were, siphons it off as interest? Of these two conditions it is the former which is fundamental, the latter being an ancillary consideration. The difficult questions relating to the theory of interest are all related to the first condition.

The second condition, i.e. what siphons off profits into interest, is relatively clear cut. It is the separation and, indeed, the conflict between the provision of capital, or, to put it crudely, the capitalist who acts as the supplier of capital, and the enterprise which demands it. We need to note in our analysis the following point. Since the supply of capital service in this sense, regardless of whether it is undertaken directly or through an intermediary, effectively comes from savings out of income, the distinction between whether the capital is lent directly to the enterprise, or whether it is deposited in a bank which in turn acts as the agent for that lending, is really immaterial. We can say that the supply of capital can be provided either by its owner or by someone other than its owner. Next, what we mean on this occasion by capital is profit-pursuing capital of a specific monetary value, which, assuming a capitalist economy, is always used for making profit, or a surplus in terms of money. Such profit-making capital does not necessarily come from savings; it can be created or supplied by banks (including all types of financial institutions). For the sake of convenience, however, supply resulting from such creation will not for the time being be included in our consideration.

Let us now engage in a little history. It is generally accepted that in earlier times capitalists operated enterprises using their own capital, hence capitalists were at the same time entrepreneurs. However, as a result of developments in the economy, the owner of capital gradually ceased to be the entrepreneur, and now the typical enterprise is regarded as being in effect a debtor. It is important to note, of course, that the main enterprise form nowadays is the limited joint stock company. Such companies differ from the above typology, but it remains the case that the owners of capital are in the main what constitutes the enterprise, albeit collectively. Nevertheless, it is not just that on the one hand enterprises even today hold very large amounts of outside capital, i.e. borrowed capital, but, on the other, as the power of finance capital has increased, banks have gradually come to control a large amount of stock. Such a situation means that in the final analysis enterprises are debtors. Even in cases where the enterprise's own capital holds the dominant position in terms of amount, in such cases the source of demand and supply must be regarded as one and the same person, and the existence of interest must be regarded as arising from the division between the capitalist and the enterprise.

Now, under a situation in which the supplier of capital and the demander, the enterprise, mutually confront each other, it is not possible for the enterprise to have as its own income its total profits. Since the profits are only gained through the provision of capital, payment is made to the supplier of the capital provided. At least the marginal return on capital is taken into the hands of the capitalist in the form of interest. Thus the separation of and confrontation between capitalist and enterprise is an organisation for absorbing profit and turning it into interest. Where we get profits, which act as the source of interest, they are then transformed into interest as a result of this confrontation. There can be no interest without the enterprise borrowing money from the capitalist.

9 CONDITIONS FOR THE REALISATION OF PROFIT – THE ADVANCE PAYMENT ECONOMY AND CAPITAL SHORTAGE

What are the conditions which give rise directly to returns on capital? I would like for the time being to consider separately the conditions which make such a thing possible, and those which make it inevitable.

I would like first to make some provisional, i.e. preparatory observations. According to the general view, or, to put it another way, if we keep to the pure economic way of reasoning, such conditions must include the following. The condition which makes possible the existence of interest is an advance payment economy, i.e. the structure of the economy is one where the price of producer goods is paid for in advance from out of capital, this being in turn recovered from the price of products. In other words, it is the structure of the capitalist economy itself. This being the case, the total price of producer goods will always be limited by the volume of capital. It can never exceed the limits imposed by the volume of capital, whatever the price of the product may be. It is this that determines the difference between expenditure in the form of the total price of producer goods and income in the form of the total product price, that is to say the profit margin. As a result of the attribution of value, the producer good price is assumed always to rise to the level of the product price. There exists a mechanism, however, which can prevent the attribution from being sufficiently reflected by the prices, producing what might be called inadequate price attribution. This mechanism is nothing but the advance payment organisation itself. This, however, is merely the condition which makes possible the creation of a surplus, that is, of a profit. By what means, then does the creation of profit become inevitable?

The answer lies in a shortage of capital. The price of the producer goods – and in this examination wages will be taken as a proxy for this – is paid for out of capital, and the total wages will be limited by the amount of capital. Moreover if we assume that, as a result of competition between those seeking to obtain producer goods, their price will tend to rise up to the level of their productivity (i.e. up to the point where marginal productivity is equal to average productivity), then the surplus will be zero when the total amount of capital is equal to the price of the producer goods. A profit will only exist in circumstances where capital fails to achieve that level.

If we accept the explanation this far, then the conditions which make inevitable the existence of profit will be self-explanatory. This can be expressed in a variety of ways, but will be referred to here as a shortage of capital. If there exists a sufficient amount of capital to enable the total price of products to be attributed to producer goods, there will be no profit. However, if the volume of capital should be inadequate for this purpose, the price attribution cannot be undertaken in full, and there will be a surplus equivalent to the difference between the two prices. How are we to determine, though, what is an adequate volume of capital? It is the amount of capital sufficiently large to allow the total price of products to be paid as the price of producer goods to all factors of production (or to the total workforce), that are involved in the production, provided that production is carried out according to the productivity of the time, that is, according to those methods of production which maximise output per unit of producer goods, hence, to borrow a popular expression, utilising those methods of production which maximise the productivity of producer goods. If the amount of capital should be inadequate for this purpose, some profit is bound to occur. Thus the amount of capital large enough to leave no margin for the existence of profit is governed on the one hand by the stage of the method of production (what in Böhm-Bawerk's eyes would be the stage of development of the period of roundabout production), and by the size of the labour force, and at the same time on the other by productivity, that is the product price obtainable per unit of producer goods.

Where the volume of capital is sufficient and produces no profit, wages are set as high as the product price. Even if certain enterprises should attempt to reduce them to a certain level and a certain amount of unused capital is available, its use will bring about an increase in the demand for labour. Then labour will be insufficient, so that an equilibrium may be regarded as being established at the original point where wages equal the product price.

However, if this phenomenon manifested in the form of a shortage of capital is looked at from another side, we find that it is nothing but the so-called productivity of capital, or, to be more exact, the value productivity of capital. Why do we get profit on capital? It is because things which can be produced by means of capital generate a product value in excess of their cost. The fact that the total value of these products exceeds cost, or, as it were, the value productivity is greater than the cost, may be regarded as a condition for the establishment of profit. Why is it, though, that the product price is greater than the producer goods price? It is difficult to dispute the fact that in production which makes use of capital the amount of product per unit of a factor of production (i.e. its physical productivity) is considerably greater. However, it is commonly held that the fact that this physical productivity is large does not necessarily mean that the value productivity will also be large. In that case, however, how can we demonstrate that the product price will be sufficiently large to produce a surplus? One method of demonstrating this can perhaps be put as follows. In an advance payment economy the whole product price is not paid to the producer goods. The total expenditure on producer goods is limited by the size of capital. Therefore, where the size of capital is smaller than the total value of the products, the product price may, as a result, be guaranteed to be larger than the cost of the producer goods per unit of output. That means that the shortage of capital itself is already a guarantee of value productivity sufficient to produce a surplus. In this sense a product value greater than the total producer goods price is effectively one aspect of capital shortage. Capital shortage is nothing but surplus productivity. It is this, then, that makes inevitable the existence of profit.

There is, however, one problem here. We assumed that, as recounted above, capital is insufficient to pay in advance for the total product price, but is not this assumption itself one which cannot essentially be valid? That is to say, is it the case that the value of the products can be controlled by the producer goods price, and hence by the scale of capital? Assuming that the laws of cost sufficiently prevail in the economy, and also assuming that, as a result of competition between enterprises, the product price will follow in line with the cost of the producer goods, then if the former should end up equal to the latter, the amount of capital paid in advance is likely to control the product price, and hence we are bound to end up with a situation where it is impossible for the producer good price, or cost, to be less than the product price. This can be expressed from another angle. Providing there is sufficient control by the laws of cost, and providing that cost and price end up equal to each other, there cannot exist a capital shortage in the sense mentioned above, nor can there be value productivity in excess of cost, and these conditions render impossible the existence of a capital shortage, value productivity, or anything like a surplus, at least as far as we are concerned with an equilibrium, or, to put it another way, as long as we are considering a situation where there is sufficient competition.

In my view, however, the laws of cost cannot govern unconditionally. This can only in general happen where a sufficient volume of capital exists. Although it is true that in a particular branch of industry cost and price (the producer good price and the product price) may become equal to each other as a result of a temporarily inadequate inflow of capital, this cannot be an enduring phenomenon, but merely a temporary one. It may be thought likely that under these circumstances capital will flow away into other enterprises which are making profits. This being the case, we cannot assert on the basis of the laws of cost that the surplus will definitely disappear. It sometimes happens that, as a result of competition, cost and price end up equal. However, this is not because the price comes nearer to the cost; rather it is because the product price is attributed to the producer goods, and therefore the cost follows the product price. In such a case, for the attribution to be carried through in its entirety, the amount of capital has to show a sufficient increase. This possibility, however, is excluded by the very premise of capital shortage. It is not possible to say that the gap between cost and price disappears because of the law of cost.

If we start from the perspective that capital has the ability to be able to generate surplus productivity, that is, that capital can produce a total price in excess of its own value, then any attempt to explain interest, any so-called productivity theory, must now be regarded as very difficult to establish. Moreover, even if we assume the actual existence of physical productivity, that is, that it is possible to produce a volume of production sufficient to cover the cost of capital invested, it is maintained that it does not mean that it will immediately give rise to value productivity. In this case we have a problem in what to take as the unit of physical productivity, which of the various different goods to choose. However, once we have taken certain standards for this, I think it is likely that physical productivity should before long imply value productivity. Let us now consider the case where only one kind of product is produced. A specific volume of these products becomes the unit of value. This being the case, where the volume of products exceeds the cost and payment made in relation to producer goods, it goes without saying that the price of the products measured according to this unit of value includes a surplus. Even where there are two kinds of product, it is unlikely to make any difference in principle. Should we wish to discuss the essential relationship, namely whether or not physical productivity is accompanied by value productivity, we probably have no alternative but to assume a static economy. Let us now assume that a specified volume of one of these two goods is chosen as the unit of value. We must also assume that all of the factors of production have the same marginal productivity, and, as long as there is a static state, the exchange rate for the two goods is fixed. In this situation, if we assume that anything over and above the volume of the two goods paid out as wages (if there are producer goods other than labour, their cost is regarded as being included as well) is produced by both goods, there is shown to be a surplus in physical productivity, that is, the capital paid out as wages has a positive physical productivity. Moreover, as long as the exchange rate between the two goods is fixed, because one of the two has been determined to be the unit of value, this implies the existence of a surplus in value, i.e. value productivity of capital. Given our assumption of a static economy, with its implication of a fixed exchange rate, our choice of just one of the two products as the unit of value means that physical productivity is also value productivity. Also, I have given elsewhere a critique of the assertion that imputation and competition negate the value productivity of capital. In short, there are no grounds for regarding productivity theory as being totally overthrown by the assertion that physical productivity is not value productivity. Just as we cannot explain interest without recognising the value productivity of capital, I think that an acknowledgement of physical productivity is likewise an acknowledgement of value productivity.

10 THE INEVITABILITY OF CAPITAL SHORTAGE – POWER RELATIONS

Even if we provisionally recognise that the conditions for establishing profits on capital lie in the advance payment economy and a shortage of capital, what is it exactly that causes these to appear? To be more exact, is it not possible to trace both of these things back to a single, common foundation? If we then assume that profit results from the capital shortage itself, then when there is no shortage of capital, we cannot have profit either. This being the case, if we are to clarify how profit will inevitably appear, we must also explain the inevitability of the capital shortage itself.

In the first place, even if profit is bound to result from a shortage of capital, if we do not make clear the reasons why the capital shortage itself becomes inevitable, we are doing no more than explaining profit as simply an accident; we are not able thereby to explain the inevitability of its existence. Now, as we well know, capital accumulation is going on continuously. Why is it, then, that as a result of this accumulation we do not get to a point where the shortage of capital is removed, and the surplus thereby wiped out? It can be thought that there are two trends which work counter to the course of capital accumulation and perpetuate the limitation on capital. These are on the one hand the development of production technology, which, in the words of our terminology, prolongs the period of roundabout production, hence increasing the volume of capital per unit of labour; and on the other a constantly increasing population. However the extension of the production period, that is the speed of technological development, is likely to be irregular, and the same will be true of the rate of population growth. Looked at in this way, it is possible to identify reasons which may under these circumstances make possible a shortage of capital. We cannot, however, identify the reasons why a capital shortage becomes inevitable. So, then, how can we explain the inevitability of the existence of profit?

Two ways have been suggested in which we can try to prove this. One view is that if profits should fall to zero, and interest should consequently also fall towards zero, then the supply of capital will show a marked diminution. This will inevitably result in a shortage of capital. The other claims that if interest should fall towards zero, the demand for capital will become of unlimited size, or, to express it from a different angle, an unlimited amount of capital will be required to enable an expansion of production up to the point where profits will disappear. The limited nature of capital thus becomes an inevitable fact. These two arguments both try and prove the inevitability of profit by looking at the conditions in which capital shortage cannot be obviated, i.e. the conditions for necessity, the former from the perspective of the diminishing supply of capital, the latter by looking at the ability of the demand for capital to increase to an unlimited extent.

When profit, and therefore interest, falls close to zero, accumulation does not merely decrease; capital begins to be used up in consumption. From this perspective it can be asserted that a capital shortage sufficient to establish a profit will become inevitable. When we consider, however, that capital accumulation is at least partly carried on to satisfy the demands of social power, it is hard to believe in such a dissipation of capital starting as a result of a decline in interest, nor is it conceivable that there could be such a conspicuous decline in accumulation. I hope to have the opportunity of explaining this separately in full in another publication. If we then take the view that as the interest rate falls the demand for capital becomes infinitely large, it may be considered that this may result in a capital shortage becoming inevitable; however, the demand for capital cannot be something which may be infinitely large. When we come to look at the number of years of roundabout production, and hence the speed of the turnover of capital and the productivity of labour, the size of capital sufficient to make impossible the establishment of profit can be clearly obtained. In short, as Böhm-Bawerk would have expressed it, the supplementary extension of the roundabout production period, that is the increase in the productivity of labour following from each additional increment of capital, is seen to be successively diminishing, and the so-called saturation point of capital, that is the limits of capital intensity, has to be ascertained for each industry respectively. Though we may accept that such a point is, of course, considerably distant from the actual volume of capital, it is not appropriate to regard the demand for capital when profits are zero as being unlimited. It has been noted that there can be marked differences in the rate of diminution in the labour productivity accorded by this capital supplement in accordance with the type of capital goods, for example machines and buildings. To embark upon discussion of this point must be a task for a later date.[10]

By what means, however, does the shortage of capital, that is to say the limitedness of the value productivity of capital, become inevitable? The foundation of this inevitability lies in the stability of wages, and this stability is in turn the inevitable result of the social position of those who are supplying the labour, and hence the power relations in the economy. According to power relations it is recognised as being appropriate for a worker assigned a specified status to be accorded a specified standard of living determined by custom in accordance with that status. Now it is regarded as appropriate to pay a worker somewhat more or somewhat less than this customary level in line with movements in the productivity of labour. This is demanded by the power of the workers, recognised by social awareness manifested in the form of opinions, customs and movements in society, and realised by enterprises complying with this practice. For that reason the volume of capital regarded as necessary for the payment of wages does not amount to workers being paid the total product of their labour. Capital will always be limited by that ceiling.

Let us now put this somewhat differently. Even if the productivity of labour increases, the price paid to labour will continue to be in line with the conventional living standard, necessitating only as much capital as is needed for that payment. Thus a shortage of capital is always promised. It can be seen that a shortage of capital will give rise to value productivity (surplus productivity) over and above compensation, and such productivity can be regarded as one aspect of the capital shortage. Thus stability of wages, capital shortage and surplus productivity are inseparable parts of the same thing. Any one of these three always signifies the other two.

In reality capital shortages are also determined by other circumstances. The development of technology, and hence the level of capital intensity in production, is gradually increasing. As a result of the increase in the working population, the demand for the capital needed to utilise it is also gradually increasing. There is, moreover, a strong mutual interaction between these factors. As a result of their stability wages exert an influence on population, the degree of capital shortage and the level of technology (roundabout production), and are influenced by them as wages are not entirely rigid. Similarly wages, population, the volume of capital, the level of capital shortage and the production period all exercise a mutually limiting effect on each other. Notwithstanding this mutual influence, it is in the final analysis the stability of wages which makes capital shortage inevitable.

I have cited two direct conditions for establishing a profit on capital, namely the advance payment economy and a shortage of capital, and have made it clear that the answer to the question of what makes inevitable a shortage of capital is to be found in power relations. A similar observation can be applied to the advance payment economy itself. What was it that necessitated the appearance of the advance payment economy? Control of the capitalist economy is divided between those who possess capital and hence the means of production, and those who do not, the latter possessing no means of income apart from selling their labour to the former. Consequently the latter do not wait for the completion of the product, providing for their basic needs through their wages, which are one element of advance payment. Such is the normally accepted view. However, must the fact that workers are separated from ownership of the means of production be said to lead inevitably to the advance payment economy? If wages should provide workers with something to spare over and above their necessities, then advance payment may not necessarily appear. Therefore it must be the low level of wages which has made inevitable the advance payment itself. Moreover the only factor which we can use to explain this low level is the status of workers, that is power relations. If we are going to attempt to deny the validity of this explanation, then we have to say that what determines the level of wages is on the one hand the volume of capital, and on the other productivity (value productivity of producer goods). That means that while we may regard the marginal productivity of labour in a certain limited sense as determining wages, this also means that the low level of wages on such an occasion arises initially from a shortage of the amount of capital, and from the low marginal productivity of labour which results from that shortage of capital. Concerning the reason, then, why it is that capital is in such relatively short supply, we find that, as I have said before, no explanation is given, if we rule out power relations from the reasoning.

In the labour theory of value, surplus value is mainly explained from the single perspective of workers' not owning the means of production. The product price is determined by the amount of labour necessary for its production. Now that of a worker is determined in a similar fashion. Therefore surplus value arises where the amount of labour required for the production of the labour force is less than that required for the product of that labour. From this perspective, since a worker does not himself own the means of production, and hence cannot himself engage in production, he has no choice but to survive by selling his labour. Thus he sells his labour according to its value, that is to say in accordance with its production cost. Why, though, is this production cost so low as to necessitate advance payment? And why is it so low as to leave behind surplus value? This can be explained by the difficulties workers have in making a living, by the urgency of their material requirements. However the value of labour, i.e. its production cost, varies according to the society and the period. It is not possible to explain this purely by reference to difficulties in making a living or the urgency of their requirements. We may then end up inevitably incorporating historical or customary factors (as Marx did), but this means accepting the elements of a new explanation. By this I mean that we end up looking for an explanation of wages in the power relations within society. In short, the formal reason of the mere lack of ownership of means of production cannot by itself prove the inevitability of low wages and advance payment. Not only that, what are the origins of this formal reason?

We may summarise by saying that the advance payment economy is founded on two premises. One is the fact that workers do not own the means of production. The second is the low level of wages. Yet the failure to own means of production, or what one might call freedom from the means of production, does not directly signify low wages. This latter factor can be explained only by power relations. I will go a bit further and say that this very freedom from the means of production can also be explained as the result of power relations.

It may, of course, be possible for a worker's status within the power relations of a society to be low due to the fact that he does not own capital and does not own any means of production. However, it is essentially because he has a lowly position in power relations that he cannot own the means of production. So-called primitive accumulation means that extra-economic power provides the starting point for capital formation. Those who have a low status within power relations in general lack the foothold needed to elevate themselves into a position where they possess the means of production. Thus conflict between those who originally owned the means of production, and those who did not, i.e. capital relations, was established on the basis of non-economic power relations. Once they had been thus established, purely economic processes, such as victory or defeat in competition and accumulation or consumption of income, led to a repeated cycle of either collapse into the proletariat or elevation to the ownership of capital. However, this conflict between the ownership and the lack of ownership of the means of production also has itself an influence on power relations, resulting in a continuation and increase in capital income and a low level of worker income. In short, freedom from the means of production has its basic origins in power relations.

The capitalist economy is bound to signify the advance payment of the means of production which are being produced, i.e. of capital goods. However, surely this does not necessarily mean advance payment of the primary means of production. For example, there are cases where land rent is not necessarily paid in advance, but paid for out of the product of the land. Seen from this point of view the advance payment of wages may be considered first and foremost as resulting from the suppliers of the producer good which is called labour needing advance payment in order for them to be able to buy necessaries for subsistence.

Now as far as the ownership of the means of production is concerned, is it not the case that since the typical entrepreneur is also a debtor, the enterprise itself cannot truly be said to own the means of production? Is it not at the most no more than the user of the means of production, possessing no more than use rights? In any case, this is certainly one point which needs to be further considered, if one wants to explain enterprise–worker relations in terms of conflict between those who own the means of production and those who do not.

Let me summarise the argument up to now. According to the normally held view, it is the advance payment economy which makes possible the existence of profit, and this in turn is made inevitable by the shortage of capital. Given the circumstances assumed by the pure economy, this is indisputably the case. As to the question as to how these two things come into being, though, can we acknowledge that there are any reasons why these things are bound to exist? Such a consideration suggests that it is power relations which act as the foundation on which they are sustained. Because power exerts an influence within the economy, and because unless it is a pure economy power economics holds sway, that alone is sufficient reason why both the advance payment economy and a shortage of capital are bound to arise. However, once we have made the basic assumption of power economics, the existence of an advance payment economy ceases to be necessary for the existence of a surplus, i.e. of profit. That is to say, in power economics the status of the worker itself leads to the existence of profit, regardless of whether or not there is advance payment.

The contention that, assuming the existence of a pure economy, profit results from a shortage of capital, is nothing but an attempt to construct a purely analytical proposition; it is no different, in fact, from saying that profit exists because there is profit. The root of the problem lies in the question of why this condition of capital shortage is bound to arise. It would appear that it is only power relations which can provide an explanation for this.

I would just like to append one final remark. In what way does the stability of wages based on power relations make inevitable a shortage of capital? This is because each enterprise sets aside as capital the amount of wages which will leave it with a surplus. This expression can, of course, be interpreted as meaning that capital is set aside so as to pay the cost of an amount that is lower than the product price. Even if capital accumulation should lead to the purchase of all labour in accordance with the given power relations, what happens when there is still some capital left over? Such a surplus of capital will always be counterbalanced by an increase in the supply of labour. The focal reason for this increase is the increase in population. There is then the requisitioning of labour which can be newly utilised (overtime work, work by women and minors, etc.). There is no reason why the size of the population should be regarded as fixed and unchanging. Once we are prepared to incorporate the idea that population does change, then however much capital accumulation takes place, there is still bound to be a shortage in the above sense. Think of what happens if power relations have no effect. As capital accumulation progresses, wages rise in line with it; there is no room for new employment, and no margin for an increase in population. Ultimately all we get is a trend of incessant wage rises. A shortage of capital can never be guaranteed by this means.

IV Disequilibrium in Factor Markets due to Power, with Special Reference to Agricultural Land Rent[1]

1 RECOGNISED THEORIES OF LAND RENT

There has long been one dominant view relating to the formation of ground rent, namely that ground rent is wholly determined by the varying gradations of the profit margin due to differentials in the quality of land.[2] The theory that ground rent should be regarded as the price of a final producer good, which, like the prices of the other final producer good (wages), is totally determined by the price of the product, i.e. what might be called the utility or productivity theory of rent, is based on the belief that rent is formed only, as it were, passively. Of course, it cannot be denied that the determination of rent is to a conspicuous extent carried out by profit margins, and hence passively. Nevertheless, any assertion that rent is determined by differences in returns from land, and hence subject to the control of the principle of differentiated returns, is bound ultimately to be subject to the principle of substitution. Now the statement that it is controlled *secondarily* by this rule, as we shall see below, is not merely restricted to the price of land use, but something which is true of ultimate producer goods in general. The fundamental question in the case of wages concerns how that part which is not subject to the principle of substitution, what might be called the primary part of wages, is going to be determined. In the same way the basic question in the case of rent is how that part of it which is not subject to the principle of differentiation of returns, what might be called the essential part of rent, is determined. In addition the product price itself is controlled by the nature of this essential part, thus the size of the differential returns is strongly influenced by it. Of course, if we carry through the considerations of general equilibrium, both the product price, and the whole ground rent, including the part due to differential returns as well as the essential part, will be determined simultaneously. However, when we consider which factor, in this complex organisation of mutual interaction, is the fundamental determinant, it is important to distinguish the essential part of the rent from the rest of it.

The crucial question here is whether or not ground rent, i.e. the price of the use of land, can be regarded as simply being determined by the product price. Any method of proof which argues that wages ought not to be considered in this way must naturally also be regarded as proof of the same for ground rent. Now this mainly applies to the essential part of ground rent, that is to say that part which is not determined by differentials in returns. Because of this part, ground rent cannot be regarded simply as being determined by the product price; its mechanism of determination becomes the same as that of wages. It must therefore be regarded as fundamentally determined by social power. From this perspective I would like to survey the mechanism whereby ground rent is determined, emphasising the points by which ground rent is essentially decided.

The present study assumes that all land within the bounds of the social economy is owned by someone. Under such circumstances, then, what will be the price at which the service of land will be provided? The service of land is not a product; its supply price will not be determined by the cost of its production. Its supply is not likely basically to require any cost. However, its supply price is nothing other than what is estimated to be obtained by the provision of land service. By what factors, then, will such an estimate be determined? As I have explained, it cannot be determined by the product price. It is true that the kinds of products to be produced and the amount of their output are determined by the prices of producer goods. It is also true that the imputation of how much of the product price is attributed to the land rent depends on other producer good prices, and hence on the prices of labour and other land services, so that they are simultaneously determined. The imputed price thus determined gives the demand price for land use subject to some modifications which will be discussed shortly. On the other hand, the supply price for each kind of land services is ultimately determined by the supplier himself, independently of the product prices. This kind of endogenous self-determination is bound in the final analysis to be a reflection of social position. The supply price for land service, i.e. the supply function, will be determined in line with the social power attributed to the owner of the land and hence to the supplier of land service. Although, of course, we need to embark on further analysis concerning the relationship between this social power and the supply price, this general viewpoint would be undeniable.

2 DISEQUILIBRIUM DUE TO POWER

Given that the service of land is also a producer good, it goes without saying that its price, too, is determined by the relationship between supply and demand. The mechanism whereby it is determined is therefore no more than one particular case out of those relating to price in general. Now I have already explained how the demand price and the supply price for land service are determined. However, we need more carefully to reconsider the way in which its demand price, and hence its demand function, is determined. The normal way of thinking would suggest that if we deduct wages and interest (or even going further to deduct average enterprise profits) from the product price, we are left with an amount that gives the maximum payable as ground rent. This gives the demand price for land service. The demand function for the use of land is determined by assuming that enterprises all share in this attitude. This perspective regards the demand price for land service as being determined by its productivity. However, a more rigorous analysis suggests that this perception cannot really be correct. It cannot explain the actual demand function of land service. The actual demand function, as in the case of that for labour, is bound to reflect the supply function. For that reason, when the productivity of the land is greater than its supply price, the former will not by itself be able to determine the demand price.

Moreover the deduction of wages and interest from the product price will not in itself be able to mark off the maximum demand price for the use of land. Under competition, the amount the supplier of land claims is likely to be able to be paid as the price of land use, even though some enterpreneurial profit and interest may suffer. In general it is thus possible to establish the standpoint that the supply price of land use determines its demand price, and hence it is the former of these which determines the price of land use.

As in the case of wages, in this case, too, such a perspective is subject to a modification by the product price. Firstly, assuming that, when the price of land service is determined in accordance with a fixed supply price, the product price cannot cover the cost of production, we will then end up with a revision of the supply price. Of course the supplier of land will be far more able than is the supplier of labour to cope with not being able to sell the total amount at his disposal. Consequently the reduction in the supply price cannot be quickly realised. Now in addition it is possible for a reduction in the price of producer goods to have a strong influence on wages or on other land use prices. And then the pressure on the land use price with which we are concerned can also be very small. Even although as a result of these circumstances it may not be possible to make any general statement regarding the degree of modification or the speed with which it is realised, there are certain things which are bound to occur. In cases where the product goods price is more than sufficient to compensate for the ground rent, the ground rent itself will, of course, be increased as a result of competition between those with a demand for the use of land. The land use itself will, so to speak, have a kind of polypoly price. Moreover that fact is in itself bound to inflate the supply price for land use. When it comes to the quantitative relationship between the increase in ground rent and the surplus in the product good price, it is not possible to make any general statement here either. It has already been made clear in the case of wages that the status of the producer goods supplier is an important factor in determining this.

While the intricacies regarding this point may not be very welcome, perhaps I may be permitted to repeat my depiction from another perspective as follows. The maximum demand price for land service can be said to be what remains after wages and interest are deducted from the product good price. Even though this can be a calculation carried out by the entrepreneur and the tenant, this way of thinking does not reach to the root of what is actually going on. However, if we come to think of how interest (or, to go further, average profits) are determined, we are faced with the need to find a different way of thinking about it. Those with a demand for land use, as in the case of labour, cannot carry out production without having those ultimate factors of production. Not carrying out production means that they lose all their profit, and on occasions there is also the loss of interest. More than that, it may result in the depreciation of very large amounts of fixed capital. If we think along these lines it may still be advantageous to purchase the use of land and continue with production even with the loss of normal profit and of some interest. Even though it may provisionally appear that the demand price for land use is bound to be determined by what remains after deducting such items as wages, interest and profit from the product price, this is so only on the surface, or only when we fail to take account of the attitude of the supplier of the land use. Ultimately what determines the demand price is the supply price set by the owner of the land; the former is, as it were, a reflection of the latter.

This point has a great deal in common with the relationship between the demand and supply prices for labour, but there remain differences, which may be suggested as follows. Even in the case of labour, where the demand at a stipulated price does not reach the supply, it is possible for the supplier to sustain the shortcomings of such a sale. This trend may in particular be assisted by the development of labour unions or the possibility of savings resulting from a rise in real wages. However, the amount of labour which is not sold cannot be very large, and the period for which it can be held back will be relatively short. By contrast, even in cases where the owner of the land who supplies the land service should not have all his land service purchased at a specified supply price, it may be generally the case that he does not feel the need involuntarily to reduce the price because he needs to sell. This is not something which stems from theory, but something which has its origins in the supplier's class status. This fact is one powerful circumstance which brings the demand price for land closer to its supply price. Looked at in this way it is the supply price which is the dominant force in determining the demand price for land service, i.e. ground rent.

There are some finished goods which cannot be increased at will by the spending of production costs. Whether these goods have already been created by producer goods, or whether they are things which do not count as products at all, makes no difference in this respect. Only in the case of goods of this kind does the demand curve determine everything. Because the volume of supply has been determined, the price is fixed at the point where all the available supply will be sold. However the present case is directly opposite to this. In this case we may regard the supply function as determining everything. The supply price of the land is determined according to the claims of its owner. The individual with a demand for land use has no choice but to fix the demand price in line with this supply price. The price is thus determined at the level of the supply price. Should the person with the demand risk not doing this, a certain part of the supply will end up by not being sold. It is unlikely, however, that the landlord will at a stroke reduce the ground rent and sell the whole supply. Landlords have the freedom whether or not to sell.

However, how do we end up with the distinction between on the one hand regarding the demand function as determining almost everything and on the other regarding the supply function as determining absolutely everything? In relation to final goods, competition among purchasers results in payment of the maximum price which the demand function allows, moreover the demand function is already fixed. In the case of the ultimate factors of production (land or labour), so long as the suppliers stand firm, the demand function has to be changed; it can change itself as a result of a loss of enterprise profit or a loss of interest. An unsold remainder is sustained when it is not possible for this demand price to go along with the supply price. Thus the price is seen to be determined by the supply price. What is it, however, that causes the owner of the land to determine the supply price of land use? As in the case of the supply price of labour, it is power relations.

3 THREE KINDS OF POWER

This point, however, requires further analysis. People will perhaps argue along the following lines. They will say that these power relations come at bottom from the actual ownership of land, so are we dealing, so to speak, with something determined in a purely economic fashion. However, a certain landlord A, for example, demands a certain price for the use of the land of which he is the owner, and this demand naturally originates in the fact that he is the owner. Nevertheless the demand which he makes is likely to be influenced by the size of his property or the size of his income. His position will be strengthened according to the scale of his income and property. Moreover his non-economic power will also have an influence in pitching his demand. If he has a powerful position, like that of a feudal lord, when it comes to relations of influence, society will even accept his issuing quite excessive demands. In today's capitalist society, of course, such feudal power does not exist. Even so, I do not believe that there can be any doubt that non-economic power relations operate in a broadly similar manner. For example, even if the labour provided by men and women is of exactly the same quality, there is a marked difference in the supply price of that labour. Can anyone believe that this structure will not have an influence on the land use supply?

There are thus three kinds of power which will determine the supply price of land use. One is the power which goes along with the actual ownership of the land itself, the second is that accruing from the wealth of the owner, and finally there is the non-economic power of the owner. The last two of these, seen from the point of view of the actual ownership of the good, are coincidental and non-rational. If we take the view that price is determined purely by ownership relations, then these both belong to the category of non-economic power in the broad sense. The supply price for land use is thus ultimately determined by non-economic power relations. It is, of course, the case that it is the actual ownership of land which acts as the basis for the supply price which can be demanded. Nevertheless, the demands made by landlords are first and foremost dictated by their power relations.

It is impossible to conceive of the power which accompanies the ownership of land as being different from the simple power of ownership of a good. This is nothing other than the simple power of ownership itself which accompanies possession of goods in general which cannot be increased at will by production. Even if we recognise that the landowner may well have power over and above the power accruing from simple ownership (for example, monopoly power), on the grounds of a scarcity of land itself, or at least a scarcity of good land, such a scarcity is ultimately likely to be no different in essence from a scarcity of other economic goods. In one sense every good which cannot be increased at will through spending on production, but which has an exchange value, will be scarce. There are two types of such scarcity. One is the scarcity that results when demand exceeds supply (to be more exact, when the demand price for the amount which is being bought and sold exceeds the supply price); the other is the scarcity that occurs when supply is at least adequate to fulfil demand. In the former case I observe polypolistic power, and in the latter only simple ownership power. However, when we look at the supply of and demand for land use, the demand even for good land is unlikely in general to exceed the supply, and this is because, as has been explained by Ricardo, the differential returns determine the supply price at the same time as determining the demand price. Even if we look at the marginal land under cultivation, it is always likely either that supply and demand will be in equilibrium, or that supply will be greater than demand. This is because if demand exceeded supply for the marginal land, the area under cultivation itself would be likely to increase. Thus the suppliers of land use do not have anything over and above their simple power of ownership. I will leave until a later stage the explanation of the establishment of monopolistic or polypolistic power in relation to land.[3]

Let us now return to the main point of our statement. It is, of course, the case that the alterations made to the ground rent determined according to social power do not always originate directly in the product price. In this case the principle of differential rent will also operate. By this means the ground rent will be influenced indirectly by the product price. That is to say the returns from each kind of land use will be differently determined according to its productivity. The ground rent for each type of land must be determined in accordance with this difference in return, i.e. the profit margin. Only in this way can equal cost achieve equal product price.

The various elements which go to make up ground rent can on no account be determined separately from each other. In that it is the price specified for the use of land, ground rent is determined in accordance with the demands made by its supplier. It is the social status of the suppliers themselves which determine these demands, and for them to sustain a lifestyle commensurate with that social status they are prepared to make specific demands. As I explained before, the ground rent established on the basis of these demands is modified from two directions. On the one hand, any disparity in demands, that is, in the supply price, will tend to be in accordance with the differential in returns. On the other hand, they will be limited, or increased, by the product price. In the normal procedure whereby ground rent is determined, our attention is drawn only to direct or indirect revisions due to the product price. Basically, however, it is the social influence of power which is dominant, as will become very clear under the kind of conditions I will describe below.

Following the downfall of the feudal system, what was it, when the use of land service became subject to sale and purchase, that first determined the ground rent for land? It was in general the very continuation of feudal ground rent. The cultivator of the land would hand over to the feudal lord a specified ground rent in the form of a contribution. Likewise, a part of the harvest more or less equivalent to the old style ground rent was paid to the landlord as the price of the service, the remainder of the harvest being assigned to sustain the livelihood of the cultivator himself. This division was wholly carried out according to the standard regarded as commensurate with the social status of both landlord and cultivator, only that, as explained above, revisions of this basis were carried out as a result of the product price. However such revisions, as might normally be expected, do not take place quickly. This is not merely because contracts relating to ground rent tend to be long term. If we look at the present situation of tenants in Japan, for example, the land which tenants can choose to cultivate is restricted to within a very small locality, and on occasions a kind of master–servant friendship ties together the tenant and the landlord. The differentials in the ground rent are still not the same as the differentials in the returns from land, and there are many cases where, regardless of any change in the product price, the ground rent is not changed over a long period. In as far as the transaction of land service takes place wholly within the money economy, though, the above-mentioned revisions are inevitable, and I would assert, moreover, that the process whereby the ground rent is pushed in line with changes in the product price has basically to be regarded as a modification of the ground rent which has already been assigned.

For us to proceed to the details of the process whereby ground rent is determined, it is necessary to analyse ground rent in its constituent parts. Of the various elements which go to make up actual ground rent, the earliest to have attracted attention, and the one which Ricardo regarded as the sole form of ground rent, is differential ground rent. This arises only in relation to land which occupies a comparatively outstanding position. The characteristic of this differential rent lies in the fact that its existence has no influence on the product price. In contrast to this, Marx also identified absolute rent (or general rent). This rent is not based on differences in land productivity, but stems from the fact that all land is owned by someone. Then the rent is not something which is, so to speak, relative, but something which exists in relation to all land, and is thus a general feature. Depending on how much is, or is not, paid, the product price will fluctuate. Where the supplier of land use service is not of any special outstanding status, the whole of the ground rent will be made up of these two components.

On some occasions the supplier of the land use will be in a monopolistic or a polypolistic position. When this is the case, as long as the purchaser is not also a monopolist (if he is a monopolist we need to analyse an additional complex series of observations), we will end up with a ground rent which is a monopoly price or a polypoly price, i.e. monopoly or polypoly rent. These can be interpreted as being significant in two ways. According to general interpretation, it means the whole of the ground rent that is established when land use is supplied monopolistically or polypolistically. Thus that part of it which can be counted as absolute rent, and as differential rent, all end up being included in this monopoly rent or polypoly rent.[4] And when our interpretation is a narrow, partial one, we can call it that part of the ground rent which arises as a result of the existence of monopolistic or polypolistic relations. Viewed in this way the total monopoly rent consists of the absolute rent and the differential rent which ought to accrue to the land, and the monopoly rent which is part of it. Polypoly rent can be thought of in the same way.

V The Twentieth Century and Secular Disequilibrium in the Economy: A Power-Theoretic View

1 MARX, KEYNES AND SCHUMPETER

What is termed orthodox, or traditional, economic theory can be said to be characterised as general equilibrium theory. If I may be permitted to go back to the confrontation between Ricardo and Malthus, it was argued that all factors of production and all products settle to a position of equilibrium as the result of competition (or as the result of the incorporation of some monopolistic elements). On the other side the demand for all commodities would be exhausted. This was understood as being because demand and supply in general moved in opposite directions as a function of price. A sideways view might be that the establishment of an equilibrium in which no factors of production are idle relates to the assumption that price moves across the board in accordance with supply and demand, or that demand and supply move in accordance with price. Notwithstanding the dominance of these ideal type laws, the difficulties which in actual fact exist, like unemployment or idle capacity, have to be explained primarily as being the result of friction. We end up with this being because there are constant fluctuations in data, and the adaptation needed to go along with them takes some time.

The 'theory of disharmony' in the broad sense which, it must be said, was a tradition stretching from Malthus through to Keynes, focuses mainly on the mediation of money. There are several essential circumstances which go to hinder the formation of equilibrium through the means of money. Long-run or repeated disturbances and idle factors of production imply such a disequilibrium. I do not propose here to give a complete exposition of the history of this theory of disharmony, merely to mention those aspects which are important for the present discussion. These relate to the stagnation and the maturity of capitalism. This is where, although the initial stages of the growth and development of the capitalist economy proceed with demand and supply keeping in harmony with each other, when it reaches a certain stage of maturity or old age it enters in a latter period of stagnation. When this period is reached, demand becomes insufficient and there is a structural surplus of factors of production.

Up to now the theory of stagnation, maturity and old age of capitalism has been outlined with three particular purposes in mind. One is to support the view of the inevitable demise of capitalism, and hence the inevitable rise of socialism. The second has been to try and explain the structural unemployment and chronic depression which followed in the wake of the First World War. The third is an attempt to explain why control, and in particular state financial and monetary policies, should be necessary to break the deadlock which exists within capitalism. The last of these three was a call for a controlled economy, or a policy demand for what might be called modifications to capitalism, while the first was significant as a fundamental part of socialist theory (especially that of Marx). The second could point in either direction, but in itself was essentially an attempt to explain recent depression. What in particular draws our attention is Professor Schumpeter's pointing out of capitalism's stagnation and the trend towards socialism, as a recent development in his theory of economic development, which can be said to have formerly been a theory of the unlimited progress of capitalism. This point was of course very much emphasised in his *Capitalism, Socialism and Democracy* (1942).

Various factors were given as the theoretical roots of this stagnation. As may be expected, it was within the Marxist school that such ideas developed earliest. However, it is not just in the contributions of Marx himself that they can be identified. They are found in the body of the classical school as well. The so-called law of declining rates of profit can hardly be said to have first been advocated by Marx. If, on the basis of the labour theory of value, we have to recognise that profit originates in surplus labour, then the rate of profit inevitably declines, provided that the distribution of net output into profits and wages remains unchanged, because the rate of capital to wages tends to increase through time. Should we reject the labour theory of value, this theory ends up being explained by falls in the marginal productivity of capital. If we consider, however, how we ought to interpret the difference in the marginal productivity of capital between the time of the apparently smooth progress of capitalism before the First World War and the stagnation which followed that war, I think that we are very likely to find it difficult to use this theory to explain the appearance of stagnation.

Within socialist thought itself there exist elements pertaining to the underconsumption theory. There are divergent views when it comes to identifying the extent to which such ideas are incorporated in Marx's own writings, and it is not easy to come to a conclusion on this. It is indisputable, however, that academic followers of Marx cluster round this point like the atmosphere round the earth. At the one extreme we have Rosa Luxemburg. The idea is also plainly apparent among those who once professed themselves to be orthodox, like Kautsky. Once we have accepted this, the inevitability of capitalism's own advance generating the phenomenon of stagnation must be acknowledged. If this is our standpoint, however, we are left with the problem of how to explain fluctuations in capitalism, especially the improvement of business conditions, and in its turn development over the long term.

External capital markets are chosen as explanatory factors in this approach, whose core is the acquisition and development of colonies. From this perspective the steady progress of capitalism is in effect the advance of the partitioning of colonies. Thus the virtually complete partitioning of territory by the end of the nineteenth century, and the fact that there was scope only for repartitioning, was equivalent to a withering and stagnation of capitalism. The occurrence of more than one major war and this withering of capitalism were not unconnected phenomena, but two sides of related phenomena, or even one and the same phenomenon. Marxism can hardly be regarded as the only doctrine to lay emphasis on this factor. Nevertheless, because it is the one most emphasised in the Marxist perspective, it should be possible to deal with it as a Marxist explanation.

North American scholars (e.g. Lawrence Klein) have recently attempted to take up the elements of changes in the composition of capital and diminution in the profit rate found in Marxian theories of stagnation and collapse, and there are many aspects of it which require theoretical scrutiny. The core element in profit in this case is interest, but it is far too difficult to explain such things as changes in interest and regional differences by means of the composition of capital. As might be expected, from the Marxist standpoint – and this was most conspicuous in the case of Lenin – it was the scarcity of land remaining to be divided into colonies which had to be regarded as the important point in stagnation theory. In contrast there are two other factors which can be counted as important for our explanation. One can be called Keynesian, the other can be connected with the name of Schumpeter. The former relates to the consumption function, the latter to the formation of new combinations within the economy.

In Keynes, just as the consumption function lies at the root of the theory of the investment multiplier, so, too, there is an implicit emphasis on the consumption function in relation to the dynamics of the economy. Keynes was not the first person to note that average consumption rates decreased with increases in income; it was Engel's law that showed this. Keynes, however, felt compelled to carry through the conclusions of this finding. He saw that the shortfall in effective demand would gradually increase as a result of the decline in the average rate of consumption. Policy actions on the part of the state were required to make up this shortfall. This meant such things as an increase in state expenditure, interest rate policy and financial policy. Alvin H. Hansen's ideas are always easily tied to those of Keynes, but Hansen's perspective is regarded as including some things not considered by Keynes, particularly some relating to North American experience, such as a diminishing rate of population growth and the progress of frontier development. Of course the question of the efficiency of capital, which focuses on the introduction of new technology, is not disregarded, but it does not have the central position that we find it has in the writings of Schumpeter. Apart from the questions of colonies and consumption trends, there is the question of new combinations, and especially the core role of new technology. There is certainly no question of the conspicuous influence exercised over the advance of the economy by this kind of large-scale, fundamental technological revolution being disregarded. For example, Kondratieff's long waves can be said in actual fact to have been found out much earlier by Cassel (1918), and Cassel himself identified a connection between the steam engine, particularly the railway, and then the spread of electricity, and these waves. Recently among those, particularly Schumpeter, who seek to explain the stagnation of capitalism by the exhaustion of new combinations, there is concern at the fact that the scope for fundamental technological changes, like the railway, electrical equipment and the use of the engine earlier on, is gradually narrowing. From this perspective the capitalist economy inevitably has within its internal mechanisms the ability to create such waves, as well as the capacity for development, and the question of the speed and amplitude of these movements will be related first of all to the scope for new combinations, and above all to the scope for technological change.

I myself recognise that each of the stagnation theories of Marx, Keynes and Schumpeter which we have had to survey here is from one perspective quite reasonable. Nevertheless, it cannot be said that they suffice to draw conclusions about the future of capitalism, or that they have grasped the fundamental movements. I will try to explain the reasons for this in the next section.

2 A POWER-THEORETIC STAGNATION THEORY

What is, then, the stagnation of capitalism? It is explained by the combination of a rise in the status of workers and one kind of wage theory. If we take this wage theory as a given premise, this stagnation becomes nothing but a change in the power relations between different classes. If we assume that the capitalist economy reaches deadlock, it is not caused by economic factors such as effective demand, the market and technology, but ultimately by extra-economic relations of power. A rise in the social status of workers combined with union solidarity increases workers' wage demands, resulting in a reduction in the efficiency of capital, and thereby what is called stagnation. Thus the fact that a capitalist economy has entered a period of stagnation signifies a shift in power relations, and does not mean that the economy itself has reached an impasse.

It is well known that following the First World War, in the long period of depression in the 1930s, money wages either did not fall at all, or else very little, at least in the economies of the major capitalist countries. This could even result in a rise in real wages. Instead enterprises contracted employment to a point where the given labour was equal to marginal productivity. Moreover interest rates were virtually pegged by controls. Under these circumstances there was no desire for anything like full employment. It was generally the case that, as in the case of a monopoly seller who has once fixed his price, there was no alternative but to entrust the amount sold to the course of the market, and hence to the condition of demand. Now if we assume a certain level of wages, that is to say no fall below a specified money wage, and no fall in interest in line with the high level of the wage, as long as an enterprise has as its target the equality of marginal productivity and wages, then even with a high rate of unemployment there will be no mechanism for reduction of wages.

It is a basic assumption of general equilibrium theory and the theories of the orthodox school that when there is unemployment a fall in wages will result due to competition within the ranks of the unemployed. However, not only does actual labour, particularly unionised labour, not enter into the competition which will engender that fall, but they will resign themselves to unemployment. Such unemployment can continue to exist for a considerable length of time, due to facilities resulting from social policy or mutual assistance by unions. Thus according to the wage theories of the orthodox school, because there is sufficient adaptation of the prices of producer goods, although unemployment can exist for a while as a transitional phenomenon, it cannot exist in principle, and therefore in any sustained fashion. Nevertheless, there are problems with this premise in itself. The belief that unemployment is bound to accompany a downward trend in wages is a fallacy common to scholars of many schools of thought.

Let us look, for example, at Marx's theory of immiseration. In this he argues that capital accumulation among capitalists is paralleled by an increase in poverty among the proletariat. The implication of this is that along with the advance of capitalism comes a material and physical decline in the conditions of labour. We may therefore take it that this theory assumes that a fall in wages will occur where there is a burden of unemployment. However, shortcomings in the recognition of this fact are unavoidable even for Böhm-Bawerk, who took quite the opposite standpoint. Though it must be accepted that there is a range of problems relating to his theory of the determination of the level of interest in the market, it is nevertheless an achievement sufficient to make his name long remembered. However, the assumptions made are far too distant from reality. When we explain the formation of an interrelated equilibrium between interest and wages, it is assumed that even in the case of labour unions supplying labour monopolistically, there will be a decline in the supply price of labour if there exists unemployment of labour. However the actual situation during the period of stagnation which followed the First World War demonstrates how far this concept deviated from reality. Keynes' concept of involuntary unemployment is rooted in this actual situation, but over the course of time Keynes' followers tended to forget the value of this significant recognition, and on occasions even harboured the idea of reconstructing Keynesian theory omitting this precious recognition. Whatever the case regarding this actual point, the assumption of perfect competition which constitutes the basis of marginal productivity theory and other wage theories propounded by the orthodox school is far from being close to reality, and in this sense a revision of the models is necessary.

Herein lies the essential reason for the second approximation, which I have advocated for many years.

If we are to understand the real situation of the contemporary capitalist economy, there are three factors of fundamental significance which have to be comprehended and explained, namely involuntary unemployment, the stickiness of wages and the long-term rise in wages. Nevertheless, I believe that we cannot discharge our responsibility of comprehending and explaining these factors without reference to power theory, whose characteristic is to incorporate into the labour supply function the influence of extra-economic power. However, it is surely the case that the most important aim in the whole area of power theory must be to understand the stagnation of capitalism.

Let us rethink the contribution of stagnation theory up to now. Take, for example, the assertions relating to the completion of the division of lands for colonisation, or the constricting of external markets. If we think of the situation of the world economy following the First World War, for those who had entrusted themselves to orthodox Marxism (scholars of the Austrian Marxist school, such as Kautsky), this was a period of steady progress, such that they could be optimistic that as the intensity of the depression weakened there would be initiated a period of the widespread dominance of cartels. There was no fundamental change in the situation regarding colonies in the post-First World War period. The colonial policies of the countries of Western Europe did not immediately demonstrate any radical alteration, while the depressed conditions of the 1930s supported the idea of the maturity of capitalism. The unchanging colonial situation cannot explain the considerable gulf between the prewar and the postwar. Of course following Lenin the principle of uneven development was offered for this. There was the problem of, on the one hand, the rise of North American capitalism, and on the other the stagnating development of Europe which went along with it. However, such uneven development was a result rather than a cause, and the addressing of the principle of uneven development in considering the present question cannot be regarded as being theoretically correct.

The next thing we have to count is the theory put forward by underconsumptionists, focused on the consumption function, in particular the set of perspectives which have followed Keynes. There are similar difficulties in this case as well. What kinds of factors restricting consumption existed in the distribution of income before the First World War and after the Second World War. Although the world entered into a period of relative stability from 1925, apart from in North America, countries did not experience any marked increase in national income compared with before the war, but as distribution came to be more favourable to workers, there should have been a rise in the rate of consumption. However, it is difficult to infer from this that a decline in the marginal rate of consumption rapidly accelerated the onset of stagnation, or else initiated it. If we finally think of the question of the drying up of new combinations or creativity, here, too, it is difficult to contend that there is sufficient basis for argument. In particular assuming an attitude that concludes that it is possible to infer from stagnation theory the shape of the future, then this becomes even more so the case.

There are many people who have recognised the accelerating trend of the development of culture; scholars such as Kant can be counted among this number. Nowadays, when the tendency of religion to act as an impediment to science has weakened and there is progressively more competition in the areas of the liberation of the individual and culture, it is difficult to conceive that the possibility of changes in the economy have grown weaker. Even if we have reached something of a pause compared with the expansion in the past of the use of railways, electricity and oil, there is still unlimited scope for creative change. Is it not the case that the era of the industrial use of nuclear power is hard upon us? If we have to think of the inevitability of stagnation while at the same time having this in mind, this must be regarded either as covering our eyes to what is truly the root cause of stagnation, or just not wanting to say what it is.

The greatest difficulty faced by the various theories developed up to now relates to the fact that they cannot explain why the condition and structure of the capitalist economy came to show a radical difference before the First World War and after it. I have already shown that this is not something which can be explained by circumstances such as diminishing consumption, innovation or the division of colonies. One could also use standpoints such as that of Fisher's theory of debt to explain this as the direct influence of the First World War, but that would mean that depression could only be regarded as a temporary phenomenon, of no use in explaining the so-called 'century of stagnation'. We are left with only one possible reason, and that must be shifts in power relations. From the middle of the First World War through to the postwar years a huge advance was made in the nations of Western Europe. The formation of the Social Democratic Party cabinet in Germany, and the ascendancy of the Labour Party in Britain were superficial political ripples, but social trends, taking the opportunity of the war and stimulated by the formation of the Soviet Union, entered into a stage which can only be referred to as a total transformation. This increase in the social status of the proletariat, with or without the organisation of unions, stiffened the resistance and demands of the suppliers of labour. This strengthening of their position can be said to be changing the face of capitalism.

At the time of the stagnation of the 1930s, the standpoint of the orthodox school provided two interpretations. One was the pegging of interest, the other the pegging of wages. Although there were some voices which, looking at the first of these two, claimed that the rigidity of interest was the cause of depression, they were not particularly prominent. This was because there were other circumstances as well (for example, rivalry between consumer demand and producer demand for capital) which made a reduction in interest difficult. However, it was also strongly asserted that the rigidity of wages increased unemployment and at the same time caused a contraction in production. This can be said to be the generally held view. It is now possible in response to this view more or less to infer the contents of the opposing theory which inevitably arose from the Keynesian school and the New Dealers. Even so, there remains among these many assertions an indisputable core, consisting of heterodox elements which up to now have proved very difficult for economic theory to absorb. It is only with a theory of power that we can explain these head on. Seen from this standpoint, stagnation becomes the other side of proletarian resistance, and hence the increase in the supply price of labour. Rather than seeking to promise to the proletariat huge amounts of wages, it does quite the opposite. In this point I would mention the injunctions asserted by competitive socialism, from which we could learn a great deal. Ultimately the so-called stagnation of capitalism is the resistance of the proletariat itself. If this resistance should increase unemployment, and should, moreover, this increase in unemployment intensify class conflict, the change in power relations will bring about socialism. The thing that will bring this about, it must be emphasised, is not productivity, but resistance. Anyhow, this view is not far from Schumpeter's perspective in *Capitalism, Socialism and Democracy* (1942).

Notes and References

Foreword: Joseph A. Schumpeter (1883–1950) and Yasuma Takata (1883–1972)

1. von Böhm-Bawerk (1914).
2. *Showa Tenno Dokuhaku Roku* (1995).
3. Schumpeter (1991), p. 179.
4. In 1910 Japan annexed Korea using methods remarkably similar to those used in Manchuria in 1931 and North China in 1937. The action could correctly be called a prototype.
5. For example Furuhata Setsuo, 'Teikokushugi Ron no Keifu' ('The lineage of theories of imperialism'), and Watanabe Hiroshi, 'Lenin no Teikokushugi Ron' ('Lenin's theory of imperialism'), both in Uno (1973), 1.
6. Morishima (1995), pp. 238–9.
7. I have written on this topic in Morishima (1988), pp. 54ff.
8. Wiles (1987) 1, pp. 643–5.
9. Pareto (1935).
10. Pareto (1991). Also see, for example, pp. xxii–xxiii of my foreword to de Pietri-Tonelli and Bousquet. From Takata's perspective, the circulation of elites was the repeated replacement of one social group with power by another. When the residue of the prevalence of the working class came into play, the power of the workers in the labour market would increase.

PART I THE FUNDAMENTAL PRINCIPLE OF DISTRIBUTION THEORY

I Preliminary Remark

1. The 'practical' person is certainly not entitled to join the ranks of those who deny all value to theory. He is constantly engaging in theory and as a rule his views simply represent the theories of 200 years ago.

II The Economics and Sociology of Distribution

1. Of course many people think that the marginal utility theory only gives a good account of the value and price formation of such goods as are present in given quantities that are not increasable through production. But I am not going to discuss this view.
2. Tugan-Baranovskii (1913).
3. One point in his observations lies outside the scope of scientific discussion and I will simply mention it here: his (negative) value judgement on

interest income. From my standpoint I can only take note with respect and sympathy of this reaction of the moral consciousness of an outstanding personality to the fact of interest on capital, without feeling myself justified in discussing it. The writer has an interesting view that is not uncommon among economists, that his moral judgement follows logically from his explanation of interest income, but this is clearly true only on the assumption of the general binding force of certain ethical principles. For Tugan-Baranovskii the expression 'exploitation' thus *ipso facto* involves moral disapproval.

4. 'Marginal productivity theory' would literally mean nothing else but a name for the marginal utility theory as applied to the distribution problem and the word will be used here in this sense. But in a narrower sense it is also employed particularly for the distribution theory of Clark's school, which is a variety of marginal productivity theory in the first sense, but which in relation to wages theory coincides perfectly with the theory of the 'Austrians' and of Marshall's followers.
5. This point of view must be judged as the result of a long process of development. One can perfectly understand that it is antipathetical to both the layman and the untheoretically-minded expert because of the measure of abstraction it involves.
6. On the significance of this fact see the work in which it is most clearly highlighted and where all the old individual problems of economics are resolved in a general theory that embraces them all, Pareto's *Manuel* (1909), or else my own *Das Wesen und Hauptinhalt der theoretischen Nationalökonomie* (1908).
7. These individual psychic amounts of value are of course 'socially conditioned', so that of themselves they can never be regarded as 'ultimate foundations' of the behaviour of individuals but rather as indices of that behaviour.
8. This has been blown up into a major theoretical contradiction, interpreted in a whole range of different ways. It is the kind of thing that fascinates economists while serious theoretical work is neglected.
9. Strictly speaking this applies solely to the methods of economic statistics, though these are often applicable outside their own domain. So as not to complicate my observations unnecessarily, I am reluctant to put any further emphasis on the matter, but I was faced with an expository difficulty. Leaving aside constantly recurring consumption loans, I regard interest on capital as a consequence of economic development, which would disappear in a perfectly stable national economy that went through the same cycle of unchanging economic periods again and again (cf. my theory of economic development). But since it is not possible for me in the context of the present treatise to give the reasons for my view, and since moreover I would prefer to adopt the standpoint of the greatest possible number of theoreticians, there is nothing for it but to accept their opinion on this point and to speak of capital and interest in the customary sense, in the sense of a stock of goods and of a net profit that is somehow linked to its role in the economy.
10. I have often thought that if we want to avoid the question which such comparisons always raise – and they cause problems however innocently

they are intended, because the kind of critic that we have always clings to such secondary matters – it is better to use the chemical analogy of the organised substance than the biological analogy of the organism.

11. A developed example of such a schematisation may be found in my *Theorie der wirtschaftlichen Entwicklung* (1912), ch. 1.
12. This circumstance has led to an 'objection' to the foundations of the theory on the grounds that is assumes that men have motives that are to an extent conscious and that they act rationally on the basis of these – something which is said not to correspond to reality (see for example Graham Wallas, *Human Nature in Politics*, 1908). But firstly a lack of conscious motives is not the same thing as a lack of motives, and secondly there is not here a reference to individuals' states of mind and personal psychology, but only to the fact that the force of necessity or something similar so forms their behaviour that it can be interpreted broadly speaking for our purposes as if the assumptions in question were valid.
13. It hardly needs stating that the economy is an activity and that we speak of 'conditions' – for example of an equilibrium state – only in the sense in which we can speak of the equilibrium state of an activity.
14. Surely then it is a mistake on Tugan-Baranovskii's part (1913, p. 76) to suggest that most theorists have ignored the simple fact that only 'a part of the social product forms the social income' while the rest serves for the restoration of the required supply of means of production. The way he applies this approach is very disturbing. He wants to use it to show that where there is increasing social productivity consequent upon technical progress, not just the real income of all economic classes may rise (which is surely correct) but also their share of the social product – at the cost of the part necessary for the restoration of the means of production! For unless less work is required, there remains more for 'social income' and all the shares in the latter measured according to the measure of labour value are increased. But is it not clear that we can equally turn this round and say that the labour value of 'social income' sinks because less direct and indirect application of labour is now necessary for its production? And that increased productivity in general only affects the size of the stock of consumption goods through the multiplication of the actual means of production, so that the relationship of the two does not need to change? If this is the 'kernel of truth' in the marginal productivity theory, and if it is the only way to demonstrate that the level of incomes has something to do with 'productivity', not much is to be said for it.
15. Once again; strictly speaking only in a stationary economy.
16. John Stuart Mill observes in his 'Preliminary Remarks' (1909, p. 21) that 'Unlike the laws of production those of distribution are partly of human institution'. But he takes the sting out of it, for he goes on (assessing the situation quite accurately) 'But though governments or nations have the power of deciding what institutions shall exist, they cannot arbitrarily determine how those institutions shall work.'
17. Only in a market economy of course. A communist economy is a 'closed' economy, i.e. it forms a single economic unit and is an economic subject.

This distribution problem is generally irrelevant to it, but the overall yield of production is for it a real income and not purely a fiction or conceptual construction like the national income referred to in the market economy, which would be fundamentally contradictory if the word 'income' were not taken only in a transferred sense – so that its distribution process would be a distinguishable operation to be subsumed under the concept of income use. What may be called individual income in a strictly communist economy would not be a true 'income' in the fullest sense of the concept.

18. But is there then no conflict between doing work and getting a wage? When they hear the word 'production' people are always too ready to think of the technical process. About this I have nothing to say, and for me production consists only in the combination of means of production, although that does take place partly on the basis of technical data. In this sense it can be said that I have nothing to do with actual work and that the special economic interest ends with those commercial operations necessary for the completion of the economic plan – and which in fact constitute it. This conflict then disappears and there remains an act of purchase which serves both the productive aim and the distributive process.
19. From the didactic point of view it would be appropriate to begin with a general sketch of the mechanism or organism of the equilibrium system, emphasising the fictitiousness of all those sharp distinctions which relentlessly impress themselves on the reader or hearer as real and push into the background the fundamental and fruitful concept of economic life as a balanced continuous process in which all the stages are always present at the same time. Erroneous views on the meaning of the passage of time in the economy, etc. have arisen out of a neglect of these factors.
20. Diehl, p. 606.
21. His concept of productivity is however an instrument that is far from flawless. It is extraordinary that having moved such a long way from the labour value principle, he should limit this concept purely to labour. This can only be explained in terms of emotional factors, and to that extent it is worrying if not too serious. But that he has not fully grasped the precise sense the word has within marginal utility theory and that he should persist in thinking chiefly of 'physical' productivity, while at the same time using this concept of productivity in discussion sometimes in place of the other and sometimes alongside the other is a more serious weakness.
22. With the most primitive forms of wage fund theory the connection arises through the mediation of savings; and Longe and Thorton (see also Hermann) were therefore wrong to regard the fact that in the last analysis wages derive from the income of consumers as an embodied contradiction of the wage fund theory – and Mill therefore was wrong in simply conceding the point.
23. The role of this factor has been subjected to a fundamental analysis by Böhm-Bawerk from the theoretical standpoint in his article 'Macht oder ökonomisches Gesetz?' (1914), and this is the only occasion on which

I will refer to that article. He too makes observations on the problem of 'artificial' wage rises, so that there is a marked parallelism between his work, Tugan-Baranovskii's, and the present work, even though the first two argue in opposite directions.

24. This requirement has unfortunately never been met by the authors who work with it.
25. Insofar as he accepts this he contradicts himself, when he portrays ground rent (1913, pp. 24–5) as a consequence of ownership of large estates and understands the income of farmers uniformly as labour income. This is one of the consequences of the neglect of the difference between functional and personal distribution, a neglect already referred to. I shall return to this again. When Tugan-Baranovskii goes on to say (1913, pp. 26–7) that differences in natural production conditions lead to differences in labour productivity and these in turn to differences in income, it seems clear that there is no point in describing the surpluses which are to be ascribed to more favourable production conditions as labour income. We appear to be jettisoning a useful instrument of analysis if we think in this way, creating artificial problems which would not arise in a natural view of things.
26. Tugan-Baranovskii thinks that ground rent expresses the dependency of the human economy on external nature (1913, p. 26). Is this dependency somehow eliminated in industry? And with ground rent and wages and interest alike, surely we are talking generally not about dependence on nature as such, but simply about the inner logic of the economic.
27. There are two different possible meanings to the phrase 'economic necessity': first it may mean that a given phenomenon must necessarily be produced by given economic causes. Secondly, that a phenomenon is necessary for the economic life or well-being of a social group. I have in mind the first meaning.
28. According to the prevailing view. However many socialistic systems obviously leave the acquisition of private interest untouched – especially those of the earlier French Socialists.
29. By the productivity theory of interest is here understood what Böhm-Bawerk designated by it, and not simply the application of the marginal productivity idea to interest – though that is also found in Böhm-Bawerk.
30. See my *Theorie der wirtschaftlichen Entwicklung* (1912), ch. 5.
31. In connection with the older theories the presence of a return never seems to Tugan-Baranovskii to be generally a problem. That every pure return is a phenomenon to be understood only in terms of the theory of value completely escapes him and therein lies the key difference between him and the marginal productivity theory.
32. In this connection 'employer's profit' is however to be understood in the particular sense attributed to it by me in my work referred to above.
33. In my review 'R. Stolzmann. Die Soziale Kategorie in der Volkswirtschaftslehre. – R. Stolzmann. Der Zweck in der Volkswirtschaft.' *Jahrbuch fuer Gesetzgebung, Verwaltung und Volkswirtschaft im Deutschen Reich*, 1912. All 'social' phraseology goes back ultimately to what is simply a very deficient form of the marginal productivity theory. There

are many such examples of the lack of substance of the power idea in the area of pure economics. It always masks some kind of pure economic thought which would be shown up as erroneous or entirely lacking in originality in the absence of such a mask.

34. 'Zur sozialen Theorie der Verteilung'.

III Foundations of the Wage Theory

1. There are not many monographs studying wage theory in terms of the marginal productivity principle, something which is related to the fact that it is a pure 'special case'. Apart from the works of the Austrian school there is a thorough presentation of the issues in Marshall and then in the work of the followers of Clark (and this quite rightly set the tone for a wider circle of disciples). Of particular interest are: Davidson (1898); Thompson (1892); Wood (1889, by the American Economic Association, where Clark also first published his wage theory). Then of course there is Pigou's great work *Wealth and Welfare* (1912).
2. There are numerous possible contradictions in this context, but in the heat of battle they are often overestimated. Thus there appears to be a very sharp contradiction between Clark and Taussig, and the latter is often generally portrayed as an opponent of the marginal productivity theory. It has to be remembered however that Clark's version of the marginal productivity theory is a rather unusual one, and that even so the gap between his and Taussig's theory is really not that big.
3. Of course it also depends on the incomes of the consumers, which in turn depend on the result of distribution. It is perfectly correct that all these exchange relations may be represented only with the help of general equilibrium theory. Here I would like to add to the above principle the words 'at a given income', without actually stating that this income would be a datum for me. In accepting certain elements as fixed and then again making them vary, I am not failing to notice their overall interdependence, but availing myself of a method of studying a system of interdependent quantities point by point.
4. The expression 'optimal' has the advantage of being an unusual one in economics and therefore not loaded with secondary meanings.
5. A surplus that has an analogy with the Ricardian presentation of ground rent.
6. Schüller, 'Die Ansprüche der Arbeiter' (1915). The secondary causal role of 'claims' is still important enough to necessitate a particular study and the merit of having initiated such a study should not be minimised. But this writer has greatly overestimated that role. More disturbing are the critical observations that same writer links to his positive affirmations in another work yet to be reviewed. For example, he argues that there is a conflict between 'prevailing scientific opinion' and the idea that where wage claims are different, to the extent that the claims of the workers are crucial for wage rates, those of the 'most demanding' of the workers necessary for the satisfaction of actual demand at the rate in question will decide that rate' (p. 389). But what theorist would ever

have doubted it? The principle is very similar to the assertion that the highest cost levels within a quantity of products are the same as the product price, a similarity which should have shown that theory cannot come to any other conclusion in the case considered by Schüller. It also holds, but on other presuppositions, that the lowest cost levels within a quantity of products are the same as the product price and on just these assumptions it would argue the same for Schüller's workers with their different demands. Which of the counter-assumptions correspond to a concrete case is a *quaestio facti* – the first assertion is valid for equilibrium conditions, the second emphasises a tendency of economic development – but there is not a contradiction between them in the sense that either one or the other is generally true. It is a direct consequence of the cost teaching of marginal utility theory that wages in an industry must keep on rising, the more profitable the use possibilities are for which further amounts of labour must be extracted if demand for labour in that one industry grows, and that all workers in the industry under consideration must be paid the wage rate necessary to attract the 'last', here thus 'dearest' workers, because withdrawn from the most profitable other use. In general it should be stressed that none of the principles on the last page of Schüller's treatise contains anything that contradicts theory or that could be repugnant to a theorist.

7. Compare Böhm-Bawerk's observations about the value of 'any saleable goods' in his 'Positive Theories of Capital' and the statements in my *Theorie der wirtschaftlichen Entwicklung* (1912), ch. 1, on the 'multiplicity of value functions' of goods that have many applications.
8. A contrary opinion will be discussed later.
9. This applies only in the case of free competition. The case of a monopoly – which is in fact governed by the fundamental principle of marginal productivity just as much as that of free competition – will be touched on later. The formation of the wage rate is of course a problem in price theory, where its solution is assumed and not further examined by those authors who like Wieser or Clark only want to sketch out the main lines of economic connections. But it is perhaps not superfluous to point out that in the case of the formation of wages 'sellers' having the equivalent of a zero own valuation of their good does not in fact create a difficulty; under free competition it simply leads to the result stated. It might be thought that the buyer's marginal utility forms only an upper limit in this case, a belief which is strengthened by the way the elements of the process are presented by many marginal utility theorists, as in Böhm-Bawerk's example of the horse market. But this is not so. Rather, if all buyers or sellers value the good the same and the latter perhaps value it at zero, the price problem is clearly settled, so that no further foundation causes for the fixing of prices need be sought.
10. Cf. on this my works: 'Das Rentenprinzip in der Verteilungslehre' (1907); also Thompson (1898). It is perhaps not superfluous to observe that residual thought is only one of the many aspects of the concept of 'rent'. Another meaning of this is 'income without work', a third

meaning 'income from naturally given means of production', a fourth is 'differential profit', a fifth 'surplus against which there are no costs', a sixth 'yield from productive expenditures, the supply of which can be varied only slowly or not at all'. None of these meanings coincides wholly with any of the others, although there are numerous connections between them.

11. Although I shall come back to this question, I must emphasise here why the fact that such 'ideal' competition never actually exists is irrelevant: firstly because there are approximations to, and tendencies towards, this condition which one can only understand on the basis of a theory of free competition; and secondly, because it is essential for diagnostic purposes to know how things should work under free competition.
12. That these distinctions are not 'frivolous' is shown for example by the fact discussed above that their neglect by an author like Tugan-Baranovskii led to an unquestionable misunderstanding in the treatment of peasant and craft income, a misunderstanding which again influenced his whole concept of the distribution process; the fact is that his exploitation theory would be quite impossible if he had analysed the case of the peasant correctly.
13. And which – a contradiction to 'profit on capital' – show no notable equalisation tendency.
14. This process is of course very complicated. The factor of investments that have been made and that cannot quickly be changed and the factor of the rise and fall of unit costs of the product with the expansion of production in the different firms are among other things that influence it, making assessment of a concrete situation difficult. It has to be worked out and combined with the necessary data. This is the starting-point for many investigations that theory will have to undertake, and here it can receive valuable help from the data available in 'private enterprise theory'.
15. E.g. from the standpoint of the Marxist system.
16. This principle has a role in Schüller's treatise, which also needs to be mentioned here.
17. But suppose the disappearance of the entrepreneur's surplus profit required an expansion of production for which the means of production simply were not there? I formulate this question for the sake of caution, but it has in fact already been answered by the above remarks. The answer runs: the situation is the same with an attempted expansion which drives the price of the means of production right up, as with an actual expansion. But suppose the necessary land and the necessary labour are available but not the necessary capital? If such a situation really applies – and not for instance only as a consequence of, e.g., the capitalists holding back on account of a panic – it can only happen because the productive organisation of society does not suit the existing stock of means of production for some reason or another, so that the economy is not in equilibrium and the prices of the means of production do not correspond to their marginal productivity. Then there will be a tendency for these prices to rise or fall and the situation will disappear with the new prices.

18. The details of the thing are of course again very complex and dependent for each sector and undertaking on the intramarginal structure of demand for capital.
19. Obviously we owe this extremely useful instrument to Marshall. I take the opportunity to re-emphasise how important it is to be clear in the discussion of economic questions that the phenomena and problems with which we have to deal tend to look very different depending on whether we consider short periods and direct effects, or long periods and those effects that first appear when the economy has adapted completely to a new situation. The confusion of the two viewpoints causes endless misunderstanding.
20. There is no point in objecting that the price of 'labour as commodity' cannot rise – as it should do on my theory – above the level given by the value of labour power. For the Marxist law of value fails in any case with 'labour as commodity'. It assumes that the commodities to which it is applied are produced rationally, but men are not produced according to rational-economic points of view.
21. It has of course been said from time to time (e.g. by Conrad, 1910) that a monopoly position for capitalists lies in capital being present in limited amounts. But this view, which blurs the distinction between 'economic good' and 'monopolised good', would also be applicable to labour as a factor of production.

IV The Social Marginal Product

1. I have written against this myself in 'The Concept of Social Value' (1909), but I have to admit that among all possible candidates for the title 'social' and for a connection with the concept 'economic productivity' (if it has any precise meaning), this consumer marginal utility is the best. In a free market economy consumers are really the forum of which it can best be said that it is the organ of social interests.
2. As happened especially with Clark and Carver.

V Critical Discussion

1. 'Die Nachfrage nach Arbeitskräften' (1916–17), pp. 37, 715 ff.
2. Remarkably, the author neglects the fact that something may be true for short periods that is false for long ones and vice versa; in addition, he does not distinguish whether there is equilibrium or no. Finally it may also be noted that many things have long since been explained by theory (e.g. cases of joint cost), which Schüller presents in such a manner as to arouse suspicions that he regards them as difficulties in the way of the application of theory.
3. While Schüller distinguishes (p. 62) between intensity of demand as measured by wages and 'real' intensity of demand, which is given by the amount of money the entrepreneur would prefer to pay rather than do without the relevant number of workers, it is obvious that this difference has meaning only for intramarginal quantities of work –

just as with consumption goods there is 'consumer rent' only *intra marginem*.

4. Cf. as particularly significant for the nature of the misunderstandings which are not avoided even by a theorist well known for his outstanding expository talent, Veblen (1908).
5. And an author like Albrecht who takes theory very seriously does not notice any of this.
6. Though he does not really seem to realise this. Rather he regards the application of this formula as a particular theory of wages, just as in the discussion of classic economists before John Stuart Mill the view emerged that supply and demand are a different cause determining price from the law of costs. Such reminiscences of outmoded views are often found in Tugan-Baranovskii, and they alone make it understandable that for example he takes the reproduction cost theory of labour so seriously and seems to consider that the 'fact that it is not produced' makes labour a difficulty for theory in general.

VI Peculiarities of the Labour Market

1. These difficulties become very obvious when one realises what a challenge to the actual state of things the concept of a free market truly amounts to. Cf. on this Moore, 'Paradoxes of Competition' (1906) and my *Das Wesen und Hauptinhalt der theoretischen Nationalökonomie* (1908).
2. Cf. Edgeworth (1907), p. 225 and *Mathematical Psychics* (1881), p. 42.
3. An analogous case would be the decrease in the intensity of saving when interest rates are rising, which I want to discuss in more detail further on, because many critics, including Tugan-Baranovskii, have based an argument against the abstinence theory on this fact.
4. But it should be stressed that this fact in no way damages the marginal productivity theory. Nor does it, despite Tugan-Baranovskii, damage the formula of supply and demand.
5. Tugan-Baranovskii is for ever repeating that a rise in productivity of labour 'must' raise the level of wages. This is not correct, not even for his own concept of productivity, which is different from mine.
6. It should be noted that my arguments relate primarily to advantage and disadvantage expressed in money terms. But a greater mobility of labour certainly has the consequence that areas of very low wage levels disappear, unless their cause lies in something other than a deficient mobility. Even if this advantage in money were outweighed by the disappearance of areas of higher than normal wages, there would still remain a gain in welfare for the workers, because the wage rise that the poorest enjoy has greater marginal utility for them than the loss of earnings for those best situated.
7. Among other things all this demonstrates the practical necessity of the marginal product concept, which unites in itself quantity of labour, output, and labour value, for otherwise we are left with several separate arguments which do not stand in any definite relation to one another.

8. The same is true of the effects of the Taylor system, which I do not specially want to go into. Cf. on that topic Pigou, *Wealth and Welfare* (1912).
9. Insofar as that is the case, workers' groups are related to each other just like different production factors. In this connection Edgeworth pointed out that the theory of the international formation of value is applicable in all the cases under consideration here: their characteristic is the relative immobility of capital and labour, and what is valid for communication between nations is also therefore often valid for communication between such groups of workers, for whom this type of price theory is thus a very important instrument.
10. There is a particular difficulty in the fact that there are not just 'artificial' differentiations (i.e. sociological rather than economic) but also equally 'artificial' falls and rises of different 'abilities' on the same level, so that very often the more able and the less able are forced into the same activity.

VII The Wage Theorem of Unilateral and Bilateral Monopoly

1. Many authors have observed that the phenomenon of marginal profits is absolutely universal. Cf. for example Hobson's idea of 'forced gains'. Tugan-Baranovskii is also of this opinion. But even if this affirmation were true, it would say nothing at all against theory as such.
2. One can readily see how well this case fits in with Tugan-Baranovskii's schema and how much he makes of combinations of this kind, but at the same time too how unforcedly the case fits with the marginal productivity theory. Perhaps this is the most important of the points at which the possibility of a complete agreement between the two in a theoretical construction is demonstrated. Whether Tugan-Baranovskii is of the opinion that this case is the rule is of no importance to me.
3. That is also the case when the monopolist is of the trust king type and carries out a complete reorganisation of the industry which pushes down the level of cost per unit so far that the monopoly price is now lower than the competitive price of earlier on, with the result that more is produced than before, perhaps so much so that more workers are employed than before. But it is still true that the monopoly price would be higher and the demand for labour lower than they would be if free competition were the rule in this new organisation of production.
4. The reader should note how little substance there is to Diehl's objections – to the extent that they are meant as such, and how completely untenable for example is his recently repeated assertion ('Zur Kritik der Kapitalzinstheorie von Böhm-Bawerk', p. 603), that Böhm-Bawerk's theory of interest is 'worked out on the assumption of perfectly free competition, like his value and price theory'. That of course applies only to the theory of the market price, but there is also the theory of the monopoly price, and anyone can apply that to wage and interest theory without the author having to do it in detail himself. In relation

to the theory of value, whose foundations have been developed from Böhm-Bawerk to Robinson, the reproach is completely incomprehensible.

5. Here emerges the difference between the two concepts: overall utilities and the amount of marginal utilities – in addition to the fact that the overall product is dependent on the general amount of labour.
6. Cf. Pigou (1905), Appendix.

VIII The Problem of the 'Artificial Rise' of Wages

1. The best discussions of this problem are to be found in Thompson (1892) and Pigou (1905).
2. A fine example of this is the fate of the wage fund theory. Cf. on this my 'Epochen der Dogmen- und Methodengeschichte' (1914).
3. Which can be shown to be correct in terms of price theory.
4. In *Giornale degli Economisti* (1909).
5. Diehl of course thinks (p. 606) that the fact that companies which have large fixed capital continue to employ their workers 'all year', even at wages which involve a capital loss, contradicts the principle that wage levels at which the entrepreneur works at a loss cannot be sustained in the long term!
6. This point is very carefully analysed in the (1914) article by Böhm-Bawerk.
7. Something that particularly needs to be stressed with regard to Schüller and Tugan-Baranovskii. Though they do not ignore this factor, they fail to give it its due weight.
8. This also applies as we have seen to the different qualities of labour in their relation to one another.
9. The most recent work on the subject is the big article by Fanno in the *Giornale degli Economisti* (Fanno, 1914) which will be included in this series as: *A Contribution to the Theory of Supply at Joint Cost* (1998).
10. The elimination of employment possibilities does not need to be regarded purely as a misfortune. For example the most obvious method to eliminate industries that are centres of social evils might simply be to establish minimum wages that ruin them, and to make provision for the workers put out of work as a result (the unskilled ones of course) so that they cannot put pressure on the general level of wages, until there are none of them left around. Of course this would require the introduction of appropriate regulations.
11. And not for the reason that the effect wage rises can have on the quality of labour was always recognised.
12. It must again be stressed that the power factor contributes nothing at all to the explanation of the success of this action; generally speaking nothing is as necessary for this explanation as a sufficient mastery of the theory of the monopoly price.
13. The introduction of a minimum wage is a special case which is made particularly complicated by the effects of wage changes for one class of workers on the wages of other classes of workers.

14. A conceivable case, but one which has only theoretical interest, would be given by an analogy with a process which can be observed on the consumption goods market, although extremely rarely: if the price of the cheapest normal food staple rises, thus for example in England wheat, and yet this staple remains the cheapest, it may happen that the workers completely give up the consumption, e.g., of meat and generally restrict themselves to bread. If they do this, it is possible that demand for bread may rise as a consequence of the rise in its price. Likewise it could happen that by raising wages the entrepreneur found it broadly advantageous to give up a range of other factors of production and increase his demand for labour.
15. Moreover if the struggle for higher wages were pointless in every sense, workers might still remain convinced that wages depend on social relations of power (1913, p. 82). For in economic as in other things the layman is very often full of quite meaningless convictions. Furthermore the technique of modern mass movements creates a tendency to call for increases in principle, which every individual penned into such an organised movement must obey, even if he perceives the pointlessness of the demand in a particular case: in fact the professional representatives of workers' (or others') interests very often have no choice.
16. It must particularly be stressed again that the socialist critique can as well be linked to the marginal productivity theory as to any other. Indeed there are enough socialists even in England and America (in Italy too) working on this premise. The sooner we bow to the inevitability of accepting it, the better for socialism; for a halt to the development of the stock of a movement's ideas can be a practical danger for that movement.

PART II EQUILIBRIUM AND POWER

I Power and the Economy: The View of an Anti-Schumpeterian

1. Schumpeter's critique of the theory of power is found initially in his first book (1908) but I am relying here on his main work dealing with this problem, 'Das Grundprinzip der Verteilungstheorie' (1916–17), pp. 1–88. [The whole article is reproduced in Part I of this volume.] It ranges very widely in the points it makes. All these points cannot be explored here, and I shall just touch on those which give the core of the argument. The order in which I have set out things is entirely my own, aimed at taking the discussion forward with the minimum restraints.

II Why Can Wages be Rigid? An Alternative Foundation for Keynes' Premise

1. Leontief (1948), p. 236.
2. A specified money wage signifies the social status of the supplier of labour. This stands, of course, on the one hand for the price of a

commodity, namely labour as a factor of production. It is on the other hand, however, the reward for the human position of the worker himself. These two are conceptually different. The spirit of capitalism lays down that wages are a commodity price. However, capitalism is realised neither in the world of the gods, nor in the world of creatures, but in human society. To that extent there is no such thing as wages purely as a commodity price. A worker accepts his wage as one manifestation of respect or lack of respect for his own character, and as long as that is the case the wage demand, i.e. the supply price of labour, will denote a gradation of honour, the price of maintaining face. Even though the real wage may fall due to a rise in prices, the supply of labour will not be impeded provided that this honour is not impaired. This explains why a cut in money wages, with prices being constant, affects the supply in labour more severely than an increase in prices, with constant money wages, will influence it. Consequently, if we are going to try and do a real calculation of utility, we will come across a situation where the marginal utility of the wage exceeds the marginal disutility of labour (Keynes).

III Why Interest Remains Positive even in Static Equilibrium: Another Anti-Schumpeterian View

1. [*Editor's Note*] As the author himself writes later, he is greatly influenced by Marx in constructing the argument of this chapter. That is, he neatly uses the labour theory of value and the formula for transformation of value into price as his two fundamental weapons for reasoning. However, he makes amendments in each of them. First, he extends the labour theory of value so as to include labour and other producer goods in the cost calculation, but he refers to the cost of production thus obtained as the value of products. It is distinguished from the price of production. Secondly, in this transformation of value into price, Takata does not accept the theory of exploitation, by means of which Marx explains profits. Instead Takata uses the concept of capital shortage as the criterion for the existence of profits.
2. When I talk here of Böhm-Bawerk's interest rate theory, I refer to the second half of his positive theory of interest, the section entitled 'Determination of the rate of interest in the market'. My own view is that there is lacking the essential theoretical linkage between this second half, and the first half, which describes the three fundamental reasons for the existence of interest. My recognition of his interest rate theory does not necessarily mean that I accept his three reasons.
3. Schmoller (1904), p. 763.
4. Tugan-Baranovskii, (1913), p. 35.
5. Schumpeter (1912), p. 326, (1926), p. 243; Takata (1924) p. 270.
6. Böhm-Bawerk (1921), pp. 316–17.
7. Schmoller (1904), p. 667.
8. Schumpeter (1912), pp. 374–5, (1926), pp. 284–5.
9. Fisher (1907), pp. 117ff.

10. The view that accumulation declines as a result of a fall in interest is widely held. However, that does not necessarily mean that there are many people who regard a downward movement of interest as bringing about sooner or later an erosion of capital. Cassel (1918) is typical of those scholars who have held this view. Conrad (1910) can be cited as a representative supporter of the view that the demand for capital is infinite.

IV Disequilibrium in Factor Markets due to Power, with Special Reference to Agricultural Land Rent

1. This chapter is a translation of Part 2 of Chapter 3 of *The Theory of Distribution*, which is Volume 4 of Takata Yasuma's *New Lectures on Economics* [*Keizaigaku Shinko*]. Takata discusses differential rent in Part 3, absolute rent in Part 4, monopoly and polypoly rent in Part 5 and the relations between these various types of rent in Part 6.
2. [*Editor's Note*] There is an implicit assumption here that we are talking about agricultural rent, and not other issues like mining rent, urban rents, etc.
3. [*Editor's Note*] This section, however, will not be included in this volume. See Takata (1940), pp. 266–80.
4. The word monopoly has come to be used in many different ways regarding the consideration of ground rent. For example, in Marx all rent was regarded as existing due to land monopoly. However, monopoly in this sense has no meaning other than the ownership of land (private property). This being the case, this view makes it easy to confuse ownership and monopoly in the true sense of the word. If we interpret monopoly in the strict sense of the word, we cannot regard the land ownership which makes possible the existence of ground rent in general or absolute rent as a land monopoly. Moreover, in many earlier works, what has here been termed polypoly rent is confused with monopoly rent. Polypoly profits from a production price which is a polypoly price, themselves end up being paid as ground rent. However, in this case there is no monopolist in the true sense of the word (either among the suppliers of land use, or on the side of the demanders, and hence the cultivators). For that reason there will be no existence of monopoly rent. Moreover, by confusing polypoly and monopoly, it is said that there is monopoly rent there. All these confusions cannot, however, be condoned.

Bibliography

Albrecht, G. 'Zur sozialen Theorie der Verteilung', *Conrads Jahrbuch*, III Folge 47. Bd.
Böhm-Bawerk, E. von (1914) 'Macht oder ökonomisches Gesetz?', *Zeitschrift für Volkswirtschaft, Sozialpolitik und Verwaltung*, Bd. 23.
Böhm-Bawerk, E. von (1921) *Positive Theorie des Kapitale* (4th edn) (Meisenheim-Glan).
Cassel, K. G. (1918) *The Theory of Social Economy* (New York).
Clark, J. B. (1889) *The Distribution of Wealth: A Theory of Wages, Interest and Profits* (New York).
Conrad, O. (1910) *Lohn und Rente*.
Davidson, J. (1898) *The Bargain Theory of Wages* (New York).
Diehl, B. K. 'Zur Kritik der Kapitalzinstheorie Böhm-Bawerks', *Conrads Jahrbuch*, Bd. 105.
Dühring, E. (1871) *Kritische Geschichte der Politischen Ökonomie und des Sozialismus*.
Edgeworth, F. Y. (1881) *Mathematical Psychics* (London).
Edgeworth, F. Y. (1907) 'Appreciations of Mathematical Theories', *Economic Journal*.
Fanno, M. (1914) 'A Contribution to the Theory of Joint Supply', *Giornale degli Economisti* to be included in this series (1998).
Fisher, I. (1907) *The Rate of Interest* (New York).
Hobson, J. A. (1900) *Economics of Distribution* (New York).
Keynes, J. M. (1920) *Economic Consequences of the Peace* (Macmillan).
Keynes, J. M. (1936) *The General Theory of Employment, Interest and Money* (London).
Knight, F. H. (1934) 'Capital, Time and the Interest Rate', *Economica*.
Leontief, W. W. (1948) 'Keynes' General Theory and the Classicists', in S. E. Harris (ed.), *The New Economics* (London).
Lindberg, J. K. (1932–3) 'Die Kapitalzinstheorie', *Zeitschrift für Nationalökonomie*, Bd. IV.
Marx, K. (1894) *Das Kapital*, Bd. 3 (London).
Menger, C. (1871) *Grundsätze der Volkswirtschaftslehre* (Vienna).
Mill, J. S. (1909) *Principles of Political Economy*, ed. Sir William Ashley (London).
Moore H. L. (1906) 'Paradoxes of Competition', *Quarterly Journal of Economics*.
Moore, H. L. (1912) *Law of Wages* (Macmillan).
Morishima, M. (1988), *Thatcher Jidai no Igirisu (Britain under Thatcher)* (Tokyo: Iwanami Shinsho).
Morishima, M. (1995) *Nihon no Sentaku* (*Options for Japan*) (Tokyo: Iwanami Shoten).
Oppenheimer, F. (1924) *Theorie der reinen und politischen Ökonomie*.
Pareto, V. (1909), *Manuel d'economie politique* (Paris).

Pareto, V. (1935) *Trattato di sociologia generale* (1916), English trans: *The Mind and Society: A Treatise on General Sociology* (London: Jonathan Cape).
Pareto, V. (1991) *The Rise and Fall of Elites: An Application of Theoretical Sociology* (London: Transaction Publishers).
De Pietri-Tonelli, A. and Bousquet, G. H. (1994) *Vilfredo Pareto: Neoclassical Synthesis of Economics and Sociology* (London: Macmillan).
Pigou, A. C. (1905) *Principles and Methods of Industrial Peace* (New York).
Pigou, A. C. (1912) *Wealth and Welfare* (London).
Preiser, E. (1949) 'Property and Power in the Theory of Distribution', *Synopsis, Festgabe für Alfred Weber*; also in *International Economic Papers*, No. 2 (1952, London).
Schmoller, G. (1904) *Grundriss der Allgemeinen Volkswirtschaftslehre*, pt. 2, 6th edn (Munich and Leipzig).
Schüller, R. (1915) 'Die Ansprüche der Arbeiter', *Archiv für Sozialwissenschaft und Sozialpolitik* (May).
Schüller, R. (1916–17) 'Die Nachfrage nach Arbeitskräften', *Archiv für Sozialwissenschaft und Sozialpolitik*, Bd. 23.
Schumpeter, J. A. (1907) 'Das Rentenprinzip in der Verteilungslehre', *Schmollers Jahrbuch*.
Schumpeter, J. A. (1908) *Das Wesen und der Hauptinhalt der theoretischen Nationalökonomie*, (Munich and Leipzig: Duncker & Humblot).
Schumpeter, J. A. (1909) 'The Concept of Social Value', *Quarterly Journal of Economics*.
Schumpeter, J. A. (1912) *Theorie der Wirtschaftlichen Entwicklung* (Leipzig); 2nd edn (1926).
Schumpeter, J. A. (1914) *Epochen der Dogmen- und Methodengeschichte, Grundriss der Sozialökonomik* I (Tübingen).
Schumpeter, J. A. (1916–17), 'Das Grundprinzip der Verteilungstheorie', *Archiv für Sozialwissenschaft und Sozialpolitik*, 42.
Schumpeter, J. A. (1918–19) 'Zur Soziologie der Imperialismen', *Archiv für Sozialwissenschaft und Sozialpolitik*.
Schumpeter J. A. (1942) *Capitalism, Socialism and Democracy*, (New York).
Schumpeter, J. A. (1991) *The Economics and Sociology of Capitalism* (ed. R. Swedbery) (Princeton: Princeton University Press).
Showa Tenno (1995) *Dokuhakuroku (The Emperor's Memorandum on the War)* (Tokyo: Bunshun Bunko).
Smith, A. (1950) *The Wealth of Nations* (London).
Takata, Y. (1924) *Keizaigaku Kenkyu* (*Studies in Economics*) (Tokyo: Iwanami).
Takata, Y. (1937) *Rishi Ron* (*Theory of Interest*) (Tokyo: Iwanami).
Takata, Y. (1940) *Keizaigaku shin ko* (*New Lectures on Economics*) Vol. 4, (Tokyo: Iwanami).
Takata, Y. (1941) *Seiryoku setsu ronshu* (*Essays in the Power Theory of Economics*) (Tokyo: Nihon Hyoron Sha).
Takata, Y. (1947) *Sekai Shakai Ron* (*On the World Society*) (Tokyo: Chugai Shuppan).
Takata, Y. (1955) *Keynes Ronnan* (*Critical Essays on Keynes*) (Kyoto: Yuhikaku).
Takata, Y. (1995) *Power Theory of Economics* (London: Macmillan).
Thompson, H. M. (1892) *The Theory of Wages*.

Tönnies, F. (1887) *Gemeinschaft und Gesellschaft: Grundbegriffe der Reinen Sociologie* (2nd edn) (Berlin, 1926).
Tugan-Baranovskii, M. I. (1913) *Soziale Theorie der Verteilung* (Berlin).
Uno, K. (ed.) (1973) *Teikokushugi no Kenkyu* (*The Study of Imperialism*), 2 vols (Tokyo: Aoki Shoten).
Veblen, T. (1908) 'Professor Clark's Economics', *Quarterly Journal of Economics*.
Wallas, G. (1908) *Human Nature in Politics* (London).
West, Sir Edward (1815) *Essays on Application of Capital to Land* (London).
Wieser, F. von (1889) *Der natürliche Werth* [(1956) *Natural Value* (New York)].
Wieser, F. von (1924) *Theorie der Gesellschaftlichen Wirtschaft*.
Wiles, P. J. D. (1987) 'Convergence Hypothesis', J. Eatwell, M. Milgate and P. Newman (ed.) *The New Palgrave: A Dictionary of Economics* (London: Macmillan), 2 vols.
Wood, S. (1889) *The Theory of Wages* (American Economic Association).
Zweidineck-Südenhorst, Otto von (1906) 'Neuere Literatur Zum Lohnfrage', *Archiv für Sozialwissenschaft und Sozialpolitik*, Bd. 23, Heft 2.

Index